Silas Cully's Tavern Tales

To Ryan
Keep 1850 Alive!

[signature] 2002

Silas H. Cully 1850

Silas Cully's Tavern Tales

Stories, Jokes and Recipes from a
Nineteenth Century Barkeeper

Bert G. Osterberg

Writers Club Press
San Jose New York Lincoln Shanghai

Silas Cully's Tavern Tales
Stories, Jokes and Recipes from a Nineteenth Century Barkeeper

Writers Club Press
an imprint of iUniverse, Inc.

For information address:
iUniverse, Inc.
5220 S. 16th St., Suite 200
Lincoln, NE 68512
www.iuniverse.com

ISBN: 0-595-18297-6

Printed in the United States of America

To Armaine (Sadie), my inspiration and love and to the "regulars" who come in to allow Silas Cully to live

CONTENTS

PREFACE

I had not planned to become Silas Cully. It happened as a matter of circumstance. After I took an early retirement from a public utility where I had risen to the position of telecommunications manager, I became a man of relative leisure. I had been a manager with a big sounding title, a fairly big staff, a big responsibility and a very big ulcer. I decided to save my life and do something else. I decided to do something I wanted to do.

At first I thought I was going to take a couple of years off and do nothing. Or, do nothing like people like me who are driven by their view of their self worth and the world do nothing. That is, I intended to write a book; to travel; to do research. I intended to remodel the house. Instead of doing those things I took a job at Dearborn, Michigan's Greenfield Village. How could I not?

My wife and I had been members of the Friends of Greenfield Village for years. The 81-acre outdoor museum of American history and American ingenuity became one of our favorite places to visit. We often took picnic lunches there after church or ate meals at the Eagle Tavern, a period restaurant on the grounds of the Village. So, when I stopped by a jobs fair at the Edison Institute, the parent organization for Greenfield Village, and saw they had an opening for barkeeper at the Eagle Tavern, I jumped at the opportunity. I asked the recruiter for the Eagle Tavern, "You mean *I* can be the bar-keeper at the Eagle Tavern? How much do I have to pay you?" The recruiter told me they'd pay me to do it, so how could I say no?

I became a barkeep, an 1850 tavern-keeper at Greenfield Village's Eagle Tavern, an 19th century eatery and barroom. I was in heaven!

The Tavern reopened in April from it annual winter hiatus. April in Michigan is often a snowy month and that April was one of the snowy ones. There were few visitors to the tavern and one blizzardy weekday I was sitting in the barroom, reading a book. My supervisor passed by and apologized for my forced inactivity.

"Bert," she said, "I'm sorry it's so slow, but it'll pick up later in the year."

I looked up from my book. "Pat," I replied, "think about it. I'm at the Eagle Tavern at Greenfield Village. I'm dressed in these wonderful period clothes, sitting by a fireplace, reading a book, and YOU'RE paying ME! What a deal!!"

That's the way it is. Even in the summer when it "picks up" I love it. Even when the servers line up at the barroom window demanding immediate service for their drinks; even when my 1850 barroom is filled with customers, and they don't understand why we don't have Diet Coke or Bud Light, I love it.

As time went on I developed stories and tales about the Eagle Tavern and Clinton, Michigan, the town where the tavern had been built. I used these stories and tales to entertain and educate my customers. A picture of Michigan in 1850 began to form in my consciousness and it became clearer and clearer.

A few months after I was hired I was awarded what I took to be a high honor. I was called "Silas". Silas was an historic name used by former bar-keepers at the Eagle Tavern and I felt its use was an honor.. Silas was the head-barkeep, the one who belonged in the barroom. I felt I had earned its use.

I took the surname of Cully from my family history. I became Silas Hezekiah Cully, the last two names being that of my own great-great-grand father. In 1850 Hezekiah's father would have been about my age and I adopted his persona.

So what follows is 1850 in Michigan through the eyes of the barkeeper at a Michigan tavern. Here are Silas' stories, jokes, memories, and tales, as well as some recipes used at taverns and inns of the time. Here are Silas Cully's Tavern Tales.

I spent five years researching life in the mid-nineteenth century in Michigan and elsewhere and have striven to be accurate in what I say and in what follows. This book is presented to inform and entertain the reader and is not intended as academic history although I believe it to be true to the feeling and substances of 1850 in Michigan. Most of the jokes are borrowed from other sources and adapted by me for the purposes of this work.

What follows is presented as if the reader is standing before me in my barroom, hearing me as I pour drinks and explain life in Michigan in the middle of the 19th Century. It is my hope that it will be both entertaining and illuminating.

The reader will please note that the food recipes I use in this book are **not** recipes used at Greenfield Village's Eagle Tavern but they are typical of recipes used in the middle of the Nineteenth Century in taverns like the Eagle.

Bert G. Osterberg

2001 (maybe 1850)

BOOK ONE: SUMMER 1850

INTRODUCTION TO BOOK ONE

The year 1850 is a time of great optimism and a little pessimism. It begins with General Taylor as President of the United States and ends with Millard Fillmore in the White House as our second "President by Accident". 1850 is the year that Henry Clay introduced his compromise bills in the Senate that he assured all would save the Union from dissolution.

1850 is also a year of social change. The Gold Rush in California continues with hundreds of people, mostly men, arriving in San Francisco every day to seek their fortune. It is the time of America's "Manifest Destiny" to subdue and rule the continent from sea to sea. Great new lands have been added to the nation as a result of the recent Mexican War. Immigration has greatly increased due to the great political upheavals in Europe in 1848 and 1849. Failed revolutions in Hungary, Italy, Prussia, Bavaria, Austria, other German States, as well as the failure of the Second Republic in France to assure freedom, has drive refugees to our shores. The Irish Potato Famine continues to populate America and Canada with thousands and thousands of poor Irish immigrants with many of those Irish coming West to Michigan and other Great Lake states. The first residential community built outside the city limits of Detroit is "Corktown", an Irish neighborhood.

The Underground Railroad brings a growing number of fugitives from Southern bondage and Detroit is a major crossing point to British North America. A sizable free African community is being established in Detroit's Third Ward, near the site of Michigan's first Jewish Synagogue, Temple Beth El.

Towns like Clinton, Michigan where I work continue their importance as stagecoach stops and mercantile centers, but the expansion of the railroads threaten their very reason for existence. Plank roads are being built and there is a renewed interest in constructing canals. The ruling Democrats in Michigan have abandoned the former notions of government building the transportation systems and have turned over the construction of such projects to private interests. The railroads have left public ownership and are controlled by private companies. Michigan's plank roads are toll roads, built by stock-stock-holding corporations. The new Michigan Constitution of 1850, the first new one since statehood in 1837, forbids the state from building roads. Privatization will give progress, it is thought.

In this time I keep bar at the Eagle Tavern in Clinton. I was there when Calvin and Harriet Wood bought the place and Calvin kept my wife and me on to help the Woods run the tavern. Calvin is a farmer, originally from New York, and his interests are divided between his newly acquired tavern and his family's farm. My wife, Sadie, and I have a room on the second floor of the Eagle Tavern so we can be there to oversee the activities of Calvin's overnight guests and see to it that things go well in Calvin's absence.

So, in my fifties, during a time when most men are dead, I have become the barkeep and resident manager of Calvin Wood's Eagle Tavern. The stories, tales, and recipes that follow are my stock in trade, my daily work. I sincerely hope that those who may have occasion to read these works of mine will do so to their general entertainment and edification.

Silas Hezekiah Cully

1850

CHAPTER ONE: DRINKS AND ACCOMMODATIONS

Well, Good-day, folks. Welcome to the Barroom of the Eagle Tavern. Can I get you somethin' to drink?

What do we have?

Everythin' we have to serve is listed on the side-bars of our Bill of Fare and all right up to date to 1850. The Temperance drinks listed in the upper right-hand corner of the Bill of Fare do not have alcohol. Everythin' else does.

Are you folks drinkin' folks?

Good. We got plenty of good drinks.

Punches? Yep, them's alcohol drinks. But, they look like temperance drinks. They're very popular with the ladies and others who want to fool the Church people into thinkin' they're not drinkin' no alcohol. The Planter's Punch—that's rum and lemonade. The Lemon Punch—that's my wife's favorite—that's apricot brandy and lemonade—very tasty. The Cherry Shrub—that really looks temperance. It's a Cherry Effervescent Drink—cherry syrup and soda water—with brandy added to it. You could be sippin' one of them and talkin' to the preacher's wife and she won't even mention it to her husband. The fourth punch—the Vanilla Punch—is my favorite. It's vanilla extract, brandy, and lemonade—very refreshing. And the lemonade makes those punches medicinal drinks because they prevent scurvy. We've been servin' lemonade here for five years and we ain't had one case of scurvy the whole time! It's done its job.

Scurvy? Yeah, that's what you get when you don't eat fresh fruits and vegetables. There's something in them things, especially citrus fruits, that prevents scurvy. An English doctor, Jeremy Lind, discovered that. He fed limes and lime juice to English sailors and stopped scurvy in the English Navy. That's why some folks call Englishmen "Limeys".

Scurvy makes your gums turn black, your teeth get loose and fall out, and your skin to hang from your body. It's something you don't want to see twice.

A lemonade? Sure. As soon as I mention scurvy, I know I'm gonna sell a lemonade.

We also got a nice Gin Fix. That's a drink made with gin and lemonade. That's medicine, too.

And you, sir?

The beers? Sure. We got a Pale Ale—a lot like the British fellahs call "bitters", an Amber Ale—a bit sweeter, Stout and Porter for dark beers—both brewed from roasted grains, and in the big mug up there I make a Half and Half, American-style—half Stout and half Amber Ale. A Pale Ale? Sure. One pint of bitters, comin' up.

Here you are, sir—one Pale Ale. Good, ain't it?

Now, what about you folks? Can I get you somethin'?

Whiskey? Scotch, Irish, Rye, or Corn?

Corn? Of course. Corn Whiskey is the most popular distilled beverage in the United States in 1850. As you can see, it's perfectly clear—never aged a day in a barrel. See? You can see my hand right through the bottle. You don't want to take the edge of it by aging Corn. This Corn Whiskey has a taste I describe somewhere between vodka and turpentine.

There you are—Corn Whiskey.

And for the lady?

No, that's all right, ma'am. I know we don't get many ladies in the bar-room, but I'll keep a look-out for anyone from the Church Temperance League and if I see any one of 'em a-peekin' in here, I'll tell you to just duck down. We don't want 'em talkin' about you, and you know they will.

Well, the Scriptures says, and it's plainly written therein, that Church folk ain't never supposed to gossip. And, of course, Church folk do not gossip. What they do is on Sunday morning they get together and say, "We gotta pray for Sister Jones…'cause let me tell you what I saw her doin' and who she was doin' it with!" But, that ain't gossipin'. That's just showin' concern. Some ladies been so concerned about, they had to get out of town.

Besides, the rule of thumb in 1850 is—we NEVER get ladies in the barroom—we DO get an occasional woman, if you get my drift.

So, I'll warn you, ma'am, if I see anyone showin' an interest in your presence here

A Stonewall? That's a man's drink, ma'am. It's hard cider—cider wine at about six-and-one-half percent alcohol with rum added. Quite powerful. I'd recommend a Jersey Lighting. That's hard cider with a little simple syrup and a splash of bitters, over ice—quite refreshing.

Yes, ma'am. One Stonewall, comin' up.

Here's the rum and here's the ice. Our ice comes right out of the lakes and rivers in the winter. We keep it in the ice-house out back built into the side of a hill. It's like a cave lined with logs and with a heavy log door. The ice lasts all summer, sometimes. Being river and lake ice you may find a fish or a frog in it. If you do, don't worry—there ain't no extra charge. People see that fish and think I'm gonna changed 'em for a meal. I just let it slip by.

Here you go. A Stonewall cock-tail with a sucker made of macaroni.

Havin' a macaroni sucker in your drink is considered rather elegant and, as you can tell, we're an elegant place. Or, we try to be so. In the big city they make these suckers outta glass, or at the big hotel restaurants or Del Monaco's in New York or in San Francisco, they make 'em outta silver with the name of the place etched on 'em. But, here in Clinton we made 'em outta macaroni. You can stir with 'em, drink through 'em, and after you're done with your drink, you can make a bit of a snack outta 'em.

If I gave glass suckers—that'd be a problem. Some of my regular customers, after a few drinks might bite through the sucker and I'd be moppin' blood all day. I'd get nothin' done in here. And silver? Out of the question! I'd be searchin' everyone before they'd leave and, once more, I'd never get nothin' done in the barroom.

Cider, anyone? Hard cider is the most popular drink in America, much more than beer. Some people call it "Johnny-Jump-Up". Cider is cheaper than beer and keeps better. It's easier to make and travels well. Beer is mostly sold within fifty miles of its point of brewing. A beer can cost five cents a pint and that ain't cheap. Five cents is nearly an hour's wages for a working man in 1850. An equal amount of cider could go for a penny. I have a barrel of cider in the barroom. If you're a regular customer I got a mug with your mark on it. So many people can't read nor write I don't put your name on it, only a mark you and I can recognize. You can dip in the barrel as much as you want and I count the dips. At the end of the night, if you're still standin', you pay your bill. If you ain't standin', I send a boy to your farm to fetch your wife and she comes back and pays your bill and hauls your sorry carcass out of the barroom like she does most every night.

Here's a suggestion for you fellows. When your wife throws you in the wagon to haul you home—leave your legs hangin' out of the back of the wagon so your heals drag in the dirt. That'll leave a nice trail so you can find your way back the next day.

Yes, sir. Two ciders.

The average consumption of hard cider in 1850 is eleven gallons per person, per year. That's in addition to seven-and-a-half gallons of whiskey. That's including women and children and the enslaved who don't get a lot to drink. That's a lot of alcohol, ain't it?

I feel the high alcohol consumption is the main reason we're livin' so long now. Life expectancy in 1850 is all the way up to 52 years!

I know whiskey's good for you. It was scientifically proved to me by my own doctor, Doc Wilson. Doc Wilson's a temperance man, but I forgive him for it. I figure everyone's gotta have some vice and temperance is Doc Wilson's vice. He inadvertently demonstrated the worth of whiskey to me one day.

In an effort to show me that drinkin' whiskey is bad for me that man of science set up an experiment. Doc set up two glasses. Into one he put water and into then other he put corn whiskey. Then he dropped a live worm into each glass. Well, sure enough, the worm that went into the whiskey curled up and died and the one that went into the water swam around lookin' all happy. Doc Wilson said to me, "Well, Silas, what does this prove to you?"

I said, "Doc, it proves to me that if you drink whiskey, you don't get worms." And I have been worm-free for most of my life.

Doc Wilson's a really good doctor. Why, a while ago a fellah came to him with a bashed in head, a bad case of belly pains, a broken leg and a terrible burn on his back. Doc went right to work on him and he still says that fellah'd be one of his greatest accomplishments—if he hadn't died.

Speakin' of doctorin'—I went into Ann Arbor earlier this year to see the opening of the new medical school. This'll impress you out-of-town people. There are now three buildings as part of the University of Michigan complex—North, South, and the new medical building. We got a new law now that says as of 1850, if you wanna be a doctor in Michigan you gotta go to college for a whole year! That's quite a burden on the young men, but they're gonna have to do it. It's a six-month long series of lectures, and then six months of watchin' doctors cut up people. After that you still gotta apprentice with a medical doctor to learn the trade.

Anyway, I was in Ann Arbor at the medical school and I met one of them professors. A professor's like a teacher, but he gets paid more. This professor showed me a whole slew of bottles on a shelf in his laboratory. Inside each bottle was a fish or a frog or a squirrel or something. The professor said his students use 'em for what he called "die-section". I figure that means they died and they section 'em up. So I looked at them bottles with the animals inside and I said, "These is all fresh killed, ain't they Doc?" He said, "no, some of 'em have been dead for a long time."

What keeps 'em from rotting, then?" I asked.

"Alcohol," said he. "I preserve 'em in alcohol that keeps 'em from rotting."

Then I went over to the butcher's shop and he had a whole line of hooks and on each one was a-hangin' a ham, or a sausage, or a turkey breast, or other meat, and they weren't rotten none, neither. I said, "You must dip these in alcohol to keep 'em from rotting."

The butcher said, "No, Silas, I take 'em out back to my smokehouse and smoke 'em and that keeps 'em from rotting."

So, I figure, between the cigars and the whiskey, I'm gonna last forever!

That's why I claim to be a healer. Corn whiskey can cure just about anything you may have and if it don't cure it, at least you'll die with a smile on your face.

Me? I've been working here at the Eagle Tavern for seven years now. I started here in 1843. That's before Calvin and Harriet Wood bought the place. The building was built here in Clinton in 1831, the same time the town got started. In 1834 Mr. James Parks made it into the Parks' Tavern to serve travelers along the Chicago Road.

Clinton? It's named for Dewitt Clinton, Governor of New York and developer of the Erie Canal. By the 1830s many people had come to Michigan by way of that canal and Dewitt Clinton was quite the hero here. We've got a Clinton River, a Clinton Township, and here, the town of Clinton. The story goes that in 1831 when they wanted to name this town suggestions were written on pieces of paper and those pieces of paper were put into the mayor's hat. Well, the mayor, himself, drew the winning suggestion and it just so happened to be the one he wrote, Clinton. He balled up that piece of paper and tossed it away so no one really knows if it said Clinton, or not. You know politicians!

So, here we are in Clinton, Michigan, a town now nineteen years old. Our population is well on its way toward a thousand folks and we have great hopes for the future as the plank road keeps a-comin' this way.

Beer? Yes, sir. Pale ale? Amber ale? Yes, sir, one Amber Ale.

Now this here beer only has four ingredients in it. That's water, yeast, malted barley, and hops. That just happens to be my wife's recipe for bread. So this beer is just liquid bread. Two beers and a piece of meat and you got yourself a sandwich.

Here you are, Amber Ale. That'll be five-cents. A half-dime. Yes, that's high, I know, but beer's rather expensive. Like I said, that five-cents is darn near an hour's wages for a working man, you know. In 1850, the average working man makes three hundred dollars a year. That's workin' twelve hours a day, six days a week. That's about a dollar a day, or so. Have you heard the expression—"Another day, another dollar"? That's us!

Brewing beer in 1850 is pretty much of a cottage industry. Beer is sold no more than fifty miles from where it is brewed. Beer don't travel well and there is no way to keep it cold during transportation. There are no national brands of beer. Local beer only and brewed according to the tastes of the local inhabitants. In Detroit there's a new brewer, a fellah from Bavaria, a Bernard Stroh. He's makin' beer for sale now and with all them Germans comin' into Detroit I bet there's gonna be a market for his lagers. If you're in Detroit and he's sellin' any stock in his company, you might wanna buy a few shares.

Beer is considered such a healthy beverage that orphanages have daily beer rations for the children. They line up for a cup of watered-down beer. It puts weight on 'em and helps 'em sleep through the night.

Yes sir, that's our spittoon over there on the floor near the fireplace. And I'd appreciate a little accuracy on your part and so would that fellah sittin' near it. He's gotta wear them clothes home and I'm the fellah whose gotta mop up here to-night.

Good-day, gentlemen. Are you with these other folks? No? Well, they seem like good people. You may want to get to know 'em. What can I get you to drink? Stone-wall? Certainly.

This here drink is called a cock-tail. A cock-tail is a rather new idea. Before 1840, or so, drinks weren't mixed like they are now. Then barkeeps began experimenting with mixing different liquors together and the cock-tail came into being. The word itself comes from the habit of an upstate New York barkeeper who mixed drinks and decorated 'em with a tail feather from a rooster. People would say "I want one of them cock's tails" and it stuck. Another great American invention.

I invented a cock-tail for one of my customers. I call it the Lilac Crazy cuz that's what the fellah does when he comes in here after fishin'.

The Stone-wall cock-tail is composed of rum and hard cider. It's a good blend. It got its name from another cock-tail called a Stone Fence. The Stone Fence is a cock-tail made of hard cider and sugar water, similar to what we call Jersey Lighting. A barkeep added rum and said "If you fellahs have a hard time climbin' over the Stone Fence, try climbin' this here Stone-wall". That's how it got its name.

Here you are sir, a Stone-wall.

And for you, sir?

One Irish.

We have both Irish and Scotch whiskies as well as corn. We have a lot of Irish people comin' in to Michigan because of that terrible Potato Famine in their homeland. They are sufferin' a lot of oppression in the East. In New York the Irish is all crowded into horrible places called tenements where there is disease, overcrowding, and hunger. Out here, in the West, we have plenty of jobs for Irish. In Detroit they're building the first community outside the city limits. It's called Corktown and its for the Irish. Just West of here is the Irish Hills, mostly Irish settlers there. In Clinton we have our own "Corktown". That's the Northwest section of town.

I don't talk bad about the Irish. If it weren't for the Irish and the Germans, I'd have nobody in my barroom.

Just kiddin' folks. Just kiddin'. I'm half-Irsish me-self, you know.

Here you go, an Irish. No ice, of course. Ice in Irish whisky is considered to be blasphemy by most Irish drinkers, you know.

Now for your over-night accommodations, folks. You'll be sleepin' no more than three or four to a bed. That's men on one side of the room upstairs and women on the other with a big sheet hung in the middle so you ladies got your privacy.

I saw the terror in your eyes, ma'am. If fact, my wife's a church-going lady and she'll be settin' up there to-night at the boundary 'twix the men and the women with a big stick, so there'll be no "sleep-walking", if you know what I mean.

I got one bed up there with only one lady in it now. She was here last night and my wife says she weren't snorin' none at all. She's a real quiet one, she is. If you snore, please wait for the others to get to sleep before you go up there and start sawin' wood.

You three fellahs will be in bed number two on the men's side. If I gotta put another man in with you I'll make sure he's real skinny. Because the other beds are filled, the rest of you men will have to sleep on the bar-room floor. No extra charge. And, from the looks of these fellahs, it won't be the first bar-room floor they fell asleep on.

We do shake out the sheets before you get into the bed so you won't have to worry about havin' any bed-bugs or any other critters in with you. That's unless you brought some along with you, of course. And, ladies, we wash the sheets at the end of each and every month! I know most taverns just leave the sheets on the bed 'til they wear out, but we wash 'em monthly whether they need it or not.

We'll bring water up in the morning so you can wash up some before comin' down to breakfast. A nice pitcher of warm water and a wash bowl. And, of course, on Saturday, you can take your weekly bath here, no extra charge.

Just like you do at home—we'll set up the bathing tub in the kitchen. Then we'll have children haul the water fresh in from the creek. They'll filter out the fish, the frogs, and the leaches and carry the water into the kitchen. We'll heat it up there and fill up the tub. After each and every ten people take a bath—we'll change the water.

The fish, leaches and frogs? Of course, we don't waste 'em. The fish we use for bait or serve for food, dependin' on their size. The leaches we sell to the barber or the doctors for their medicinal use. And the frogs? We sell them to a French family in town I think they eat 'em!

And in your bath, there ain't no charge for the use of the soap. We make out soap just like the ladies do at home. We save our meat grease while cookin' and when we got a full bucket we strain it. Meanwhile we put an ash barrel with holes in the bottom of it in a big tub. Then we put twigs and branches in the barrel and fill it with ashes from the fireplaces. Next we pour buckets of water through the ashes and that leaches out the lye. After that we take the ash water and the grease out back and cook it up in a big caldron over a fire. The mixture cures into lye soap. If its soft cure it's soft soap good for washin' floors. If it's hard cure it's hard soap. That's good for bathin'. It'll get the dirt off you and kill any bugs you might have in your hair.

The only trouble with usin' lye soap to wash your hair is that after a while your hair falls out. That means if you ladies are lookin' for a man of maturity to marry, be sure to pick one with some scalp showin' through on top. It means he's been clean all his life. If you find a man of advanced years with a big bushy head of hair, you know he ain't been washin' through the years.

In the winter we don't usually offer baths. Most people don't bath in the cold weather because it ain't healthy. I don't want to use the "N word" in front of ladies but we don't get "all undressed" in the winter. We wash our hands and face daily—them's the only parts hangin' out of your clothes to get dirty. We wait 'til the spring for an all-over bath. That's where we get the tradition of havin' a June wedding. That's right after everyone's spring bath so the wedding party is relatively clean. If you get married in March—the church can get a bit gamy.

Besides, you don't get that dirty in the winter. You're not plowin' your fields, or nothin'.

If any of you folks are travelin' west, toward Chicago, your next overnight could be Walker's Tavern in the Irish Hills. It's seventeen miles from here but that could be a day's travel for you. Most of the time on a clear and dry road you go fifty miles, or so, in a day. You stop every ten miles to change teams of horses. That stop may give you a chance to get out of the coach to stretch your legs, straighten your spine and, maybe, find a tavern to get a couple of drinks to give you the courage to get back into the coach. But, in the Irish Hills, you may go no more than fifteen or twenty miles a day. Your coach will pull to the bottom of one of them rollin' hills and stop. All the passengers have to get out and walk up to the top of the hill to meet the coach up there and get back in. That slows you down considerable! After the Irish Hills you're back to makin' fifty miles a day, if it don't rain none. If it rains, I ain't promisin' nothin'.

The Walker's Tavern is a good place to stay but I'd be careful about eatin' anywhere in Cambridge Junction where it's located. Last year a Cambridge Junction caterer was accused of puttin' horsemeat in his rabbit stew! Can you imagine that? Well, he denied it all year and he was finally taken to court over it. And, of course, when you get before the judge you gotta tell the truth, unless you're a Washington politician, I hear. And the judge asked the man and he said, "Your Honor, I *do* put *a little bit* of horse meat in my rabbit stew." Well, the judge was from Michigan, so he was used to that sort of equivocation talk. He asked, "What do you mean by the words, 'a little bit'"?

"Half and half", the caterer answered.

"And what do you mean by 'half and half?'"

"One horse and one rabbit," was his reply.

Well, you don't have to be worried about that here. Whatever we say you've a-gettin'—you get. And if you have the beef that's on our menu, rest assured that I count the number of horses that come into the barn each night and the ones that come out in the morning. I make sure it's the same number. I gotta eat here, too, you know.

If anyone's headed east, you should be able to make Detroit in one day. It's only fifty miles and that'll take you ten hours. That's if it don't rain the first ten miles from here to Saline. That part of the road's still dirt road—mud road if it rains. After that you'll be on a plank road and make Ypsilanti (ten miles) in two hours. From there, it's ten more miles, or two hours, to Derby's Corners, ten more miles, or two hours, to Dearbornville, and then just two more hours to Detroit. Those towns are all pretty interesting.

Saline is a place of about two-hundred people. It's right on the Saline River. The river was named that for the natural salt deposits along its run. The town was plotted by a fellah named Orange Rankin who was a surveyor for the government. He was surveyin' for the military road that we call the Chicago Road. Saline now is where the plank road ends that comes this way out of Detroit. Rankin liked the area along the Saline River so much he bought it and founded the town of Saline.

From there you travel on to Ypsilanti which was named in 1825 by Michigan's Judge Woodward for a personal hero of his, Dimitrius Ypsilanti. Ypsilanti was a hero of the Greek war of independence from the Ottoman Empire. On April 21 of 1825 the town was formed and the founders heard there was a party of Indians comin' their way. I was there at the time 'cause they were givin' out free food and cider. We quickly armed ourselves only to find that the Indians where comin' to celebrate with us. We had quite a party, I can tell you.

Ypsilanti is one of the ways we Michiganians know if someone's a newcomer to our state. The town's name is pronounced as it was *IP*-SA-LANT-TEE. Outsiders always say *YIP*-SIL-LANT-TEE and give themselves away.

The next town east is Derby's Corners that some folks want to rename Wayne, Michigan. It's named for the prominent tavern in town, Derby 's Tavern. It used to be Johnson's Tavern, but Johnson got himself hanged for killin' his wife. That was before Michigan became a state and did away with capital punishment. Johnson was lucky. If he had waited a year to kill his wife, he'd be in prison still instead of in the history books. Ezra Derby plotted the town and named it for himself.

There there's Dearbornville. That town of 248 souls is named for Henry Dearborn, a general and hero in the War of 1812 and the American Revolution. Fort Dearborn that became Chicago was named for him, too. Dearbornville sits at the Rouge River; part of a series of branches, all named the Rouge River. The French called the river that for their word for red because of the red clay along its banks. And that river's clean enough to drink out of. Before it was called Dearbornville, the place was Ten Eyck after Conrad Ten Eyck's Tavern that was located there. It was part of Bucklin Township named for an early settler, A. J. Bucklin. It was also called Pekin but was renamed Dearbornville

The biggest employer in Dearbornville is the Army. There is an arsenal on the north side of the Chicago Plank Road in Dearbornville that protects the western approach to Detroit. We're not about to have our supply lines cut again as we did in the War of 1812.

And, with all those solders in town, there's gonna be a need for more barrooms. Dearbornville will get even bigger.

There's a young fellah I know there. His name is William Ford. He lives with his family and farms just outside of town in Greenfield Township. Will Ford's family came to American just three years ago, in 1847, from County Cork in Ireland. Their hometown in County Cork is the town of Fairlane. There's a terrible famine going on over there and the Fords were one of the many Irish families which came to America because of it. Theirs is a farmin' family and William's a fine young fellah. He's thinkin' about the day when he'll have a family and a farm of his own. And, like I said, Dearbornville is named for *Henry* Dearborn. William Ford is so taken with that name, he says if he ever has a son, he'd like to call him either Henry Ford, or Dearborn Ford. He ain't quite made up his mind.

I told him to stick to the shorter of the two names. Save the boy a little writin' over his time. Besides, Henry Ford sounds more like the owner of a company rather than the dealership!

From Dearbornville to Detroit is only another ten miles—two more hours. But, it's too late to make the trip to Detroit from here to-day. There ain't enough day-light left and you can only travel in the day-light. The roads are nearly impassable in the day and impossible at night. No— night's for sleep—day's for travel.

Dearborn was at one time called Pekin for the Chinese town. There were three places in Michigan named that way—Pekin, Nankin, and Canton. The last two are still there. The folks who named those places just did it 'cause they liked the names, not because they had any connection to China.

When you get to Detroit you'll find quite a city. The population of that town has grown to 20,019. Just thirteen years ago, in 1837 when Michigan became at state, Detroit only had eight thousand people living in it. Now it's grown considerably. It's a town of business with warehouses, shops, hotels, taverns and many cigar-rollin' facilities. Most people don't think of Detroit as a cigar center, but it is. Most of the best cigars in the West come from Detroit. The cigars are made from tobacco brought to Detroit from elsewhere and rolled into fine cigars by immigrant women and children in small factories.

One of the most famous cigar-rollin' facilities in Detroit is one owned by T. C. Miller. By all accounts it is a building just about as wide as this here tavern and about as long. It's a two-story building with the tobacco stored upstairs and the rollin' of cigars occurrin' on the first floor. And, also on the first floor, without any separation, is the stable. The, shall we say "horsy material" gets mixed in with the tobacco that gives Miller's cigars a particular "horsy" smell and taste. It became so popular the other cigar rollers stop by stables and barns to pick up some "raw material" to mix in with their cigars to "keep up with the competition". So, if you ladies think the cigars stink in your town, just imagine how they are in Detroit!

Detroit itself is a large place, almost a mile square. It's bounded by the Detroit River on the South, Grand Circus Park on the North, Dequindre Avenue on the East, and Eighth Street on the West. They're building the first residential community outside the Detroit city-limits—it's called "Corktown" and it's for the Irish.

Yes, sir? An other ale? Certainly. Here you are—one more slice of bread.

Now, for your overnight accommodations, I got you three fellahs in bed number two on the men's side upstairs. You ladies will be in bed number one on the ladies' side. You fellahs over there will be together in bed number one on the men's side.

You bar-room sleepers can sleep on the floor or on the bench over there. It ain't too uncomfortable. If you'd rather, you can sleep in the barn, out back. And, from the looks of things upstairs—the barn's gonna smell a lot better.

Another Stone-wall, Ma'am? Certainly. Here, I ain't gonna give you a clean glass—I didn't give you a clean glass the first time.

Rum. Hard cider. Ice. A Stone-wall. And, a macaroni sucker, of course.

Now, you notice when I put one of these macaroni suckers in your drink I always break a piece off an end. That's so it won't be so long you could accidentally tip over your drink with it. But, you *never* break a sucker in half. That's 'cause "you never give a sucker an even break"!

I made that up.

So where is it that you folks are travelin' from?

Chicago? Well, that's convenient with us being on the Chicago Road and all. Chicago's a big town now—almost thirty thousand people live there. Just some twenty years ago there were only ninety-eight people in what is now Chicago. There was only Wolf Point and the old Fort Dearborn. Then they started building the great Illinois and Michigan Canal and Chicago just grew like mad. At first they laid out a plot for the town that looked like a checker-board. There were going to be blocks for houses, blocks for commercial buildings, and blocks for parks—all in equal numbers. Then they found out how much people were willin' to pay for the land there and they decided they really didn't need all them parks after all.

It's quite the city now, 'though. The new John Deere Plow Company's there in Illinois not far from Chicago and Cyrus McCormick's Reaping Machine Company is right in town. We have a fellah, Dan'l Brown, who often stays here and he's a sales-agent for McCormick. If anyone here is lookin' to buy a new reaper—see Dan'l. He'll do well by you. Just don't play Euchre with him.

Chicago's gettin' a lot of emigrants movin' in from other places—Irish and Germans—just like the rest of us. In fact there was an Irish family comin' through here the other day on the way to Chicago. Their name was—O'Leary. I'm sure they'll be a fine asset to the community. I sold

Catherine O'Leary a lantern and told her to keep it steady—it leaks along one edge. Her and her kicky-foot cow.

So you Chicagoans might want to remind Mrs. O'Leary of that when you get back home.

You can get to Chicago in six days from Detroit, if every thing goes right—if the horses all stay alive, the stage don't break down, and it don't rain any, that is. Usually, one of them things happen, so count an eight day trip to Chicago and be prepared for a ten day one.

Now, if a horse dies along the way, that's good news and bad news. The bad news is—you'll be late to where you're goin'. The good news is—you'll have a fine stew when you get there—and plenty of it!

There's a Doctor Evans in Chicago who's investin' money in land to the north of the City—maybe he'll let you in on his ideas. It might be worth a small investment.

Chicago's got a rail-road now—the Galena and Chicago. It don't go all the way to Galena yet but they still call it the Galena and Chicago anyway. But there's more rail-roads a-comin' to Chicago. Your Senator Douglass, Stephan A. Douglass, just got a bill through Congress to construct a rail-road south from Chicago through central Illinois all the way down to Mobile, Alabama. That'll be the first North-South rail-road in America. That'll sure bring more business to you Chicago folks, let me tell you.

Of course Senator Douglass has everyone convinced that donatin' government land to the rail-road as a right of way won't cost us nothin'. He reasons that if we build a rail-road through government owned lands that'll make the land we don't give away more valuable and it won't cost us nothin'. I'd like to see that—a government program that don't cost us nothin'!

You're a-buildin' plank roads, too, just like us in Michigan. The Southwestern Plank Road is open to Doty's Tavern and now the Northwestern Plank Road is opperatin' 'tween Chicago and Oak Ridge along Milwaukee Avenue. They're hopin' to build more, too. Ain't a bad place to be—Chicago.

And you folks? Are you from Chicago, or are you from some civilized place?

Lansing? I thought you said civilized!

Lansing, Michigan is our new state capitol. It's only two days from Detroit. To get there you take the stage to Detroit, ten hours, and spend the night there. Then take the Detroit and Howell Plank Road. It's planked all the way to Howell, so you can make Howell from Detroit in ten hours, or so. You'll change horses at Greenfield, then at East Farmington, or Farmington, dependin' on in which town your stage company has its barn. Then you change again in Novi or Hickville. The next stop is the New Hudson Station. From there you go through the town of Kensington and stop at Brighton. Howell's you next stop and your overnight. The next day, it's Cedar, LeRoy, Williamstown, Hamilton, and Lansing by night-fall.

When they moved the state capitol from Detroit two years ago, in 1848—from Detroit to Lansing—that was good news and bad news for Detroit. The bad news is—they lost a lot of business because of the capitol movin'. The good news is—they got rid of all them politicians!

I like the governor, John Berry. He's the only man in our history who got elected governor of Michigan for two, non-consecutive terms. We kept forgettin' how bad he was.

He's done a good job this time, 'though. He's developed plans to lure Germans and other immigrants to Michigan. He's got people plantin' sugar beets in the Saginaw Valley, somethin' that may catch on.

So, if you Lansing folks run into Governor Berry, be sure to say "Howdy" from me, will you?

Now, as for your meals. Your fifty-cents will get you two meals and a place in the bed—or on the floor for you fellahs. You can have dinner and supper, or supper and breakfast. Your choice. Dinner's bein' served soon, the big meal of the day. Supper's later—usually left-overs from the dinner. At home most women just put doilies over the dinner food to keep the flies off and leave it on the table for supper. Here, we'll scrape the left-overs onto platters and you can help yourself at supper.

Before you choose your meals be aware that we're a little short on meats for breakfast tomorrow—we only got four. You'll have your fried sausage, fried bacon, fried hog jowl, and fried pork chops. Because that ain't enough meat for most people, we'll fry your potatoes, onions, and pancakes in the bacon grease so it'll be good and healthy for you.

Breakfast is served promptly at six in the morning. That'll give you at least an hour before the first coach leaves the tavern. You can sit out on the porch and hold you belly and moan for a while.

Yes, Ma'am?

Me? You wanna know about me?

Well, I ain't nothin' special. I was born in Kentucky in the later part of the last century. My Pa came to America from Ireland where he was recruited to join the English Army to come over and fight the Boys of Freedom here. He was in a pub—that's what they call a bar-room over there—in Dublin when he took the "King's shilling".

The English Army recruiter offers you a shilling as your first pay and if you accept it—that's enlistment. In Ireland they used to drop a shilling into a beer mug and buy prospects a beer. You drain the mug and as soon as the shilling touches your lips, "you're in the army now"!

That's how my Pa got "recruited". From then on he always drank beer out of glasses or mugs with glass bottoms.

He came to America, "Ameri-kay" he called it, to fight the Boys of Freedom but at one of them battles he saw all the guns that Washington had pointed his way and he decided that becomin' a Continental sounded like a good idea. That night he changed sides and we've been Americans ever since. My Pa changed his last name from McCully to Cully just in case the English won the war and the king was lookin' for him. We've been Cullys since then.

After the war my Pa married my Ma, an English girl, Isabel Currier originally from Kent in England. So, I'm the product of a "mixed marriage". Both sides of the family disowned 'em. Both the English and the Irish thought their children were "marryin' down."

My folks moved to Kentucky where I was born. We lived near the capitol of Danville, but in 1800 we moved to Indiana for the Harrison Land Act. Government land was for sale and my Pa wanted some. But when we got to Indiana we found land cost over three dollars an acre! No one could afford that so we worked for another family until 1805 when the New Land Act went into effect. It provided land for $1.20 an acre with ten years to pay the government for it. That's when we became official Hoosiers.

"Hoosier" No one really knows what people from Indiana are called that. At first it weren't no complement. It was a word much like "Hillbilly". Some say it was because so many newcomers came in from 1800 to 1805 that every time you rolled by a new place you'd call out "Who's here?" That became Hoosier.

Anyway, I grew up on the farm near Vincennes, which was the capitol of Indiana in those days. In 1811 I was part of the force William Henry Harrison led to attack the huge Shawnee encampment along the Tippicanoe River. The Indians came out to attack us, but we whipped 'em.

That was a victory, but it only made the Shawnees mad. They joined up with the English in 1812 to fight us all over again. Their leader was the great war chief, Tecumseh, a man I feared and learned to respect. You know, you come to respect your enemies after a while, or you should.

In that war I was part of the force that crossed the Detroit River at the outbreak of the war in 1812 to take Canada for America. Our commander in Detroit, General William Hull, heard about the beginnin' of the war before the Canadian garrison in Sandwich. Sandwich is called Windsor now, just to make it sound fancy, I suppose. Anyway, we crossed the river in long canoes and the Canadians thought we were comin' over to gamble with 'em, or somethin'. We occupied the place for about five weeks during the summer of 1812. Then we heard there was a force of regular British soldiers comin' from York—it became Toronto recently—to challenge us and we looked around and decided we didn't want Canada after all. We went home.

After the war I was mustered out in Indiana. I didn't want to go back to the farm like my brother did and I sure didn't want to be a soldier any more. So I just traveled a bit, endin' up at Wolf Point—that's Chicago now. There I fell in love with a barkeeper's daughter and he said I couldn't marry his girl unless I had a good profession. He taught me his and I've been a barkeep ever since.

My wife? Yes, she's here with me. This November we'll be married thirty wonderful years! Thirty out of thirty-three one ain't so bad.

Just kiddin', I hope my wife can't hear

Anyway, we moved to Michigan in 1830 and by then had our three children with us. I barkeeped in Pontiac, Michigan and, later in Detroit and Ypsilanti. I've been here in Clinton since 1844, six years ago.

Yes, sir? An other ale? Certainly.

And you, ma'am?

One more Stone-wall, comin' up.

I hope you folks have had a good time so far in my barroom. You're table's ready for your dinner, so you'd better get to it. The first ones there get the first choice of the food, you know. I'll take you in to our dining room now. If you come back to the barroom maybe we'll sing a few songs before supper and bed.

Drink Recipes for Chapter One

PLANTER'S PUNCH

Pour 1 to 1 ½ ounce of dark Jamaican Rum into an eight-ounce glass filled with shaved or cracked ice. Add ½ ounce of simple syrup. Fill with fresh squeezed lemonade and add three shakes of Angostura aromatic bitters. Add a macaroni sucker.

To make simple syrup—heat ½ water and ½ white sugar until the sugar is dissolved.

Angostura bitters is a mixture of alcohol, barks and vegetable flavorings. It is readily available at most food stores.

STONE-WALL COCK-TAIL

Pour 1 to 1 ½ ounce of dark Jamaican Rum into an eight-ounce glass filled with shaved or cracked ice. Fill with hard cider. Add a macaroni sucker.

Hard cider is fermented apple cider. The best for a Stone-wall is a medium dry one at about 6 to 6½ % alcohol. It is available in many food stores and wine shops.

JERSEY LIGHTNING or STONE-FENCE COCK-TAIL

Fill an eight-ounce glass with shaved or cracked ice. Pour in 1 ounce of simple syrup and fill with hard cider. Shake four shakes of bitters. Add a macaroni sucker.

CORN WHISKEY COCK-TAIL

Fill an eight-ounce glass with shaved or cracked ice. Add 2 ounces of corn whiskey and fill with simple syrup. Add three shakes of bitters. Add a macaroni sucker.

VANILLA PUNCH

Fill a twelve-ounce glass with shaved or cracked ice. Add 1 to 1 ½ ounce of brandy, 1 ounce of vanilla extract, and 1 ounce of simple syrup. Fill with fresh squeezed lemonade. Add a macaroni sucker.

LEMON PUNCH

Fill an eight-ounce glass with shaved or cracked ice. Add 1 to 1 ½ ounces of Apricot brandy. Fill with fresh squeezed lemonade. Add a macaroni sucker.

CHERRY SHRUB

Fill a twelve-ounce glass with shaved or cracked ice. Add 1 to 1 ½ ounce of brandy. Add 3 ounces of sweetened cherry syrup. Fill with carbonated water (soda water). Add a macaroni sucker.

SHERRY COBBLER

Fill an eight-ounce glass with shaved or cracked ice. Add one teaspoonful of powdered sugar or one-ounce of simple syrup. Fill with a dry medium dry sherry.

MULLED CIDER A LA SILAS

In a large pot of cider mill apple cider, add one orange cut in half. Into a muslin or linen bag put five sticks of cinnamon, ten cloves, three whole nutmegs and one whole allspice. Tie the bag and add to the cider. Bring to a boil then lower the heat to simmer for an hour or two. Add ½ cup of honey. Serve hot in a mug with 2 ounces of dark Jamaican rum. Add a cinnamon stick, if desired.

CHAPTER TWO: DINNER

I'm glad you found your way to the table, folks. Your meal'll begin with soup and bread. To-day we got a great soup—It's Butternut Squash Soup.

Yeah, yeah, I know for them's that not eaten squash soup it sounds terrible, but let me assure you, our squash soup is a real treat. It's rich with cream and thick enough to fully coat your spoon and stay there if you turn the spoon upside down over your bowl. It's sweet and real good to eat. It's served quite hot, too.

After the soup you'll be gettin' Chicken Pie. That's served like a chicken stew with a crust over it. It's not baked in the crust like a potpie. That's not a bad way to make a meat pie, but the crust gets all soggy and, sometimes, you think you're bitin' into a piece of meat and really you've got a piece of crust on your fork. I hate that, myself.

So we cook a nice chicken stew, then put a separately baked crust on top it on your plate. It's good eatin'.

After the Chicken Pie you'll be offered the meat. We got a nice cut of beef, roasted 'til it's tender and tasty. It's served with a sauce like a gravy. The sauce has a nice touch of red wine in it. Mrs. Wood used claret, like we serve in the barroom. That enriches the sauce and gives it a good flavor.

Oh, sir, I'm sorry, most of the alcohol cooks off it so you'll still have to order a drink.

With the meal comes vegetables, both hot and cold, and fresh baked breads. All our vegetables come from Mister Wood's farm and the breads are baked fresh every day right here at the Tavern. Whatever bread we don't use goes into the puddings or is fed to the birds outside. We never reuse our breads on the table.

Speakin' of pudding, we got a good one for you to-day. It's a Suet Pudding served with a vanilla sauce or with marmalade. You'll love it. It's thick baked with the best ingredients—eggs, chopped suet, bread crumbs and milk. Other things are in there, too, but that's ladies' business.

Now, for the rules of the dinin' room.

That there little bowl on your table is filled with salt. It ain't sugar. Don't put any of it in your coffee unless you like salty coffee. And don't use your fingers to pick it out of that little bowl, either. I don't know where your fingers have been. Use the tip of your knife if you haven't used your knife. Just dip it into the salt, then sprinkle the salt onto your food. If you've already used your knife, then use the heel of your fork. Just keep them fingers out of the salt.

If you need pepper, we got it. Pepper is very expensive. It comes all the way from Malibar in the Spice Islands. We keep it locked up in the kitchen. If you require some, let us know and I'll unlock the cabinet and get you some. Use as much as you want, but if you walk out of here sneezin', I'm gonna have to have you searched!

Nothing personal, sir.

Please notice your knives and folks and how they're placed on the table in front of you. The knife if above your place with the tip facin' to the left. The fork is placed to the left of your plate with the tines down. Miss Catherine Beecher brings this setting to us from Connecticut in her recently published book. She is the sister of Harriet Beecher Stowe who now is teachin' with her husband at Bowdoin College and also the sister of the Reverend Henry Ward Beecher, who holds America's premiere pulpit at the Plymouth Congregational Church of Brooklyn, New York. Comin' from a family like that you know she knows how to set a proper table.

Miss Beecher says that simplicity is elegance. That's why we set things like they are on the table. You can pick up your fork in your left hand and pick up your knife in your right and just start eatin'. No fuss. No changin' hands. That works to your advantage when you're eatin' at must taverns. Most of the time a platter is put on the table and everyone shares the food on it. The fastest ones get the most food and to have your eatin' utensils at the ready really helps.

Oh, and by the way, here at the Eagle Tavern we don't do you that way. We give everyone here a clean plate to start. Many taverns have tin plates that are nailed right to the table. When you're hungry, you stand behind someone who's eatin' and when he's done you replace him, usin' his plate and utensils. At the end of the day they tip the table on its side and mop it clean. But here we use soap and water to wash the dishes in between each and every use.

And we wash our dishes even when they don't need it. If you use your bread and wipe up all your gravy and your plate don't need washin'—we wash it anyway! That how fancy we are.

And we don't do it like a lot of you folks do it at home—just by havin' a dog lick it clean. We use soap and water—most of the time.

Now, you don't see any spoons on your table. Once we bring out the soup, you'll be gettin' some spoons. And if you want coffee or tea, we'll bring spoons out for that, too. It's just that Miss Beecher says that spoons just clutter the table and we don't want clutter to disrupt our simply elegant presentation, do we?

If you want coffee or tea, they are available and hot. Pots of each are hangin' over the fire as we speak. We got a nice Mocha Java Coffee. That's not chocolate flavor, you know. Mocha in 1850 means rich and Java is the island in the Dutch East Indies where the coffee beans are grown. It's expensive to get in Michigan, but well worth the price.

We have two teas. One is Gunpowder Tea. No, there's no gunpowder in it. It's Chinese Green Tea brewed from the unfermented green and yellow leaves of the tea plant. Black tea comes from fermented tea leaves and is quire different. It like the Gunpowder tea with milk, but you can drink it by itself, or with sugar, if you wish. Ask for sugar if you need some and we'll bring it out. The Spanish embargo of molasses shipments to America has forced up the price of sugar. In Michigan we get most of our sugar from maple tree sap boiled and processed into a good sugar. They're plantin' sugar cane in Louisiana so that'll be a domestic source of sugar and molasses.

The other tea is a nice Mint Tea. It's made with black tea and mint leaves brewed together. It's quite refreshin'.

Oh, one caution about the Gunpowder Tea. We can't give you more than one pot of it. After more than one pot of Gunpowder Tea you start shootin' off your mouth!

That's an old Eagle Tavern joke.

So am I.

Now, as far as wines with your dinner—we got three table wines. The first is a Hock. That's a German wine. The first German wines to America came from the Hochheim, a region of the Rhinegau. By 1850 "Hock" is a generic term for any German white wine. "Hoch" which is pronounced "hock" means "high" in the German language and more than a few people feel that was after a few glasses of Hock.

For Hock we serve a Rheinhessen Leibfraumilch. It's not the best German wine but not the worst, either. Leibfraumilch literally means "Love Lady Milk" because it was first made at the Leibfrau Kirsch, the Church of Our Lady of Love in the Rhinehessen. It goes well with some chicken dishes, fish, some pork and lots of cheeses.

I had a fellah come in here when Mister Wood was serving some imported cheese all the way from Switzerland. The man looked at that cheese and frowned. "I hate cheese with holes in it," he complained.

Mister Wood told him, "Then just eat around the holes."

As Claret we are servin' a rather new wine from France, a Cabernet Sauvignon. This is a new grape that was planted about ten years ago in France. It's now replacin' the Cabernet Franc because it travels better than that wine. It takes at least two months to sail from France to America so you need a wine that can travel good in the hold of a sailin' ship. This

Claret is one. It's a dry red wine that goes well with red meat, especially beef. It's also good with hearty pork dishes, some chicken, well-seasoned veal, and hearty cheeses.

The final wine is the ever-popular Cider Wine, our hard cider. It goes with anything you're eatin'. It's fermented apple cider at about five percent alcohol and has a great tingle on your tongue as you drink

Most of the drink you carried in here goes good with food, too. Cocktails gets your taste buds ready for the repast and punches settle your stomach to receive the meal. The Stone-wall will help you eat something you don't like and the Corn Whiskey will disguise the taste of any food that's gone bad. Not that you'll be gettin' any of that here.

If anyone wants fish, we have a good pan-fried Trout we can bring out. Mister Wood's down at the Raisin River just about every day fishin' for trout so we have plenty. We fillet it and then dip the fillets into seasoned flour. After that it's pan-fried golden bronze in a big pan of butter. Mrs. Wood finishes the Trout with a lemon sauce that's her specialty. If you like fish, you'll love this one. Just let us know and we'll start fryin' one for you.

Mister Wood? Yeah, he's quite the fisherman. And quite a good salesman, too. The other day he was down at the river fishin' and a city fellah dipped his line in the water. Well Calvin looked over at the other fellah and asks, "What kind of a fish mirror are you usin' to-day/"

The city fellah looks at Mr. Wood and asks back, "What's a fish mirror?"

Calvin holds up a little round mirror and tells the man that you tie it on the end of your line and the fish sees it at a distance. Thinkin' it's another fish and being a sociable kinda creature, the fish swims to say howdy and that brings it right up to your bait. "You catch more fish that way," Calvin said.

"I never heard of that, but it sounds reasonable," the city fellah said. "Where can I buy one?"

"Well, it just so happens, I sells 'em," Calvin smiled. "They're five cents each."

So the city fellah bought one from Calvin and tied it on his line. "So, sir, how many have you caught to-day?' he asked.

"You're my first one!" Calvin replied.

That Calvin is quite the jokester, you know. But he does catch good fish.

So, I hope you enjoy what we have to eat and I'll see you in the bar-room when you're done. I'll have Ilene, Calvin and Harriet's daughter, come over and take your orders.

Excuse me. I don't want to interrupt you dinner none but I got real good news for you two ladies. You know I had you assigned to the bed tonight with that one lady who was here from last night. The quiet one? Well, it t urns out she weren't sleepin'—she's dead! That means, after they haul the body outta the bed, there'll be more room in the bed for you two to-night.

And, it weren't like she was coughin' or nothin' so she didn't pass of Cholera or Consumption or anything else you gotta worry about. I think she just died of old age. She was almost sixty, you know.

I'll let you ladies know when it's safe to go up to bed. Out of respect for the dead, we ain't gonna take the body down through the dinin' room. Instead we'll throw her out of the window in the back. So, as soon as you see the body drop past that window, you'll know it's all right to go up to bed.

And, rest assured we'll shake the sheets out before you get in the bed.

Change the sheets? Oh, no. We don't need to. She weren't leakin' or nothin'.

Enjoy your meal.

Excuse me, again.

Bad news, ladies—she ain't dead! We grabbed her by her ankles and pulled her out of the bed. Her head hit the floor and she started to moan. So we put her back in the bed. She'll be in with you tonight, but she won't cause you no trouble 'cause she's real sick.

It might work to your benefit if it's cold up there tonight. She's feverish, you know.

Now I'm gonna give you, ma'am, a little mirror. If you could hold it under the sick lady's nose from time to time to check on her breathin', we'd appreciate it.

How's the food, so far?

Glad to hear it.

Ladies—she's dead, again. We had the coroner check her and he says she ain't just ninety percent dead. This time she's one hundred percent dead. So, it'll be fewer people in your bed, after all.

Oh, you people at that other table—there's an openin' in one of the ladies' beds, if you plan to spend the night with us.

Recipes for Chapter Two

SUET PUDDING

Sift together one-cup of flour and one-teaspoonful of baking soda. Blend in one-cup of finely chopped breadcrumbs, one-cup of finely chopped suet, and one cup of sugar. Mix in two well-beaten eggs. Then add enough milk to make it sticky. Turn the pudding into a well-greased pan. Cover with a napkin (foil if you're in the Twenty-first Century) and steam in a steamer for two hours. If you don't have a pudding steamer, you can steam the pudding over boiling water or in a larger pan with water in it. Add water, as needed. Serve with syrup, vanilla sauce, jam, or marmalade.

Suet can be obtained from your butcher. It is the pure white fat that occurs around the kidneys. Any leftover is appreciated by birds in the winter.

BUTTERNUT SQUASH SOUP

Peal and core one butternut squash. Cut the squash into one to two inch pieces and boil in just enough water to cover them. Drain when the squash is well-cooked and mash, and then puree the cooked squash. Mix in two tablespoonsful of butter and one cup of cream. Cook, adding chicken broth or vegetable broth, as needed. Season with salt and pepper. Add sugar, if needed. Add nutmeg and, or mace to taste. A little of those goes a long way to season the soup. Serve hot with sour cream, if desired.

Mace is a spice taken from the outer shell of the nutmeg and has a similar flavor.

CHICKEN PIE

Pluck a well-cleaned chicken. Burn off the pinfeathers and wash inside and out. Cut into pieces for boiling. Boil in enough water to cover. Skim off the fat as it rises. Add carrots, celery, and onions, cut into large pieces. Cook it all until the chicken is falling off the bones. Meanwhile, either boil other carrots, onions, potatoes, and celery or roast these vegetables. Chop them into small pieces when they are soft.

As the chicken cooks, prepare a pastry crust. The crust should be made like piecrust but cut into six-inch rounds or squares. Bake these crispy.

Drain, saving the both. Press the cooked vegetables through a sieve into the broth. Discard the vegetables (put them in the slop bucket for the hogs).

Cool the chicken, then remove all the meat from the bones. Discard the bones and cartilage (slop bucket, again). Chop the meat into small pieces. Chop the separately boiled vegetables and mix them with the chicken meat. Season with salt and pepper. Add freshly chopped parsley and mix well. Heat together with the broth in the fireplace or on a stove if you are fortunate enough to own one. Make a slurry with water and flour. Stir this into the chicken stew to thicken it. Cook over a low flame.

To serve put a goodly helping of the chicken mixture on a plate and top with a pasty crust.

If you are rich and buy your chicken from the butcher already killed and cleaned you may not know how to properly prepare a chicken without help. The chicken must be killed in a humane manner, then gutted. Put the chicken into boiling water to loosen the feathers. Cool and pluck the feathers from the bird. There will be little hair-like "pin feathers" left behind. These may be removed by holding the plucked chicken over a flame to burn them off. The house may smell like burning hair when this is done but the stench quickly dissipates. Wash the chicken well. Salting will help draw out the blood. Rinse well after salting.

ROASTED VEGETABLES

To roast vegetables coat the vegetables with a fine oil. Olive oil is the best, but it is expensive. Place the oiled vegetables in a shallow roasting pan. Place the pan in a very hot oven. Roast until well-done. Season with salt and pepper.

CHAPTER THREE: BACK TO THE BARROOM

Well, I certainly don't need to ask how you people enjoyed your dinner. I can see the satisfaction on your faces. Weren't it good? Glad to hear you liked our victuals.Let's get back to the drinkin'.

An after dinner drink? Perhaps, a nice glass of Port, or a Rainwater.

Port? It's a fortified wine. Ports and Sherries are fermented from grapes. Then some of the wine is distilled into a brandy and that brandy is added back into the wine to bring up its alcohol content. It's stronger than wine but not as powerful as brandy. It makes a 'two, one aged seven years—a Ruby Port that's sweet and one aged fifteen years—a Tawny Port that's dry. Ports originated in Portugal. They were shipped from the port of Oporto there and that's how they got their name. The rainwater is Madeira. Madeira is an island where they grow the grapes for this fortified wine. It's sweet and makes a good after dinner sip. We call it "Rainwater" 'cause it had the color of rainwater in the rain barrel—a golden hue. Yes, whiskey's good after dinner, too. Here you go—a corn whiskey.

And for you, sir?

One Rainwater, comin' up.

Are there any ladies here?

No? Then we can talk politics.

The big issue at our country faces is Henry Clay's Compromise. You fellahs have strong feelin' about it?

I sure do. The bill that would end the slave trade in our nation's capitol is certainly long past due. Northerners and foreign dignitaries have to endure seein' human beings bought and sold right across the street from the White House. It's an abomination! The least thing we can do it to outlaw that.

You agree, right? Sure you do.

Then there's the bill to make Utah and New Mexico territories without regard to slavery. That would be up to them that live there. That sounds fair, but why take the chance of extendin' the horror of human bondage when we have a choice.

Yes, I'm an abolitionist, like so many in Michigan. I know many fine free African men and the thought of my friends in chains is appallin' to me.

Then there is the problem in Utah of how many wives a fellah can have at one time. Until two years ago Utah was a province of Mexico called Deseret. We won it from Mexico in 1848 as part of the Mexican War. Brigham Young is the Territorial Governor and it's mostly Mormons out there. They're fine people. I gotta respect a man who can put up with more than one wife at a time. I have enough trouble with one!

Besides, with every wife comes a mother-in-law!

Another issue is payin' Texas ten million dollars for 'em to give up their claim to New Mexico. We annexed Texas as a state five years ago in 1845 and that ten million dollars was their former national debt when they were a republic. If they fix the boarder where we want, we'll pay their debt. It's quite the good deal for the Texacans. There ain't nothin' in New Mexico worth ten million dollars!

The two other ideas that are part of Senator Clay's Compromise of 1850 I oppose wholeheartedly. The first one is a new Fugitive Slave Act. Until now, if a fugitive made it to a free state he was, effectively safe. Yes, the slave catchers could, and did, come North, but their cases for return were tried in local courts with local judges who, often, opposed the dastardly work of slave catchin'. Delays were imposed and many slave catchers went home without their prey. The local magistrates could find many ways to delay a hearin', you know. As each new adjournment was announced, the slave catchers would have to decide whether to stay in Michigan or go home empty handed. The delays also gave the quarry time to escape to Canada.

The new Fugitive Slave Act will move the jurisdiction to the Federal Courts where there are a lot of Southern and Southern-sympathizin' judges. The act also pays the magistrate more to return a fugitive than to refuse return. It ain't right. This means the work of the Underground Railroad becomes all the more important.

The other issue I oppose is makin' California a state! That would be a terrible thing for our country.

Think about it. Two years ago, when California was a province of Mexico called Alto California it had a total population, not countin' Indians, of only ten thousand people—top to bottom! Yes, now there's a hundred thousand people out there, but that's because of the Gold Rush. Those extra folks are mostly in the Sacramento Valley and once the gold peters, they'll go home and California will have a population of less than ten thousand people. If we make them a state, they'll have two Senators and at least one Congressman, that's in the Constitution, and a population of half of Detroit! Detroit's population is 20,019. Why not make Detroit two states?

It ain't fair.

Besides, the whole territory of California is uninhabitable. The top part is nothin' but mountains and the big trees that are so big around you can't cut 'em down and make anythin' useful outta 'em. And the south part is nothin' but desert and hostile Indians. Havin' Texas in as a state was a mistake. This is gettin' ridiculous!

But, everyone's entitled to his own opinion.

There's a fellah here in town who hopes to make his fortune with takin' folks out to California. Our local cooper (that's a barrel-maker for you city people), Latimer Booth, is assemblin' a crew to go west in the spring. He figures on takin' mail-order brides out to the men in the gold fields and get paid for his efforts. Latimer is also takin' musicians out there to start a whole new industry in California—the entertainment business. Right now, he says, the gold miners don't have nothin' to spend their money on except whiskey and gamblin'—not that there's anythin' wrong with that.

Latimer figures he'll introduce musical entertainment and make some money off that. If you know someone who plays a musical instrument, or sings and is lookin' for adventure, have 'em look up Latimer Booth. And the girls to be mail-order brides gotta be at least 14-years-old and have most of their teeth.

I asked Latimer 'bout the requirement for the women to have teeth and he told me them miners need someone to chew there good for 'em. I don't know if that's true, or no but Latimer's insistin' on it.

Latimer Booth will be leavin' for St. Joseph, Missouri soon. He's already acquired Conestoga wagons there and will be for California from St. Joe. He's also hirin' muleskinners if any of you men need a job.

I just hope Latimer Booth pays his bar bill before he lights out for California.

But back to politics.

Senator Clay says this Compromise will save the Union. I sure hope he's right.

How 'bout local politics? Anyone here in favor of more rail-roads in Michigan.

Yes? Well, I'm not. Rail-roads ain't safe. And I'm not just sayin' that 'cause it's our competition, us bein' in the stagecoach stop business either. Rail-road trains can hit speeds up to thirty-five miles an hour! Science don't yet know what happens to the human body when it goes that fast. It may be safe, but I don't advise folks to take a chance with their health like that.

There's a scientist in one of the German countries who just published a new book about science this year called "Cosmos". His name is Alexander von Humboldt and his book explains everythin' there is to know about things. In it he proposes an idea held by others that all matter, includin' human beings, is made up of little bitty things called atoms. I understand he got the idea from the old Greeks.

Anyway, von Humboldt says these atoms are held together by a force he can't quite fully explain. My personal theory is that the faster you go the weaker that bond gets. If you were to reach thirty-five or forty miles an hour, you'd just be a pile of dust on the seat when you got to your destination. Too horrible to contemplate, ain't it? It's best to stick to the stage-coach, folks.

Beside the stagecoach is a more natural way to travel. A rail-road train spews out filth, smoke, ciders, and stream. The rail-road scares the children, confuses the women. It startles the cows into stop givin' milk and the chickens into stop layin' eggs. If a rail-road goes by your farm, it ruins the soil. If a stagecoach goes by, pulled by a full team of horses, your ground's a little more fertile than it was in the first place, if you get my drift.

I just happen to have a petition here about the rail-roads. If any of you fellahs are Michigan voters, I'll appreciate your signature on it. Here, let me read it to you:

"A PETITION to the HONORABLE JOHN BERRY, GOVERNOR of the STATE OF MICHIGAN, to whit—

That no STATE money be spent to build or extend any rail-road within the State of Michigan and

That no rail-road be allowed to build within one-half mile of any milk cow or egg-layin' chicken."

I think that's fair. They can still built their filthy rail-road with their own money. But it ain't right to spend the money they collect from Mr. Wood from his stagecoach stop business to build our competition. That ain't right. And the second part protects our agriculture.

Anyone to sign?

Thank you, sir. Yes, here's a pen and a bottle of ink for your use.

If you can't write your name, just make your mark. I don't know if the Governor can read, anyway.

Have your wife sign? Oh no. Just voters, sir. Just voters.

I thank you fellahs for your support.

Think about it. All this racin' around is useless. What's you hurry. If we put a rail-road all the way through from Detroit to Chicago, you could make the trip in a day and a half rather than the six or eight days it takes by coach. But, why the rush? Chicago's still gonna be there when you get to it. It's not likes Chicago's gonna burn down, or nothin'.

Oh, gentlemen! A lady has just stepped into the barroom. That means there will be no spittin' on the floor and no foul language. If she leaves you can start spittin' and cussin', again.

And, men, if there ain't no place for a lady to sit, a man's gotta get up and give her his seat. (You walked into the wrong century, didn't you?)

Ma'am, what can I get you to drink?

A Sherry? Certainly. See, fellahs, I told you she was a lady.

Here you go, ma'am, a nice Golden Sherry.

Sherry comes from Spain, from the port of Jerriz. That's where we get its name, an English sort of a way to say that town. It's another fortified wine that goes well with cheese and either before or after dinner. It's a good stomach settler.

Oh, while we're talkin' about drinks, here's a list of drinks that was displayed last year at the El Dorado Saloon in San Francisco. That's where the great bar-keep, Professor Jerry Thomas pour drinks.

This is called "THE TODDY TIMETABLE"

"Good Morning"

6 a.m.—Eye-opener	4 p.m.—Social Drink
7 a.m.—Appetizer	5 p.m.—Invigorator
8 a.m.—Digester	6 p.m.—Solid Straight
9 a.m.—Big Reposer	7 p.m.—Chit—Chat
10 a.m.—Refresher	8 p.m.—Fancy Smile
11 A.M.—Stimulant	9 p.m.—Entre Act
12 m.—Ante-lunch	10 p.m.—Sparkler
1 p.m.—Settler	11 p.m.—Rouser
2 p.m.—A la Smithe	12 p.m.—Night Cap
3 p.m.—Cobbler	"Good Night"

That sounds reasonable, don't it?

Check your pocket watches, gentlemen, and see what drink is due.

Sir? A corn whiskey? Certainly.

So where you from?

Kentucky! That's where I was born. We're probably cousins, you know. And being kin of mine, I'm gonna make you pay in advance.

Just jokin', sir. Just jokin'.

Well, well, well. Look who's here. Lady and Gentlemen, this fellah who just came into the barroom is John Madigan, the only man who ever took me for a free drink! That's quite an accomplishment.

How are you, Johnny?

How did he do it? Well, let me tell you. Remember, John? He came in here last year durin' a very hot day in August and the barroom was filled with flies. John comes up to the bar and was honest about it.

"Silas," he said, "I ain't got no money, but I sure could use a drink. You got any work for me to do?"

I looked around at all them flies and said, "Sure, John. If you could kill all these flies, it'd be worth a free drink."

"I guarantee it," says he and, stupid me, I poured the drink before he did the work. We he drank down the Irish I poured him then stepped out of the door, onto the porch. He put up his fists and shouted back in, "Send 'em out one at a time."

That's why John Madigan pays first.

What will it be, Johnny? Irish? Of course.

Here you are, one Irish Whiskey—ten cents.

We're servin' Bushmills Irish. They've been distillin' Bushmills since 1608 in Northern Ireland. It's a Protestant whiskey, but a good one. Right, John?

John here plays the fiddle and I see he's brought his fiddle along with him. Anyone want to hear a tune? Maybe we can sing along. I've got songbooks here. Here, let me distribute 'em.

If you can read, please sit or stand next to someone who can't.

John Madigan will lead us in some popular tunes. We have Stephen Foster music and others, too. Sing loud enough for then to hear us outside to get 'em to come in, but not so loud they'll call the police.

Let's start with O Susanna! That's a great tune, ain't it? Everybody sing out now.

All right. That was pretty good. Now turn the page to Old Style. That's one of my favorites. That's a Steven Foster tune, too, you know.

Next is Shady Grove. I particularly like the last verse, but that's a personal preference.

Camptown Races is another Foster tune. Let's sing that next. It's just published in 1850 and I'm interested to hear if you folks like it, it bein' a new song and all. Let's go.

Now for Ring, Ring the Banjo. That's an earlier Steven Foster song. I like it. It's a happy one and, in this version, mentions a barkeep.

That was great, folks. You're all in good voice. I guess that's the effect of our drinks.

Stephen Foster wrote some of them tunes. He just got married this year in Pittsburgh, Pennsylvania. He and his new wife are movin' to New York. I guess he figures he can sell more music there. Three years ago he wrote the first song we sang—Oh Susanna! The song has become one of the most popular songs even written. Durin' the presidential campaign two years ago, in 1848, all three major candidates for President used the tune for campaign songs. A lady in the work of the Underground Rail-road, one Sojourner Truth, as she now calls herself, wrote a freedom song to the tune. "Oh Susanna, don't you cry for me. I'm gonna up North to Canada where all the slaves are free." They sing that song as they "follow the Drinking Gourd" north from slavery.

Foster sold all future rights to the song to Christy of the Christy Minstrels for the sum of $100.00. That's no small amount, bein' a third of a workin' man's annual income, by Christy goes on to make ten thousand dollars off it! That's a million dollars in your time's money.

But, I suppose, people will remember Foster long after they forget who Christy was.

The other song we sang was Old Style. That's a very popular barroom hymn in 1850. It recalls the old days when our fathers came to the West and links us with 'em. I like it.

Yes, sir?

The privy? Sure, it's inside. Go to the front door to the Tavern and turn left. That's that side of you. There's two. One says "MEN" and the other says "WOMEN". If you can't read, yours is the one with the least number of letters on it.

People don't realize it, but indoor plumbin' has been possible since the 1790s. Invented in England, the "water closet" allows the "outhouse" to be indoors. It's a system of piping that has a box filled with water on the wall over a seat where you do what needs to be done. The water can be flushed through.

Even after more than fifty years since its invention, it's still not very popular. There are two reasons for that.

First, indoor plumbing is very expensive. You have to have water pressure to make it work and the only way to do that is to build a cistern on top of your house and collect rain water in it to use to fill the water closet. Otherwise, you'd be pumpin' and pumpin' all day. Even in the cities, where there is a water system, there's really no pressure to the houses. In Detroit, for instance, this year they just put in a 120 horse power steam pump that pumps raw water from the Detroit River through Tamarack logs that are burrowed out in the center to serve as pipes. The water come to the houses but people still have to pump it in.

The other reason no one wants indoor privies, is a social one. That's just not the kind of thing you want people doin' inside your house! I mean, you've got to eat and sleep in your house. You don't want people doin' THAT in there.

Besides, if a lady start headin' that way, everyone will know what she's goin' to do! How embarrassin'! Most fellahs don't even think ladies do that sort of thing.

No, it's best for most, after dinner to take a "constitutional" walk and head back to the house by way of the outhouse. No one's the wiser.

We moved ours indoors last year out of necessity. The boys kept tippin' over the outhouse. They either tipped it over, or moved it over, just a bit. That would be disconcertin' if you walked out there at night and took a wrong step. Of course, that would mean you get a place in the bed to yourself that night—and for a few nights to come!

I heard this story about a farmer down the road—Johnson—who got his outhouse tipped over. He called in his son, Johnny, who was the primary suspect in the case. He questioned the boy. "Johnny," said Johnson, "before I ask you about that outhouse incident, I'm gonna tell you a story from history. When George Washington was a little boy he chopped down his father's cherry tree. His father called him in and asked him, 'George Washington, did you cut down my cherry tree?' George Washington said, 'Father, I cannot tell a lie. I cut down the cherry tree'. Well, his father was so impressed with his son's honesty, he didn't punish him. So, rememberin' that story," he said to the boy, "did you tip over the outhouse?"

The boy smiled and stood up straight. "Father," he said, "I cannot tell a lie. I tipped over the outhouse."

Well, the old man grabbed his son and pulled down his son's britches. Then he began to give the boy the wailin' of his life.

Little Johnny started screamin', "What about George Washington?"

The old man said, "George Washington's father wasn't IN the cherry tree at the time."

It makes a big difference, you know. The worst thing they can do when they tip over the outhouse when you're inside is to tip it over with the door facin' down. That gives you only one way out and it ain't a really happy one.

There's been more than one fellah shoutin' out of that hole for help.

Johnson's quite a fellah. I was over to his place a while back and I found he was a-keepin' a pig inside the house. Johnson," I said, "that ain't healthy."

"Nonsense," said he. "I've been a-keepin' pigs in the house for years and never had one of 'em die on me."

Drink up, folks. We may do some more singing.

Any of you folk Canadians? We get some through here from time to time, you know.

You are, sir? Well, welcome to Clinton and to the United States. I don't know if you was here when I was talkin' 'bout my experiences invadin' Canada during the War of 1812, but all is forgiven, I hope. Things sure are goin' good over in your country now. What we called the Patriot War and the Upper Canada Rebellion is over and the Crown won. Queen Vickie has appointed Lord Elgin to be your governor-general and he looks like he's doin' a good job. The fellah's got Upper Canada and Lower Canada talkin' to each other, at least. The combined Parliament now meets in Montreal. Government's been formed by Louis Hippolyte Lafontaine, a Frenchie, and Robert Baldwin, an English. If those two fellahs can get along, I guess there's hope for the rest of you.

So, where, in Canada are you from?

Windsor? Sure, that's where I was in the War. It's Windsor now. It's been called Sandwich, The Ferry, Richmond, and South Detroit.

There was trouble over there in Canada last year. The Baldwin-Lafontaine government introduced a bill to compensate those who lost property in the Rebellion of '37 and it caused some hard feelings in Lower Canada. If fact, some men set fire to the Parliament building in Montreal but the trouble's over now. Two men in Parliament used to be enemies during the Rebellion but they're gettin' along with each other now—Johnny MacDonald and Georges Etienne Cartier. Cartier was for the uprising and had to hide out in Vermont for a while. MacDonald was a loyalist lawyer from Kingston.

Yep, things are lookin' good for you Canadians. The only trouble I see is that William Lyon Mackenzie has been pardoned for his rebellion in Toronto and he's headed back there. With Mackenzie in town, things might get hot, again. It'd be best to stay away from York for a while, I think.

The trouble he started was back in '37 when Mackenzie led a group of disgruntled farmers who had experienced crop failures and were upset over patronage goin' to the rich families. In 1834 Mackenzie had been elected the first mayor of the newly created City of Toronto. But before 1837 he had been defeated for election to the House of Assembly. So, he and his pack of fellahs came down Yonge Street all armed with pitchforks and rifles. The militia which was better armed and better trained stopped them. In that militia was a young fellah named John A. MacDonald. Yep, Johnny MacDonald was there!

The revolt was crushed and both McDonald and Mackenzie survived it. Mackenzie was exiled and MacDonald went on to greater things. Now the Earl of Elgin has pardoned Mackenzie and he's back to Toronto, the scene of the crime.

The Earl of Elgin? Yeah, he's the Governor-General. His name's really John George Lambton, but them earls and dukes always called themselves after their title. It's s'posed to impress us, you know.

Let's see, who else do I know of other there? Oh, yes, another Frenchman named Louie Papineau. This man fought against joinin' Upper Canada and Lower Canada. He was 'fraid the French would be overwhelmed by the English. I don't know if he's right, or not. Them French of Lower Canada seem to be a strong and proud people. I doubt if anyone could overwhelm them.

Papineau fled to France in '37 when some of his followers made a ruckus, but he's back in Montreal now. A member of the combined

Parliament, he is. I guess he figures he can better affect change from the inside than from the outside.

There's one young fellah, a Canadian boy of about fourteen, or so, who came in here a while ago. I don't know if you know him, sir. He wanted to be a carpenter until I told him things 'bout your history and politics like I've been a-tellin' these folks. Now he wants to go into politics. I can't think of his name…oh, yes—Willie—Wilfred…Wilfred Laurie?

Oh, it's pronounced Laurie-eh?

That was the problem. A Canadian told me the boy's name and I thought he said it was Wilfred Laurie, eh?

That's a Canadian joke. It works well in Michigan's Upper Peninsula, too…eh?

Oh! I just heard. You folks who are spendin' the night and havin' breakfast with us are in luck. Mrs. Wood's makin' Hopple-Popple tomorrow. You'll love it. Hopple-Popple is a blend of potatoes, onions, and eggs. It's quite the treat.

Stay in the barroom 'til supper. We'll sing more and I'll tell some more stories.

Music is important to us in the 19th Century. We look forward to someone like John Madigan here bringin' in a fiddle and entertainin' us with a tune. We enjoy sittin' around the barroom singin' and raisin' a glass of cider.

There's plenty of music around, too. In Detroit there's a new German singin' club called the Harmonie. They get together and sing all kinds of German tunes, some old and some new. They present German Christmas musicals in December and lots of folks go to hear 'em sing. And not just Germans, either.

From time to time I go in to Detroit and hear some music performed. I heard the Harmonie sing some opera music. I liked some and hated some. There's a new composer over in the German countries name

Richard Wagner. They say his name's pronounced "Rickart Vagner", but what do they know?

All I know is he writes some dandy tunes, but he seems to get carried away with the task. It takes forever for him to get to the end of one of his operas, sometimes.

I liked the Flyin' Dutchman and Tannhauser. There was plenty of singin' and some good tunes. There was some action, too.

But Wagner's latest one, I didn't like. He just published a new opera called Lohengrinn. I was really disappointed. I thought it was gonna to be a comedy—you know "Low 'n' grin"? But, it weren't. What it was five hours of fat people all singin' in German. I didn't understand a word of it and there weren't no laughs, at all.

But it did have a few catchy tunes in it. I bet some brides might be walkin' down the aisle to the tune of the weddin' march Wagner wrote for that one someday.

Another opera writer is an Italian fellah named Joe Green. Well, he say it's Guiseppe Verdi, but he speaks Italian, you know.

He's writin' some good tunes, too.

Like Wagner's music, Verdi's music is all caught up in politics. Both Germany and Italy are all divided up into a whole bunch of countries and them who'd like to see 'em united have adopted the music of Verdi and Wagner as their themes. Every time there's a performance of Verdi's Chorus of the Hebrew Slaves from his opera Nabucco, there's darn near a riot in the theater. The Italian patriots stand and cheer and shout slogans against the Austrians and other enemies of Italian unification and the Austrian tell 'em to sit down.

Wagner's music, too, inspires those who fought in the revolutions of 1848 to get rid of some oppressive kings and dukes. Those revolts failed, but they sure got folks' attention. A couple of them kings left their thrones over it. Ludwig in Bavaria is out of work and he lost his mistress, Lola Montez, because of his unemployment. They got a new Emperor in Austria, Franz Josepf von Hapsburg. This one's a young fellah and I think he'll last a while. The Prussian King, Frederick Willhelm IV, kept his throne but it was nip and tuck for a while in '48 in Berlin, let me tell you.

Musical taste here in America is pretty diverse. We like opera. We like what you might call folk songs. We like the music our parents or grandparents brought with 'em from the old countries. We like minstrel shows.

Now that's a hard thing for some folks to understand. Even the people who are fightin' hard against the abomination of slavery enjoy goin' to a minstrel show where white men dress up in blackface and sing songs of Southern plantation life. I guess folks aren't always logical, huh?

Father Kemp's Old Timers, The Kentucky Ramblers, and many other troops go from town to town to entertain people. Family singin' groups are most popular, too. The Hutchinson Family is the best in America right now. But, they're gettin' themselves in trouble by includin' anti-slavery songs in the act. Often now there are riots breakin' out during their performances as the men for slavery fight the men against in the audience.

Here at the Tavern we have people play instruments for our enjoyment—Johnny Madigan here among 'em.

I remember once we had John playin' just about all night. He played tunes of Ireland and American tunes, too. He played soft and he played loud. There, finally he put the fiddle down. A man in the bar asked him, "Is that all the music you know, John?"

"No," Madigan replied, "I know a lot more, but that's all my fiddle knows."

Remember that, John?

Another time John got hooked up with another musician. That one played the guitar and the two of 'em were playin' for some folks. Well, I'm told that musicians can't really tell how they sound to the listeners when they're playin'. You have to be out where the folks are to hear how it sounds. So, part way through the impromptu concert, John puts down his fiddle and goes out into the audience to listen. He listens for a while, then returns to the guitar player.

"How's it sound?" the guitar player asked him.

"Good, but too much guitar," John reported.

Another time I sent Johnny and a couple of other so-called musicians over to old Hattie Harris' place to play for her. Mrs. Harris was feelin' poorly and I thought a little music would cheer her up. The fellahs gathered outside Hattie's window and commenced to play. Hattie opened up the widow and listen for a while. The men stopped and John said, "Mrs. Harris, we hope you get better."

Hattie looked at the three pitiful musicians and replied, "I hope you get better, too."

Gentlemen, let's refill them drinks!

Two Breakfast Recipes

HOPPLE-POPPLE

Peal and slice potatoes into ¼ to ½ inch slices. Chop onions. Fry bacon in an iron skillet and drain. Chop the bacon into rather large pieces. Drain some of the bacon grease from the pan, but leave enough in which to cook the potatoes and onions. Add water to the bacon drippings and stir it into the pan. Add the potatoes and the onions. Cook covered until the water had cooked off. Add more bacon grease, if needed. Add the chopped bacon and cook in. Then pour on several well-beaten eggs. Cook until the eggs are firm. Turn the Hopple-popple onto a large platter and serve. Sprinkle it with chopped parsley, if you want.

KENTUCKY SCRAMBLE

In a skillet over a medium flame, sauté' corn kernels and chopped onion in plenty of butter until the corn in slightly brown. Add well-beaten eggs and fry until the eggs are set. Turn it onto plates or a platter and serve with toasted bread.

TOASTED BREAD

Toast is easy to make. Simple slice bread from a loaf and hold before your cooking fire in a toastin' rack or on a stick. Turn when it browns.

SONGS FROM CHAPTER THREE

OH SUSANNA!

(a song by Stephen Foster)

I come from Alabama with my banjo on my knee.
I'm goin' to Louisiana my true love there to see.
It rained so hard the day I left—the weather it was dry.
The sun so hot I froze to death. Susanna don't you cry.
Chorus:
Oh, Susanna! Oh don't you cry for me. I'm come from Alabama with
my banjo on my knee.
I had a dream the other night when everythin' was still.
I thought I saw Susanna acomin' down a hill.
A buckwheat cake was in her mouth, a tear was in her eye.
Sez I I'm comin' from the South. Susanna don't you cry.
Chorus
I soon will be in New Orleans and then I'll look around.
When I find Susanna, I'll fall upon the ground.
But, if I do not find her this roamer* sure will die.
And when I'm dead and buri-ed, Susanna don't you cry.
Chorus
* the original word was "darkie"

Note on Foster's music—Steven Foster wrote what he called his Ethiopian music, minstrel songs like "Ring, Ring the Banjo" and "Oh Susanna". He used words that to us are offensive but in the context of his time, were not intended to be so. One of the great paradoxes of the mid-Nineteenth Century is that even ardent Abolitionists enjoyed this kind of lyric and attended entertainment where white men wore black face to sing "Negro Songs".

For the purpose of the Tavern I have changed these words to "roamer", or in one case "barkeep" so as not to offend my 21st Century customers. I feel this does not hurt the meaning.

OLD STYLE (the tune is Old Lang Sine)

Should good old cider be despised
and ne'er regarded more?
Should plain log cabins be despised
our fathers built of yore?
For the-a good old style, my boys.
For the-a old style.
Let's take a mug of cider now.
For-r the-a old style.

RING, RING, THE BANJO

(another Foster tune)

Ring, ring the banjo. I like that dear old song.
Come again my true love. Oh, where you been so long?

The time is getting weary and the barkeep never roams.
The ladies never weary for the rattle of the bones
Oh come again, Susanna, the gaslight never dims.
I'll play the old piano and sing some barroom hymns.

Ring, ring the banjo, I like that dear old song.
Come again my true love. Oh, where you been so long?

Oh, never count the bubbles when wading 'cross a stream.
Never got our troubles—we got this song to sing.
The beauties of creation will never lose their charm.
I roam the old plantation, my true love on my arm.

Ring, Ring the banjo. I love that dear old song.
Come again my true love. Oh, where you been so long?

CAMPTOWN RACES

(This is just published this year, 1850, by Stephen Foster, and I think it
may catch on)

Oh, the Camptown ladies sing that song—
DOO-DAH, DOO-DAH.
The Camptown racetrack, five miles long—
OH, THE DOO-DAY DAY.
I went downtown with my hat caved in—
DOO-DAH, DOO-DAH.
I came back home with a pocket full o' tin—
OH, THE DOO-DAH DAY.

CHORUS:
Goin' to run all night—goin' to run all day.
I bet my money on the bobtail nag—somebody bet on the bay.

The long-tailed filly and the big black horse—
DOO-DAH, DOO-DAH.
They fly the track, but they cut across—
OH, THE DOO-DAH DAY.
The blind horse stuck in a big mud hole—

DOO-DAH, DOO-DAH.
Can't touch bottom with a ten-foot pole—
OH, THE DOO-DAH DAY

(Chorus)

FOLLOW THE DRINKING GOURD

(A Song of the Underground Railroad)

When the sun comes back
And the first quail calls.
Follow the Drinking Gourd
For the old man is waiting for to carry you to freedom
If you follow the drinking gourd.

CHORUS
Follow the drinking gourd. Follow the Drinking gourd
For the old man is waiting for to carry you to freedom
If you follow the Drinking Gourd.

The riverbank makes a very good road.
The dead trees will show you the way.
Left foot, peg foot, traveling on,
Follow the Drinking Gourd.

(Chorus)

The river ends between two hills
Follow the Drinking Gourd.
There's another river on the other side.

Follow the Drinking Gourd.

(Chorus)

When the great big river meets the little river
Follow the Drinking Gourd.
For the old man is waiting for to carry you to freedom
If you follow the Drinking Gourd.

(Chorus)

Note on the "Drinking Gourd"—The Drinking Gourd refers to the constellation Ursa Major or the "big dipper". Despite the season of the year Ursa Major is always in the Northern sky. Hollowed out gourds were used as water dippers and thus the name. Escaping fugitives from slavery would travel by night and if they kept the Drinking Gourd in the sky in front of them they would be traveling North—toward freedom.

CHAPTER FOUR: RELIGION

John Madigan is quite the light for the Roman Catholics here in Clinton.

I know. I know. You're not supposed to talk religion with folks. But the churches are an important part of life in 1850. I can't ignore their presence and importance.

Here in Clinton we got several churches. There's a Congregational Church, a Methodist Church that has a nice new brick building, and an Episcopal Church, St. Patrick's. The Roman Catholics don't have a church building of their own, yet. They meet in homes with a supply priest who comes up from Adrian to celebrate Mass with his flock here.

Churches are why cities and towns have become overlappin' patchworks of ethnic neighborhoods. You come to America from a foreign country, or move to Michigan from the East and you move to where your kind of church is. In Detroit's Third Ward, for instance, there are two "colored" churches, the Baptist Church on Cognan Street and St. Matthew's Methodist Episcopal on East Lafayette. Most of the 600 or so African people in Detroit live near those two churches. Both of those congregations risk much in their work cooperatin' with the Underground Rail-road.

Nearby those Colored churches, Temple Beth-el was just organized this year as Michigan's first Jewish Synagogue. They needed ten Jewish fellahs to come together to form a temple and they did. They don't have a building yet. They meet in peoples' homes to worship.

There are German churches there, too. On the south side of the Fort Gratiot Plank Road there is St. Joseph's Roman Church for the Bavarians.

Another new German Roman Catholic Church is just built nearby. It is St. Mary's on Cognan Street. They want to have a girls' school with it someday.

On the north side of the road there are two German Protestant churches, Trinity Lutheran and St. John's German Evangelical. The Germans still divide themselves North and South due to their religions, just like at home,

On the West Side of Detroit there are English and Scottish churches like the Presbyterian churches and others. There is also old Ste. Anne's. That's Detroit's oldest Roman Catholic parish. It was French, but now is almost all Irish.

There are lots of French on the Eastside, too. That's where they had their ribbon farms and some of the streets there still bear their names. There is a Beaubien Street, a Rivard Street, a Dubois Street, all named for the farms they replaced. Madam de Beaubien is still an important lady in Detroit society. She just donated money to build St. Mary's Hospital for the poor women.

In Detroit they got a brand new church that was built for sailors. Two saintly ladies, sisters, named Charlotte Ann Taylor and Julia Ann Anderson, left money when they died to build a church for the sailors of the Great Lakes in Detroit like they got back East. The place is called Mariners' Church and it is located in a beautiful stone building right at the foot of Woodward Avenue at the waterfront. The bottom story of the building is rented out to provide income to the church 'cause them sailors don't always have a lot of money for the collection plate nor to pay for the pews.

There's a new French Church in Grosse Pointe Township, St. Paul's. The pastor is a fellah from Belgium where they speak French, too.

Grosse Pointe was founded a long time ago by the same French folks who started settlin' in Detroit. It was originally part of Hamtramck Township, but two years ago, in 1848, it was separated to form its own township. Everythin' east of the Fort Gratiot Plank Road outside of Detroit is now the Grosse Pointe Township. It's mostly farms with lots of woods and some swamp.

I know there are swamps in Grosse Pointe because just about every time I get a lady here from Grosse Pointe she's a-wearin' bitches. Swamp people, you know.

Other towns are founded around a church. Missionary families from Franconia, a province of Bavaria, founded Frankenmuth, the new town on the Cass River in the Saginaw Valley.

What happened to found that town is quite the story. It seems there was a Lutheran missionary in the area who wrote home beggin' for help to show the Indians the Way. Common people, farmers, mostly, heeded the call, sold their farms in Franconia and headed for America. They had a terrible crossin', storm-tossed most of the way and almost shipwrecked several times. When the got to New York, the train they took toward Michigan was derailed. They then took a vote as to whether all the trouble they were endurin' was of the Lord or of the Devil. They decided because they were on their way to do the Lord's work, it must be the Devil who was workin' against 'em.

They pressed on and were helped in Michigan by other German Lutheran pastors. They settled in the Saginaw valley and founded St. Lorenz Church there. Others followed and now there are the settlements of Frankentrost, and Frankenlust, too.

These are brave and faithful people to whom the church is very important. The work among the Indians had worked out good, too. They learned the Chippewa language and taught the Indians to speak German.

Here in Clinton we have a new pastor at one of the churches, the Reverend Mister Culpepper. Here is quite the preacher. I was at his church the other evening. They were havin' a special service to raise money to put a new roof on the building and the choir was singin'. I went for the entertainment value.

What happened was Culpepper did such a good job of explainin' the need for the money that durin' the pledge time I stood up and pledged ten dollars. That's no small amount, you know. Ten dollars is about a week's income for me.

Well, the pastor looked out and he recognized me. "Silas," he said, "I know you're honest in your offer, but I can't take your money for the church—it's barroom money."

One of the regular parishioners stood up behind me and said, "Pastor, you might as well take it. It's mostly our money, anyway!"

The Reverend Mister Culpepper gained respect as soon as he took the pulpit at his church. Right after he was called there he faced the biggest dilemma I ever heard a preacher face. That was when one of the Cathcart brothers died.

Who's that? Oh, yes, you're not from around here.

The Cathcarts run a store here in Clinton. They are the most despicable, dishonest, ornery, nasty fellahs I ever met. The kind of store they run is the kind where if you go in to buy a pound of meat, you pay for a half-pound of thumb on the scale. Nobody liked 'em.

Well, one of 'em up and died and the survivin' brother when to Culpepper with a proposition. "Pastor," he said, "we've never had much to do with your church, and you church people never liked us much, but I want my brother put away right. So I got a deal for you. I will pay the church three hundred dollars on two conditions. One—you preach my brother's funeral. Two—sometime durin' the eulogy you gotta say that he was a saint"

Well, three hundred dollars is a year's income for a workin' man and that's hard to turn down. But, a preacher needs a reputation for honesty. In spite of that Culpepper took the job. Just about the whole town turned out to see how he was gonna do it. It was one of the biggest funerals we've ever had.

Old Culpepper started preachin'. "You all knew this fellow Cathcart who died," he said. "He was a despicable, dirty, low-down thievin', cheatin' dog. But, compared to his brother—he was a saint!"

So the church got three hundred dollars and the preacher's reputation for honesty is still intact.

Culpepper's onlyest fault is that he's kinda long on his sermons. Preachers, like barkeepers, can be a bit long-winded. Well, one Sunday he was a-preachin' away and a fellah stood up and started for the door.

"Where you goin', Brother John?" Culpepper asked him.

"Pastor, I'm gonna get myself a hair-cut," he replied.

"You should have gotten your hair cut BEFORE you came to church," Culpepper said.

"BEFORE I came to church I didn't need one." the man said.

That might be a bit of an exaggeration, but he does go on.

Culpepper's a good man, 'though. He is a Temperance fellah, but I forgive him for it. I figure that's an occupational hazard. Bein' a preacher, he's gotta be temperance.

In fact, the onlyest time when he got criticism in church while he was preachin' was when he was preachin' against drinkin' and such. Culpepper was holdin' forth in his strong way and, right down in front of him was Old Lady Maude Graham. She was lookin' up at the preacher over her glasses, amenin' everythin' he was sayin'.

"Brothers and sisters," said Culpepper, "I'm here today preachin' against those people who are sinnin' by drinkin' alcoholic beverages."

"Amen," said Maude.

"And those people who are sinnin' by stealin' other people's property."

"Amen!" said Maude.

"And those people who are lyin' and cheatin' and philanderin'."

"AMEN!" said Maude.

"And people who are dippin' snuff."

Maude jumped up from her seat and shouted, "Now you've stopped preachin' and started meddlin'!"

It depends upon who's ox is bein' gored, I guess.

Yes, sir. An other whiskey? Of course. Here you are.

Anyone else before I go on?

Yes, sir. Two more beers for you and your euchre partner.

Yep, them fellahs are playin' euchre, the "national game of Michigan." If you don't play euchre, you don't do business. It's almost a religion by itself.

Last month we had four euchre-players playin' right there at that table and at about noon a funeral procession pasted the Tavern. One of the men jumped up, took his hat offa his head and held it over his heart at a perfect stance of attention until the procession passed. Then he sat down and started playin' euchre, again.

His partner remarked, "I've never seen someone show so much respect for the dead."

"Yep," the man said, "next week we woulda been married twenty-two years."

That's a fellah that loves the game.

Speakin' of religion, John Madigan, here, had quite a problem last year with Father Leo at Adrian. John was down on his luck then too, and asked the priest if there was any work he could do for money. Father Leo told him that the church building needed a-paintin' and if John would do it, he'd pay him. "Here's three dollars," the priest said to John. "Go to the mercantile store and but two buckets of paint for a dollar each. Paint the church and keep the extra dollar for yourself"

Well, a dollar for a day's work is pretty good wages, especially for Irish, and John jumped at the opportunity. But, on the way to the store the Devil started to speak to John and he came up with the idea that if he bought only one bucket of paint and thinned it down to make two buckets out of it, he's make an extra dollar on the deal.

That's what John did. He painted the church with that thinned paint and, sure enough, it started to rain. That thin paint just poured off the building and Father Leo came out and saw it.

John felt ashamed and knelt in front of the priest. "Father, forgive me," he said.

"Of course you're forgiven, son," Father Leo said. "Repaint and thin no more."

Right, John? Yeah, we know you'll never do it again. (Father Leo won't let him).

I get along real good with the Roman Catholics and the Lutherans, They seem to have a sensible attitude toward drinkin'. I ain't got nothin' against the Temperance people. I don't agree with their philosophy nor their politics, but I think they got every right to be wrong.

There are really several different positions there. Temperance usually refers to the idea of drinkin' in moderation. Many Temperance people still drink wine, cider, and beer. Some drink whiskey, but not as much as others.

Then there are those who don't drink alcohol at all. They're called "Tee-total" because they are for "total Temperance". They're a problem in town but not as much of a problem as the Prohibitionists.

Prohibition is a political idea that maintains we should pass laws to keep everyone from drinkin' alcohol, not just them that don't want to. That don't seem right to me. It's bein' considered in Maine and in Ohio. There are actually some fellahs in Michigan who have accepted that notion. Dangerous men, they.

It's not that heavy drinkin' don't cause problems. It does. Men drink up all the money they have. Drunken husbands beat their wives. Drunken workers do poor work. But, there should be some better way to stop those things than to keep those of us who know how to drink to forget how.

One of John Madigan's friends, Terry Lowe, is a drunk. One day old Terry's wife looked in the cupboard and yelled, "Terry, all we got in the cupboard is ten jugs whiskey and two loaves of bread!"
Terry yelled back, "What are we doin' with all that bread?"

Terry's wife was so upset about Terry's drinkin' that she went to extremes to stop him. One day she sewed up a Devil costume and dressed in it. When her husband came home, drunk again, she jumped out at him to scare him from drinkin'.

"I AM THE DEVIL—COME TO GET YOU!" she said in a scary voice.

Terry smiled and stuck out his hand. "Put 'er there, pal." He said. "I think I married your sister."

After that Mrs. Lowe got more desperate. She went to see Father Leo about it. The priest asked her how she handles it now.

"I beat Terry with a broom stick and call him names when he comes home drunk," she said.

"Try somethin' else," the good father suggested. "Treat him with kindness and try to shame him into doin' good back."

So, the next time Terry came home drunk, his wife met him at the door in a pretty dress and holdin' a fresh-baked pie. "Come in and sit down and have a piece of pie," she smiled.

Terry blinked and smiled, too. "I might as well, 'cause when I find my *real* house, I'm gonna be in trouble anyway."

Hey! Hey! You euchre-players. Calm down. There's no fightin' in here—this is a barroom!

Sorry, folks. Sometimes them fellahs just get carried away with that game.

Religion? I think it's important. I was on a sailin' ship once and one of the sailors explained to me how the ship works. The sails make it go and the rudder makes it go where you want it to go. A ship without a rudder just goes hither and yon. Religion's like a rudder to folks, I think.

Religion brought a lot of people to America, you know. They came here to practice the kind of faith they couldn't practice back home. We are a land of immigrants. Except for the Indians, just about everyone here is someone they didn't want back home. They were the wrong religion, the wrong politics, the wrong race, or the wrong color. They were too poor or they had land that was too good not to take away from 'em. They were all losers or some kind.

But, bring people to America. Give 'em political freedom and economic opportunity and watch out! We make winners outta losers real quick.

American is seventy-four years old this year. 1776 to 1850. We're still goin' strong and, despite our differences, we're still one country. Let's keep it that way, all right?

Michigan had, and has, a lot of people here 'cause of religion. Why, the very first road built in Michigan was built by some religious folks—the Moravians—from the Clinton River to Detroit. That's right. It's the Fort Gratiot Plank Road now. It was first called the Moravian Trail 'cause of the folks that built it. That was way back when I was being born in Kentucky in the late 1700s.

The Moravians are gone now but the road they started is still there. One of them which stayed in the Moravian Village after the Moravians left was an Irishman named Richard Connor. He was originally an O'Connor, but he changed it. He married a girl named Margaret Boyer who had been held captive by the Indians and treated by the chief as his daughter. Their daughter, Susannah Connor, baptized by the Moravians, was the first English-speakin' child born in Macomb County.

Susannah Connor married a fellah named Elisha Harrington and they lived at the Moravian Village near what was then called High Banks.until they died in 1847 and 1848. When Army surveyor Christian Clemens saw the land there he plotted out a town which he called Mount Clemens, after himself. Now that's a growin' town with plenty of churches in it.

And folks are pretty religious about goin' to church, if you excuse the pun. Just last week Misses Crater and her husband were goin' home from services in their wagon and Rebecca Crater asked her husband if he had noticed that "awful" hat that Misses Johnson was wearin'.

"No, dear, I didn't," Elmer Crater replied.

"Well, you certainly saw that terrible old dress Misses Phelps had on," his wife asked.

"No—can't say that I did," Elmer answered.

"What about the tie Brother Browne had 'round his neck. You saw that awful thin', didn't you?"

"Nope," the man said.

"I don't even know why you go to church, Elmer," Rebecca said in a disgusted tone of voice. "You never get anythin' out of it!"

Yes, sir? A punch for the lady? What kind?

One Vanilla Punch. Here you are. That'll be five cents.

A half-dime. Thank you.

And this is for me? Thank you, again.

Yes, being generous with them who's alone with your food and drink is always a good idea, no matter which century we're talkin' about.

They say "TIP" comes from "*To Insure Promptness*" I don't know if that's the truth, but I'm sure prompt with them's that generous. But, of course, I'm prompt with them that's cheap, too. That's just my nature. I don't judge folks by their wealth or by how much of it they spread around.

I suppose that's like the Bible story 'bout the widow woman who gave a mite to her church and the rich fellah who gave a whole bunch more. The Scripture says she was the one who gave the most 'cause it was all that she had.

I find some folks are generous and some folks ain't. I figure some of 'em that ain't is because they just don't have it to spare. That's acceptable with me. All my customers are important, not just the ones with a lot of money. I remember the days when I was without, you know.

Besides, you never know what's gonna come back to bite you. A kind act toward someone's who's down and out now may bring a blessin' to you later. You never know. This is America, as I said, and one that's got nothin' now may come back rich later. If I treat a poor person bad now 'cause he's poor, when he's wealthy he'll stay at someone else's tavern and spend his newly gained fortune there.

I bet all them fellahs who made fun of Cornellius Vanderbilt when he was hustlin' passengers for trips on his little sailin' boat in New York harbor now regret what they said to him.

And what about them men who laughed at John Jacob Astor when he came to town with a bag of furs to sell. They're sure not laughin' now at

Astor's heirs. I sure wish I was there to serve one of them two fellahs a drink when they were on the way up—tip or no tip.

The onlyest trouble with some rich folks is they forget where they came from. Like this rich city lady who came in here one day. She said she'd like some milk for her tea but she wanted it fresh. "I can't imagine how you poor country folk keep milk from spoiling without iceboxes like we have in the city," she said in a haughty tone.

"We do alright," I smiled.

"Then tell me, where do you keep milk so it doesn't spoil?"

"In the cow," I told her.

Another drink before we change the subject?

Of course. You're drinkin' Ale, right? Here's another for you. And, if I may, I propose a toast.

Folks—to America—May we be ever free and united.

Recipes for Chapter Four

BEEF BARLEY SOUP

Begin with a meaty beef shank. Brown it in fat in a large pot. Drain the fat. Add water to more than to cover and bring to a boil. Skim any fat that rises and lower to a simmer. Add large pieces of celery, carrots, and onion. Add a half handful of peppercorns and three whole cloves of garlic. Keep the skin on the garlic and onions. Add salt.

Let the soup simmer for several hours until the meat is very soft. Then remove the meat and cut it into small pieces. Extract the marrow from the shank bone and chop it, too. Drain the broth of the vegetables. Press the cooked vegetables' juices through a sieve or strainer into the broth and discard the pulp. You can give the pulp to the birds or the hogs.

Add the chopped meat and marrow to the broth and simmer some more.

Chop more carrots, onions, and celery, this time into small pieces. Add them to the broth and skim as it cooks. Many cooks add chopped tomatoes, too.

The marrow will rise, but after a while it will cook in to enrich the soup. Any undisolved marrow is a great treat.

Add a handful of barley and simmer for an hour.

Add salt and ground pepper to taste before serving.

SQUIRREL SOUP

Wash and quarter three or four goodly sized squirrels. Put the squirrels in a gallon of salted water and bring to a boil. Reduce the heat to simmer. Add vegetables as for any soup—corn, potatoes, tomatoes and lima beans.

Strain the soup when the meat is shredded and remove those troublesome little bones.

Return the soup to the pot and bring it to a boil. Thicken with butter mixed together with flour to form a ball. Add celery and chopped parsley.

Serve this soup over a thick slice of toasted bread placed in the bottom of a bowl.

Yes, you may substitute dark meat of chicken for the squirrels, but why would you want to?

CLAM SOUP

Clean and chop fine twenty-five clams. Put the liquor drained from the clams with a cup of water into a pot. Add the chopped clams and boil for a half-hour. Add salt and pepper to taste. Add a piece of butter the size of an egg in the soup to enrich it. Add one quart of milk. Then stir in a tablespoonful of flour that has been blended to a cream with a little cold cream or milk.

Add a little mace and lemon juice to taste.

Note: the French will thicken this soup by means of what they call a *roux*. This is flour that has been cooked in butter for a few minutes. It does a fine job of thickening white soups without adding a flour taste to them.

Chapter Five: Death and Taxes

I suppose a lot of you folks are here in Clinton for the big funeral. A few days ago Brother Fellows died. He was a man of advanced years—I think he was sixty, or so—and he had a lot of friends in the area. Mister Fellows was a fine fellah. He's first name was "Odd". Ain't that somethin'? "Odd Fellows" He's parents musta had a sick sense of humor when they named Odd.

Well, as you could imagine, Brother Fellows grew up a-hatin' that name. You know how cruel children can be about that sort of thing—and adults, too. In fact Odd's final request is they don't put that name on his tombstone. They kept his request. Sure enough, yesterday they buried him in the Congregational Cemetery and there's nothin' on the stone. It's blank.

People go by. They look at that stone and say, "That's odd."

Sometimes you can't win for losin'.

Speakin' of death, we've got a lot of that around here. Funerals are an important social function. People have customs to remember the dead like wearin' memorials of the departed. Rings, bracelets, and other pieces of jewelry are made from a dead person's hair and worn as a remembrance.

In fact, the other day I saw Mrs. Trace, a local woman, walkin' to church and she had what looked like a memorial pin on her blouse. I stuck my head out the window and asked her about it.

"Oh, yes," she said. "This is a small picture of my husband, Harold, and a lock of his hair. I want to remember him how he was."

"I didn't know he was gone," I said.

"Oh, he ain't gone," Mrs. Trace smiled, "but he's hair is."

To each his own.

I lost one of my regular customers last month. Robert H. Harris died. He was a man who regularly drank corn whiskey, and in great quantities. When he died his wife had the body cremated Rob burned for a week and a half!

A nice, low blue flame.

His wife kept tryin' to stomp out the fire. She couldn't, but she enjoyed the stompin' part.

That's Rob's ashes up there on the fireplace in that tin container. Sometimes people will flip their cigar ashes in with him. If you do that, Ole Rob won't mind none. That'll just add to his bulk in a way he'd find pleasin'.

Then, when poor old Harold Froman was a-dyin' he was layin' up in his bed and he called to his wife, Polly, who was in the kitchen. She joined the dyin"man and he said, """ on my way out, I know that. But I can smell them pies you're a-cookin' in there. I'd sure like a bit of your wonderful apple pir for a die."

Polly said, "Can't do it, Harold. "Them pies is for the funeral."

Told you funerals are important things.

We had a strange occurrence in the Roman Catholic cemetery the other day. One of my customers, David Paul Wilson, was walkin' home. He was well into his cups and staggered through the cemetery on his way home. Well, sure enough, he fell into a newly dug grave.

It was cold and he started shiverin'. "Help me! It'coooold down here," David said. "It's cooooooold down here."

My friend, John Madigan, was also takin' a short cut through the cemetery and he was bent, too. John came upon that open grave with David down inside it. He heard David cryin', "Help me. It's cold down here." And John picked up a shovel that was stuck in a pile of dirt nearby.

"No wonder you're cold," he said as he started to throw dirt down into the hole. "You done kicked off all your covers."

That was a close one for David, but it didn't stop him from drinkin' none.

And it didn't slow John none, neither.

And then, when Martha Smith's husband died there was quite the fuss, too. He was quite the miser and just before he passed, he told Martha to put all his money in a chest in the attic above his bedroom.

"That way, when I go I can grab the money on the way up and be rich in heaven."

Martha what he said and after the funeral she went back home to see if the money was gone. "It's all still here," said the widow Martha said as she inspected the money chest. "I told him we should put it in the cellar."

We had a bear maulin' that killed a fellah last month. David Paul Wilson ran into the Tavern screamin', "A bear just bit off one of Nelson Frank's legs!"

"Which one?" I asked him.

"I don't know," David said. "All those bears look alike to me"

Nelson died, despite the doctor's best efforts. He cauterized the wound and bled Nelson, but there was no savin' the poor fellow. Remarkably, Nelson's brother lost both of his legs in a fight with a bear.

He was a fine fellah who helped everyone, despite his condition. He was fitted with two wooden legs that took him just about everywhere he wanted to go.

One day he came upon a brush fire that coulda spread into town and burn us all out. He went right to work and stomped out that fire with those wooden legs of his. He saved the town, but *he* burned to the ground!

Gentlemen, please notice that the lady has left the barroom. It is now acceptable, again, to talk politics.

Taxes are a concern now. The only taxes most people pay are property taxes and that's only if you own real estate. The money goes to the state or local governments for their use. Right now there are no federal taxes. The federal budget is about $36 million, that just over a dollar per person per year, and none of it comes from taxes. It's all from tariffs and the sale of public land. With all that land we got from Mexico at the end of the War two years ago, there will NEVER be a need for a federal tax.

We did have quite the discussion the other week due to taxes. The country was suggestin' we have a tax to build a new road in the county. A local fellah, Ollie Jonson, a Swede, came in supportin' the road building. Ollie was going table to table, man to man, tellin' everyone to vote yes on the new road.

Ollie came up to Henry Busch who was standin' at the bar and he was lobbyin' him, too. Henry, a bean-countin' German man, asked Ollie why we should build a new road.

"It'll bring in new business to Clinton," said the Swede.

"But, who'll built the new road?" Henry asked.

"The government. The government's gonna build the road," Ollie replied.

"Ollie, do you know who the government is?" Henry asked.

"No."

"We're the government—you and me," explained Henry.

"I didn't know that," Ollie said. He left and came back the next day, tellin' everyone to vote no on the road bill.

"Why?" someone asked him.

"'cause if they build it," Ollie said, "they're gonna make Henry Busch and me to do all the work. That's why."

We have a lot of Swedes in Michigan. A lot go to the Minnesota Territory. That's the only place in America that's cold enough for 'em, I guess.

They get to Minnesota and write back home—"You come to Mean—e—sota. It's yest like Svenden." Is that a plus?

Taxes is a touchy subject. No one likes payin' taxes, it seems.

One day the local tax collector caught Mister Wood and wanted his property taxes. Calvin was all down in the mouth and the tax collector told him, "Calvin, with all the government does for you, you should pay your taxes with a smile."

Calvin smiled and said, "Good. I thought you wanted money!"

That's Calvin Wood, you know. Calvin Wood originated in New York, like so many people in Michigan. New York's quite the place. The governor is a fellah named Hamilton Fish. He's gettin' a good reputation out here in the west. Their Senators are Daniel Dickerson, a Democrat, and Willam Seward, a Whig. Seward is a lawyer and a leader in the anti-slavery actions in Congress. He is a Whig but has split with Millard Fillmore and the less radical Whigs over slavery and other issues. If any of you fellahs are from New York, say howdy to Senator Seward from us the next time you see him.

New York gave us the women rights notion in great force. It started in Seneca Falls, New York two years ago and had spread since then. New York is also the origins of the Spiritualist idea that is now sweepin' America, A couple of sisters in New York, the Fox sisters, heard rappin's in their home and they interpreted 'em as messages from dead folks. Well, now there are folks that hold "seances" where they sit in a circle, hold hands, and talk to the dead! It's quite the phenomenon.

I'm not too much in love with that sort of thing. I had an impulse once to contact my brother-in-law who died owin' me fifty dollars, but I never liked talkin' to him in life, why should I go to all the trouble to talk to him now?

The way I see this Spiritualism business if this: If it's true that it's all hokum, humbug, and a bamboozle, why should I be interested in it? If it's true—I don't want anythin' to do with it!

But, there are them that do. That's for sure.

Hattie Harris, a prudish and judgmental woman here in town, went to one of those spirit circles. I supposed she gave her poor dead husband such a hard time in life she wanted to give him a little more in death.

Well, Hattie held hands in the dark and called out the name of her husband. His voice was heard and Hattie began scoldin' him for not takin' the sweater she had made for him to Heaven so God could see how good she was at knittin'.

"We don't need clothes here, Hattie," her husband said.

"You mean everyone in Heaven's naked?" the woman gasped. "I'm not sure if I wanna go to a place like that!"

"Then I got good news for you, dear," her husband's voice said. "I understand, you ain't invited."

Did you hear the one about the politician who went to Heaven?
You never will!

A fellah once told me about how there was a line to get into Heaven and Saint Peter, himself, was checkin' the list and makin' accommodations. He looked at the first man in line and he says "Oh, you're the Pope. We were expectin' you, your Holiness. I'm sorry to tell you that we're a little crowded right now, so I'm gonna give to a walk-up room down in the valley, if that's acceptable.

The Pope says it was acceptable and off he goes.

The next man in line is a politician and Saint Peter gives him a big palace up on a big hill that overlooks all of Heaven, with servants and all. The third man is stunned. He says to Saint Peter, "Now let me get this right—the first man was the POPE and you gave him a little room in the valley and the other man was a politician and he got the palace on the hill?"

"Yep," Saint Peter smiled, "You see, we have over a hundred popes up here. That was our first politician!"

But we need politicians. If we didn't have politicians, we'd have to cuss at our wives.

Yes, sir? An other drink. Let's see, you're drinkin' stonewalls, right? Here you go—one more.

What's for dinner tomorrow? I'll ask Misses Wood, but I'm sure we're havin' veal pie. I saw her doin' a bit of preparation for it, already. You'll like it, if you like veal. We're also havin' potato biscuits.

Anyone else want some more to drink. Supper's comin' up and you'll soon be goin' into the dinin' room, again for your final repast of the day. The food will be the leftovers from your dinner plus stewed pears.

We were talkin' about taxes. All jokin' aside, taxes are one of the costs of livin' in a free country. Unlike the taxes imposed on folks in other lands, our dues are set by the will of the people, or so it should be. In other lands taxes are imposed by a king, or a duke, or some other fellah who may have little regard for the ability of his people to pay.

When we pass a tax here, it's the people who own property who vote yes or no on it. That seems fair. If a tax is imposed directly on us be a legislature, at least it's the men we elect who did it. And we can always "unelect" 'em.

America's never had a President assassinated and, I believe never will. That is because in Europe if you want to get rid of the king or other royal big fish the only way is to wait for him to die, or help him along that path. But, here in America, we can vote the rascal out. And, we've done that, too.

"Old Kinderhook", Martin Van Buren got us in a heck of a fix and we went to the polls and elected President Harrison in Van Buren's stead. That was in 1840. By the way, that's how "OK" came into our lexicon.

The Democrats that supported Van Buren were called "OK Democrats" because Martin Van Buren was called Old Kinderhook from his place of birth in Kinderhook, New York. Prior to that there was a Boston newspaper which used fanciful abbreviations for words and phases. One was "OK" for "All Korrect". It was only a Boston expression until the election of 1840 when it became a national one. Now people are still usin' it. Maybe "OK" will really catch on. Who knows?

That was the election I told you about when hard cider helped win it for the Whigs.

Van Buren ran, again, durin' our most recent presidential election in 1848 as the candidates for the Free Soil Party. He won no states but drew enough votes from the Democrats to put Taylor into the White House.

"White House" Now that's an interestin' term. That's the place where the President and his wife live. It's officially called the "Executive Mansion" but because it's big and painted white, people call it the White House.

The English will tell you that it was first called that after they burned the place in the War of 1812. That is not true. People were callin' the Executive Mansion the White House for a couple of years before that war.

When I have English guests I remind 'em that they did, in fact, once capture our capitol, burn down the White House, and chase the President and the First Lady out of the place. I pause and looked at the English. "And some of us would like to see you do it again," I add.

President Taylor and his wife, Margaret, ain't everyone's favorite, you know.

"First Lady" that's another interestin' term. She's really called the Presidin' Lady, or simply, the President's wife. Her duties are to run social affairs of the White House and to stand beside her husband as he performs his duties. Most Presidents' wives have done a good job in their duties.

Margaret Taylor, General Taylor's wife does her best. She is not always in good health and her daughter does many of her hostessin' tasks.

Both Margaret Taylor and her daughter are good cooks and they oversee the work of the White House kitchen staff.

There is a local man who knows all about White House operations. That's George de Baptist. He is a man of African descent who served as the White House steward to President Harrison. In fact, General Harrison died in George de Baptist's arms.

Mr. de Baptist is now in Detroit and runs a small restaurant and owns a ferryboat that operates on the Detroit River. The boat is called the "F. Whitney" and he uses it to ferry payin' passengers back and forth between Detroit and Canada. That is during the day. At night George uses his boat to get runaway slaves to freedom across the river. He's involved in the work of the Underground Rail-road, you know.

Good men like George de Baptist, Seymour Finney, the Richards family, and others in Detroit are "Station Masters" in the work of the U.G.R.R. and have already rescued many Africans. Seymour Finney is a white man who owns a hotel in Detroit. He often hides fugitives in his barn as he entertains slave catchers in his hotel. He talks to the slave catchers and finds out their plans. That way Finney can warn those sought to get to Canada in a hurry.

I can't be too specific about the work of the Underground Rail-road around here, 'cause I don't want to give away any of their secrets, but I can name a few people who are open about being involved.

There's a Quaker lady to the south of us, in Adrian, Michigan, named Laura Haviland. She's quite the hard worker in the cause.

In Detroit, with de Baptist and the others, is William Lambert. Lambert's a tailor of African descent who has formed several secret anti-slavery societies and is a leader against the abomination of human slavery. If you shake hands with that Lambert you'll be expected to give him a special kind of handshake. There are different codes in those shakes that identify people as part of the struggle.

Recently there have been raids into Michigan to recapture runaways and the people of our state have stood proud against 'em. Kentucky slave catchers rose into Cass County a few years ago and were just about killed by the white people there to keep 'em from kidnappin' their African neighbors.

Marshall, Michigan, down the road from us, a family named Blackburn, were the targets of a slave-catchin' raid and their neighbors surrounded their home to protect the Blackburns. The Blackburns escaped to Canada and their neighbors were fined for their efforts. Some of those brave men will lose their farms because they have to pay thousand dollar fines. But, I think, they'd all do it, again.

Abolition is the only part of the Progressive agenda with which I agree. Temperance and Women Suffrage are the others and, as I said, I disagree with 'em.

As I said before, the women of America had their first big conclave in Seneca Falls, New York two years ago, in 1848. Mrs. Elizabeth Cady Stanton and her friend, Lucrecia Mott sponsored it. Those ladies were corrupted by readin' a book that was written by Margaret Fuller who edited and wrote for the Dial in Massachusetts. Fuller went off to Italy to marry an Italian count and fight in the Rome Revolution there last year. She drowned this year on the way back to America.

That was quite the tragedy, you know. She was a lady who needed to get hanged. The women won't learn nothin' from a drownin', but a good hangin' might teach 'em somethin'!

Oh, I'm sorry, ma'am. I didn't see you step back into the barroom. Don't get me wrong. I ain't got nothin' against the ladies' cause. In fact, I talked to my wife about this suffrage stuff last week, at great length and considerable volume—they could hear my half of the conversation outside—and the way I see it is this—my wife tells me how to vote now. If we gave her the vote, she'd have two votes and that wouldn't be fair!

My wife didn't quite follow that line of reasonin', but science tells us that the male and female brains are quite different when it comes to understandin' logic. There remains some dispute about which one is better at it.

I was just tellin' these gentlemen about Elizabeth Cady Stanton and Lucrecia Mott.

You don't know of 'em? Good, then you can stay in the barroom.

They are two ladies who went to England to represent the American Anti-Slavery League and the English wouldn't seat 'em in London in the world convention. Men, only, they said. They didn't want to upset those who were against slavery but not for women's rights. That made the two ladies mad and they returned to America to cause all kinds of trouble.

Now other ladies are involved in the great conspiracy, too. Among them are Susan B. Anthony of Massachusetts, Lucy Stone of Ohio, and the so-called doctor Harriet Hunt. Hunt's a lady who never went to medical school, but practices medicine away. Of course, most male doctors do that. She sometimes dresses like a man and cures folks. You go to her, get healed, then find out she's really a woman. You are really ashamed you got better.

I'm sure glad you don't know any of those ladies, ma'am. My customers will feel more secure for it.

There's some of that women's rights feelin's in Michigan now. Some ladies in the Western parts of our state have been caught up in it as well as some in Detroit. But, generally men are safe here. Or, as safe as their wives let 'em be.

Grand Rapids, Michigan is quite the growin' area. The town of Grand Rapids was founded just nineteen years ago when Louis Campau, a trader who built a tradin' post there in 1826 bought the whole downtown business district for the sum of $90.00. I was there at the time and he wanted me to put up $45.00 and go into partnership with him. I turned down Louis Campau's offer of partnership because I didn't see much future in a town there, what with the rapids and all.

But his theory was that the trappers and others goin' up and down the Grand River would have to portage around the rapids. That would bring 'em right through his town and, those men bein' mostly Frenchmen, that meant a lot of barrooms would be needed. Well, he must have been right 'cause he owns a town and I'm still keepin' bar.

Louis Campau is the same fellah who built a tradin' post on the Saginaw River in 1816 and plotted it as the town he called "Sagina" in 1823. A fort was built there and now, in 1850, the town of Saginaw, Michigan has over 900 people livin' in it. And Grand Rapids has a population of 2,686! That makes Grand Rapids Michigan's fourth largest town behind Detroit (20,019), Ann Arbor (2,870), and Monroe (2,850).

I guess old Louis Campau was on to somethin'!

Another Michigan town had an interestin' start. is Kalamazoo. Kalamazoo was founded as Bronson and named for Titus Bronson who settled there in 1829 from Connecticut. I knew him too, of course. In fact he left the area owin' me ten dollars, so if you ever see Titus, please remind him of the debt.

After Bronson left the people in the town chose a new name for their settlement. They chose an Indian word, kikalamazoo that means shinin' or boilin' water because of the active and clear river there. The name became just Kalamazoo in 1836. It has 2,507 people livin' there in 1850.

Battle Creek, Michigan also has a funny way it got its name. Most people assume there was some famous battle there. There weren't. The name was given as a joke because when the surveyin' crew was there makin' maps in 1824 two of 'em got drunk and had a fist fight with two local Indians by the creek. Captain John Mullett, the surveyin' chief, made fun of those fellahs by referrin' to where they had the fight as the "battle creek" and it stuck.

Lady and gentlemen! Supper is served.

Recipes for Chapter Five

VEAL STEW

Start with a brisket or breast of veal. Cut it into small pieces or slices and put them in a pan with the meat that's still on the bones. Cover with salted water and heat. Skim off the fat as it rises. Cook until the meat is tender and falling off the bones. Drain and remove all the bones. Save the water.

Butter a tin or deep cooking dish and line with a pie pastry. Half fill this with the meat and put bits of butter over the meat. Add pepper, and then enough flour to make it white on the top. Top with the water in which the meat was boiled and cover with a crust. Slit the crust, trim, and bake.

A half pound of corned pork cooked with the veal adds to this dish.

An alternative is to cook as a stew with celery, carrots, onions, and potatoes. Serve on a plate as a stew, topping with a separately baked crust.

POTATO BISCUITS

Boil six goodly-sized potatoes in their jackets. When fully cooked, drain the potatoes and remove the skins. Mash the potatoes well, free from lumps. Add one tablespoonful of butter, one egg, and one pint of sweet cream. When cooled, beat in one-half cup of yeast. Add enough flour to make a stiff dough and mixed thoroughly. Let rise in a warm place, covered with a towel.

When risen, form into small cakes and let rise, again. Bake a nice light brown and serve with butter. These are wonderful with stews and meat pies.

STEWED PEARS

Peal and cut pears then into halves. Leave the stems on and scoop out the cores. Place the pears closely together in a saucepan. Cover with water, a cup of sugar, a few whole cloves, some cinnamon sticks, and a tablespoonful of lemon juice. Cover and stew gently until the pears are tender

Carefully removed the pears and serve them on a platter. Boil down the syrup until it is quite thick. Stain and cool enough to set it up. Pour over the pears.

Brandy may be added to the syrup and it may be colored by adding a bit of beet as the syrup cools.

CHAPTER SIX: FOLKS IN TOWN

Enjoy that supper, did you?

Good.

Let me tell you about a few of the people you might meet here in Clinton if you choose to stay a while. We have some real interestin' folks around here.

There are two fellahs you often see in the same place at the same time. That's the David Paul Wilson I told you about, and James Kilroy. After dealin' with these two men for a while my wife asked 'em how long they've been friends.

James Kilroy answered, "That assumes it's happened yet."

The two may not be friends but they do drink together a lot. And, they've been known to associate, too.

One day James and David were out in the woods, doin' some huntin'. They came upon a deep hole in the ground that looked like an old well, or mineshaft. James wondered aloud how deep it was.

"Let's find out," David said. He picked up a rock and dropped it into the hole. He listened for the sound of the rock strikin' the bottom, but there was no such report.

"We need a bigger rock," James offered and he dropped a much larger one down the hole. There was still no sound.

"Here," David said. He pulled an old rail-road tie over to the hole and threw it down. "That'll do it," he said.

As the two men were waitin' for the report, a goat came runnin' over and jumped right down into the hole. The two men were still ponderin' that when an old farmer came upon 'em.

"Did either of you two fellahs see a goat around here?" he asked.

"Yes. One just ran over and jumped into this here hole," David said.

"No. That can't be my goat," the farmer said. "I had my goat tied up to an old rail-road tie."

The same two men were walkin' toward town one day when they came upon Farmer Smith who lives just down the road from here. David turned to James and remarked, "That fellah's a great farmer."

"How can you tell?" James foolishly asked.

"He's out standin' in his field," was David's reply.

If it weren't for a pun, David Paul Wilson would have little to say

Farmer Cryus Smith is quite a fellah, too. Once he put up a large bell, one of those big triangles, right outside his house. He told his son and his wife to ring the bell in case of an emergency.

The very next day, while Cryus was in his fields, he heard the bell and went a-runnin'. He reached his house all breathless and asked what was wrong.

"Oh, nothin' wrong, dear," his wife said. "I just wanted to ask you what you want for dinner."

"No!" the man protested. "The bell's for emergencies only."

The next day, Smith heard the bell, again, and went a-runnin', once more. When he got home his son told him he just wanted to let his father know he was back from school.

"Emergencies. Emergencies," he insisted. "Ring the bell only in an emergency."

The very next day that bell rang, again. This time, when Cyrus Smith got up over the hill and could see his place he saw that his house was on fire!

"That's more like it," he smiled.

Some folks are real sticklers for the rules, you know.

Who's for another drink?

Yes, ma'am. A sherry? Of course.

And for the gentleman?

Beer? Pale Ale? Certainly, sir.

Here you are, folks—a beer and a sherry.

Let's see who else I can tell you about.

There's Doc Wilson. I already mentioned him. He's my personal doctor and a pretty good man, too. He really fixed me up the other week. I had the miseries and went to see Doc Wilson about it. He looked me over and aid, "Silas, I know what's wrong with you and I can cure you, if you do exactly what I say."

I said, "Of course I will, Doc. Anythin' to get better."

"Doc said, "I'm gonna make you up some medicinals and you take 'em like I say. First take one of these here red pills with a full glass of water the first thing every mornin'."

"I will," I said.

"There's more," the doctor said. "Just before breakfast take an other red pill. Then just after breakfast take a green one."

"I will," I said.

"More—just before dinner take a red pill and just after dinner take a blue one."

By now I'm writin' it down.

"And just before supper take a red pill and just after take a green pill. Then just before bed, take a blue one."

By then I was gettin' a little concerned, what with all this medication, and all. So I asked, "My Gosh, doctor, what's wrong with me?"

The doctor smiled. "You ain't drinkin' enough water," he said.

Old Doc Wilson will find a way to cure you, one way or the other.

I heard that Doc Wilson was once outside his office playin' checkers with his dog. A man passin' by noticed and said, "Doc! Did you really teach that dog to play checkers?"

"Yep," the doctor said without lookin' up from the game.

"That's gotta be the smartest dog in the world!" the passerby remarked.

"He ain't so smart," Doc Wilson maintained. "I already beat him two games outta three."

Speakin' of dogs—the other day we had a city fellah get off the coach in front of the Tavern. He had a dog on a leash with him and stupid dog was barkin' and pullin' at that leash and the city fellah was havin' a terrible time controllin' it. Then he saw little Jed Ferguson comin' toward him. Jed, a boy of about ten, had his dog with him. Jed's dog was under complete control without no leash. If Jed said "sit" it sat. If Jed said, "stay", it did,

The city man saw that and remarked to Jed, "How can a stupid country boy like you control a dog like that?"

Well, Jed Ferguson didn't want to insult the man back so he just looked at him and his dog. "It helps, sir," said he, "if you're a little smarter than the dog."

That showed the rude man.

We got another doctor in town now. That's young Harris Tweed. He's set up a practice but isn't doin' well 'cause he's afraid of the sight of blood. This is a bad thing for one who'd be a doctor.

Harris is a fine young man who unfortunately just lost his finance. She didn't die—she broke off their engagement. She told Harris she needed a man more stable. Harris agreed sayin', "You're right. I don't know much 'bout horses."

So young Harris is lookin' for a wife, again. If you know a girl who's desperate enough to marry a doctor, let Harris know about her. Most girls don't want to marry no doctor. Them docs is always hangin' 'round sick people and you never know where their hands have been.

Oh, Vickie, the blacksmith's daughter was here last night. You know her—she's what they call a midget, one of them little folks. She's an African girl and a real nice one. Her Pa puts her to work for Mr. and Mrs. Wood from time to time. She's only been in trouble here once. That was when some cookies was missin' from the cupboard and someone accused Vickie of takin' 'em. She denied she did it and pleaded that her diminutive size made it impossible to get to where the cookies were stored.

Mrs. Wood agreed and she got off even though there were cookie crumbs on Vickie's chin.

How's she do it? I suppose some one put her up to it.

Vickie told me her brother is an inventor.

"Did he invent anything important?" I asked her.

"Yep," she replied. "He invented an acid so strong thatg it can eat through anything. Now he's trying to invent something to keep it in!"

That could be a problem.

Like I said, Vickie's one of them midgets but compared to P.T. Barnum's friend, Tom Thumb, Vickie's a giant. Tom Thumb, they say, is the smallest person alive. Barnum has him perform at his a mertican Museum in New York from time to time.

Oh, last month a funny thing happened in here. It was a slow day and only one man was drinkin' at the bar. Another man came in and he struck up a conversation with the first one. Soon he asked him, "So, where do you hail from?"

"Ireland," the man replied.

"Ireland? I'm from Ireland me self. Let's drink to the old sod."

So they both have a drink to Ireland.

"And in Ireland, where?"

"Dublin," was the first man's reply.

"I'm from Dublin, too," the second fellah declared and, sure enough, there was a drink to Dublin. "And in Dublin, did you go to school?"

"St. Mary's," the man said.

"I'm a graduate me self. Let's drink to the old school." And they did.

"Which class?" was the next question.

"Class of 1836," was the answer.

"That's my class, too. Let's have a drink to the class of '36."

As the men were havin' that drink, another man came in. "What's new, Silas," he asked.

I replied, "Oh, nothin' new. Just the O'Brian twins gettin' drunk, again."

Another time an Irishman came in and ordered three drinks for himself.

"No." I said. "I don't do that. I pour one drink at a time, but I'm fast in pourin' a new one."

"No, it's not that,' the man insisted. "It's like a family tradition. I always drink one drink for me brother who's still in Ireland and one drink for me other brother in New York and one drink for me self."

Well, I thought that was a touchin' tradition so I poured the three drinks. The man drank each one, paid, and left. He did that just about every day for a month.

Then he came in and said real sad-soundin' and all, "Silas, I only need two drinks today."

"Oh no," said I. "Did one of your brothers die?"

"No," the Irishman said. "My doctor told me *I've* got to stop drinkin'."

I love the Irish. Like I said, I'm half-Irish myself—this half on this side of me. The other half's English. My body's always at war with itself over it. That's why I'm clumsy, I suppose. My right hand doesn't know what my left hand's doin'. And don't care to find out.

England is quite the country now. We get an occasional Englishman comin' through here and I loved to talk about their homeland. Their big fish is Victoria. This is the thirteenth year of her reign and she's still goin' strong. She and her husband have just have their seventh child, Arthur. So I guess they're still gettin' along.

We have a lot of respect for Victoria and Albert. And, the English shouldn't be ashamed—a lot of people here marry their cousins, too.

The English are takin' over just about every place in the world that's got water lappin' up against it. They hold Gibraltar, Malta, South Africa, places in Central America and South America. They are fightin' the Zulus in Natal. The Zulus are led by the grandson of their great king, Shaka. The English are sendin' troops into India to take that place over, too. They own Singapore and have a hundred-fifty year lease on Hong Kong in China. They own Australia and New Zealand and lots more. Australia was started as a penal colony for folks that did bad in England. They are given their choice of bein' hanged in London or bein' transported to Australia. And, some of 'em actually choose to go to Australia!

That's all right, 'though. We started as a place for England to send the folks they didn't want, too, and look how we came out.

It's about a year's sailin' time to get from America to Australia so few take the trip. You'd have to go to New York, first. Then to England—that's about a two-month sail in itself. From England you sail to South Africa, then to India and on to Australia.

Back to people here in Clinton.

I told you about the Reverend Mister Culpepper. Father Leo from the Roman Catholic Church and the new cleric, The Reverend Mister Schies from the German Church, joins him. When Schies showed up the other two clerical fellahs took him fishin' to get aquatinted.

They rowed our in a lake and all threw down their lines. After a while Father Leo needed to go to the shore. The good priest got up and stepped into the water and literally walked to the shore from the boat!

The Rev. Mr. Schies was amazed but didn't say nothin'.

Then Culpepper walked across the surface of the water to the shore, too.

Well, not to be outdone in faith by those two fellahs, Schies stepped out of the boat and immediately sunk into the lake and almost drowned!

"I have faith, too," the good German preacher insisted as his colleagues helped him out of the water. "Why couldn't I do what you did?"

"It helps," Father Leo said, "to know where the rocks are."

Father Leo almost got himself in trouble a few years ago. He went to Detroit and bought a keg of wine to bring back to Clinton. When he got to town he was stopped by the sheriff who reminded the priest that there was a tax on alcohol.

The priest was a bit strapped for money so he lied, hopin' the Lord would forgive him for it.

"It's water in the keg," he said.

"I'm sorry, father," the sheriff said, "but I gotta check. He took a sample from the keg and keg and tasted it. "This is wine," he said.

"By Golly! He's done it, again!" Father Leo proclaimed.

You saw that one comin', didn't you, sir?

We're gettin' a few people from France in Michigan to join the French who are here from the old days. They had a revolution over there two years ago. In 1848 they kicked out the King, Louis Phillipe of the House of Orleans, and started a Second Republic. That Orleans—they pronouce it "OR-LEE-OWN 'cause they ain't speakin' English no good in France. The revolution's fine with us. The more republics, the better. But, then what did they do? They elected Louis Napoleon to be their president. He's the nephew of the former Emperor Napoleon Bonapart. This is not so smart. Every time one of those Napoleon fellahs sees an empty throne they wanna see if his backside fits on it.

So this Louis Napoleon is crackin' the whip on folks who want to speak what they believe and some are comin' over here. The more the merrier, I say.

The war, sir? You were in the War of 1812, too? Really? Where?

Yes, I served under Harrison, too, out here in the West. A fine fellah, wasn't he?

I grew up on a farm in Indiana and joined with Harrison's militia in 1811 to fight the Shawnees at Tippicanoe. After the war broke out I served as a messenger for General Harrison's staff and a private soldier.

I remember the day I joined up. A recruiter came to town and talked a bunch of us young men into joinin' the fight. Some of my friends joined the Army, some the Navy, and some the Marines. I recall the recruiter sayin'. "I want all you boys to go back to your farms and say good-bye to your families. Get your guns,"—in those days we had to supply our own weapons, you know—"and reassemble right back here on the green at four this afternoon. For you army men, that's sixteen hundred hours. For you Navy men, that's four bells, for you Marines—that's the big hand's on the twelve and the little hand's on the four".

Just jokin'. You Marines are so touchy, ain't you? I got a lot of respect and give great honor to the Corps. You fought bravely in every war we've had, and protected us when we weren't at war. You fought the Barbary pirates at "The Shores of Tripoli" and, in the recent Mexican War, you led the way into "The Halls of Montezuma". There's a song in there, somewhere, I think.

The "Shores of Tripoli"? That was back when Navy Lt. Steven Decatur was sent over to North Africa to put an end to the attacks of the Barbary Pirates on American ships in the Mediterranean Sea. Decatur recaptured an American man o' war that them pirates captured and put it to the torch. Then an ex-Army man named Will Eaton led some fellahs from Egypt to Tripoli. This rag-tag group of Arabs, Greeks and Americans included eight United States Marines and it was them Marines who led the charge that took the pirates' second-largest city, Tripoli. No longer would American seamen be captured and enslaved by them pirates of North Africa and when, later, them pirates tried it again we went to war with Algiers and under the guns of two United States Navy squadrons them pirates were defeated.

Since them the French and the Italians took over in the area and they now control North Africa.

"The Halls of Montezuma?" That refers to Mexico City that we captured during the recent Mexican War. Generals Scott and Taylor led our forces and the Marines which landed at Veracruz led the way to the Mexican capitol.

I give honor to all our arms services. The brave fellahs who fight our country's wars have kept us free for seventy-four years now and, I except, they'll be keepin' at it for a while longer.

On the Fourth of July we honor 'em when we mark our country's birthday. We'll be "shootin' the anvil" and the politicians will be givin' their speeches.

"Shootin' the anvil"? Don't you do that where you come from?

What you do is to put an anvil atop a keg of gunpowder and see how far up in the air you can blow it.

You've got to be real careful, 'though to avoid the temptation of catchin' the anvil on its way down. That could prove disastrous.

Anyway, in the war I served under Harrison and fought out here, in the West. We invaded Canada at the start of the war. We wanted to take over Upper and Lower Canada for America. Our forces occupied Sandwich, that's called Windsor now and it's right across the Detroit River from Detroit. We stayed there for about five weeks during the summer of 1812. Then we heard there was a force of British regulars comin' down from York—that's called Toronto now—to challenge us. We looked around and decided we didn't want Canada after all and went home.

The English and their Shawnee allies captured Detroit and we had lots of fights around here. After Perry's victory over the British squadron at Put-in-Bay in Lake Erie, the English had to withdraw to York because we cut their supply lines to the West. Our forces caught 'em at the Thames River and that's where the Shawnee war chief, Tecumseh, fell.

That ended the alliance between the Shawnee and the English and things got a lot more peaceful out here.

After the war I didn't want to go back to the farm, like my brother did, and I sure didn't want to go on being a soldier. So I moved around a bit, then ended up in what is now Chicago.

In those days Chicago had about fifty people in it. It was just Wolf Point and the old abandoned Fort Dearborn. The mouth of the Chicago River was a tradin' point for the fur trade with the Indians and there was a small cluster of taverns and barrooms there. That's where I met my wife, Sadie.

Sadie was—and is—a beautiful woman. Her Pa was that barkeeper I told you about who taught me my profession.

Sadie and I have three children, Hezekiah—we call him Hez—, Dorcas, and Margaret. Hez is a travelin' salesman for a harness manufacturer. His circuit is mostly in Ohio, but he comes up to see us from time to time. He has two children, Ashley and Michael Dorcas married a man from Georgia and she's down there with him and their four youngin's. Those grand-childrens' names are Miranda, Karen, Hannah, and Devon.

Margaret lives here with us in Clinton. She's a widow with one child, my granddaughter, Nettie.

That gives Sadie and me seven grandchildren. That should be enough to take care of us in our old age, right?

Sadie and I have been in Michigan for thirty years now. We came here in to live 1830 when Michigan was still a territory. I had visited Michigan prior to that and saw potential here. It was an interestin' new start for us. I kept bar in Pontiac for a while, then in Detroit. We moved to Clinton ten years ago, in 1840 but because we've already reserved a cemetery plot in the new Elmwood Cemetery in Detroit, we'll be endin' up there.

It was in Pontiac that I met Alexis. He was a French fellah, some kind of a count, or somethin', I'm told. Alexis de Tocqueville was his full name and he was a nice man. He and I had a long talk about politics and opportunities in Michigan. He seemed impressed. Alexis spoke English pretty good—a little better than me, sometimes. He told me that in Europe they think of we Westerners as bumpkins and ignorant backwoodsmen. He was impressed at how much we knew and how well we were able to express our thoughts.

Alexis de Tocqueville said the Western farmer was an Eastern gentleman in rugged attire. He said we may reside in rude surroundings, we aspire to better things and will someday construct 'em here.

I liked him, a lot.

That's more than I can say for another foreign visitor I hosted on another occasion. That man was an English fellah who was so arrogant and uppity he made me feel like he didn't like anythin' he had seen in our country. All he did was to complain about everythin'. Nothin' was good enough for him. The beds had bugs in 'em. The sheets weren't clean. The food was too simple.

And, you know, he writes good books despite his bad attitude. I read a couple—*A Christmas Carol* and *David Copperfield.*

Yes sir, Dickens—that's the fellah. Did you meet him, too?

No? Well, that's no loss to you.

A Christmas Carol? Yeah, that's his book about that Scrooge fellah who finds a good attitude about Christmas.

Yes, we celebrate Christmas well here. It ain't a big holiday, but it's gettin' to be. The Germans and the Irish who are pourin' into America are bringin' festive traditions of that holiday with 'em. So are the Swedes and the other Scandinavians.

There are still a lot of people of the Puritan tradition who refuse to recognize Christmas. The see it as a Roman Catholic observance and make quite the point about being our workin' in public every December twenty-fifth.

Now, Mister Wood ain't that way, so we mark Christmas here at the Tavern. We have special meals and we decorate some. No, we don't have no Christmas tree. That's a German idea and this is an American barroom.

But we serve a great figgy pudding and we sing Christmas songs.

Figgy pudding?

That's a great pudding made with figs. It's got apples and nuts in it, too. Misses Wood made one that you'll remember all the new year.

Figgy pudding is mentioned in the song "We Wish You a Merry Christmas" that the children sing in England and America. It tells about the treats people give to the singers who go from house to house singin' holiday songs. It is akin to "Here We Come A-Wassailing".

Wassail is a punch made during the Christmas season. Singers go door to door singin' their songs and are offered some wassail as a reward. The word Wassail comes from the early English "Was Heil", or "to health". That's a toast, you know.

People also give the singers other treats like figgy pudding. If you come back around Christmas we'll give you some pudding and you don't even have to sing for it.

But, you can sing, if you want to.

I was talkin' about that French fellah, de Tocqueville—well, he was a nice man. He came to Michigan in 1831 as part of his general visit to America. Here he wanted to see the wilderness. Three years later, in 1834, he published a book about his American adventures, called *Democracy in America*. It's a pretty good work, I understand. The Michigan part of his visit didn't get into the book, but I hope he'll publish it someday. I know it'll be favorable.

We met in Pontiac, as I said, where I was keepin' bar. We talked at length about life in the "wilderness" of the Michigan Territory and the differences between America and Europe. "In France and the rest of Europe," I told Alexis, "land is dear and labor is cheap. Here, it's different. Land is nothin' but labor very expensive. A day's wages can buy an acre of land! In Europe, land, if it can be purchased, goes for many times that exchange."

He was fascinated and asked me many questions.

"How much capital does it require to begin an enterprise in the wilderness?" asked he.

"At least one-hundred, fifty dollars," I replied. That's half a year's income for the workin' man. But it can lead to great reward.

Lady and Gentlemen! Let's refill them glasses for those of you who are stayin' in the barroom. For them that's going outside for your evening constitutional, be sure to come back in here for your nightcap before retirin' to your beds.

Recipes for Chapter Six

FIGGY PUDDING

Grease a mold or casserole dish. Blend ½ cup of shortening with ½ cup of butter. Add one cup of milk, one cup of brown sugar, four egg yokes, grated orange peal, grated lemon peal, one pound of chopped figs, one pealed and chopped apple, and ½ cup of rum. Grind five cloves with ½ teaspoonful ground of cinnamon and ¼ teaspoonful of ground ginger. Add this to the mixture. Beat the whites from the eggs you separated for the yokes until they are stiff. Carefully fold in the egg whites.

Pour it all into the pan and put it into the oven inside another, larger pan.

Fill the large pan half with hot water and steam like that for about three and a half to four hours. Replace the water, as needed to keep it half-way up the pudding.

Serve with a hard sauce or custard sauce.

A Christmas Pudding like this is traditionally presented decorated with candied or brandied fruit and covered with a sauce. Additional sauce maybe provided in a bowl.

CUSTARD SAUCE

Scald two cups of milk in a pan and let it cool. This is important. The sauce will not be good unless you used scalded milk. When the milk is cooled, mixed one egg, ¾ cup of white sugar, two teaspoonsful of vanilla extract, one tablespoonful of white flour and the milk. Cook until thickened. Take off the heat and stir in a little butter to enrich it.

HARD SAUCE

Scald the milk as for the custard sauce. Let it cool. Make a roux in a pan with butter and flour. Cook it for two minutes. Add the cooled milk and vanilla. Stir in ¼ cup of brandy or rum. Let it cook until it's nice and thick.

WASSAILS

Wassails are traditional warm punches made from cider or wine. The following are only two of many.

CIDER WASSAIL

Bring a pot of apple cider to a boil. Add spices as for Mulled Cider (see Chapter One's Recipes). Simmer. Add one whole bottle of applejack. Serve in a bowl with sliced apples and raisins.

Applejack is a brandy made from hard cider.

WINE WASSAIL

Boil a pot of red wine with lots of sugar and raisins. Simmer and add cinnamon sticks and cloves in a bag. Add a bottle of vodka or gin. Serve in a bowl with slices oranges or apples.

Songs for Chapter Six

HERE WE COME A-WASSAILING

Here we come a-wassailing among the leaves so green.
Here we come a-wassailing so fair to be seen.
Chorus:
Love and joy come to you and to you, your wassail, too.
And God bless you and send you a happy New Year.
And God send you a happy New Year.

We are not daily beggars that beg from door to door.
We are your neighbor's children whom you have seen before.

(Chorus)

God bless the master of this house, likewise the mistress, too.
And all the little children that round the table go.

(Chorus)

WE WISH YOU A MERRY CHRISTMAS

We wish you a Merry Christmas.
We wish you a Merry Christmas.
We wish you a Merry Christmas.
And a Happy New Year.

Oh, Bring us a figgy pudding.
Oh, bring us a figgy pudding.

Oh, bring us a figgy pudding.
And bring it our here.

Good tiding to you
and all of your kin.
Good tidings of Christmas.
And a Happy New Year.

JINGLE BELLS

(This is a new song in 1850. It's about a sleigh ride. See if you like it)

Dashing through the s now, in a one-horse open sleigh,
O'er the fields we go, laughing all the way.
Bells on bobtail ring, making spirits bright.
What fun it is to ride and sing a sleighing song tonight.
CHORUS:
Oh! Jingle bells, jingle bells, jingle all the way.
Oh what fun it is to ride in a one-horse open sleigh.
(Repeat)

A day or two ago I thought I'd take a ride,
And soon Miss Fanny Bright was seated by my side.
The horse was lean and lank; Miss Fortune seemed his lot.
We got into a drifted bank and we, we got upshot!

(Chorus)

Now the ground is white, go it while you're young.
Take the girls to-night and sing a sleighing song.

Just get a bobtail bay, two-forty for h is speed,
Then hitch him to an open sleigh and crack! you'll take the lead.

(Chorus)

DECK THE HALLS

Deck the halls with boughs of holly,

Fa la la la la la la la la

'tis the season to be jolly,

Fa la la la la la la la la.

Don wc now our gay apparel,

Fa la la la la la la la la

Troll the ancient Yule-tide carol,
Fa la la la la la la la la

See the blazing Yule before us—etc.
Strike the harp and join the chorus—etc.
Follow me in merry measure—etc.
While I tell of Yule-tide treasure—etc.

Fast away the old year passes—etc.
Hail the new, ye lads and lasses—etc.
Sing we joyous, all together—etc.
Heedless of the wind and weather—etc.

CHAPTER SEVEN: THE NIGHTCAP

Well, I see you all survived your walk. Now, let's get back to the drinks.

Yes, ma'am?

One more Stonewall, certainly.

And for you gentlemen?

Beer, a Vanilla Punch, another Irish, and a Scotch. Coming right up.

And what else?

Some more stories? Well, I'm just about storied-out, but there may be a few more things I could tell you. Let me get your drinks, first.

Here you are fellahs, some beer, the punch, an Irish and a Scotch.

Now for them stories.

Let's see…I suppose I could tell you folks more about your absent host, the owner and caterer of the Eagle Tavern, Calvin Wood. Calvin's quite the fellah. He ain't bad to work for, if you can put up with his odd ways.

Like, the other day when he and I were putting up a flagpole out front. We laid it out on the ground and painted it all nice and white and all. Then, after the paint dried we put it up. Then Mister Wood told me to shinny up to the top of the pole to drop a light line to see how long of a halyard we needed to raise the flag.

I said, "Mister Wood, if we needed to measure the pole why didn't we measure it when we had it laying out on the ground?"

He said, "Silas, you darn fool, I wanna know how *tall* it is, not how *long* it is!"

That's Calvin.

Another time he was in the barroom drinking. Now Calvin Wood really ain't no drinker. He says he drinks only to steady his nerves. Sometimes he gets so steady—he can't move.

Anyway, Calvin was in the barroom, paintin' his tonsils real good and there was no way he could make it back to his house in the condition he became. So he went up and got into one of the beds upstairs. That was fine, but pretty soon I got scared 'cause I saw smoke comin' down the stairs.

I ran up and found Mister Wood, sound asleep in the bed with his lit cigar still in his hand and the bed was on fire! Well, I pulled him outta that burnin' bed, put out the fire, and started to scold him.

"Mister Wood," I said, "you shouldn't drink so much that you fall asleep in the bed with a lit cigar. You coulda killed yourself and burnt down the whole place.

"That's how much you know," say he. "The bed was already on fire before I got in it!"

That's drunk!

One other thing I gotta tell you about Mister Wood. He's careful with money. That means, he's cheap. You know how that goes—I'm careful with money—he's tight-fisted—you're cheap. It's all the same thing, but the way you say it depends on who you're talkin' about

Mister Wood is all three. But, most of us in 1850 ain't exactly free spenders. We saw the great Panic of 1837 and 1838 just about destroyed this country, especially our here in the West. Almost all the banks closed and the money they issued became worthless. People hoarded any gold or silver coins they had and business was conducted by barter a lot. It was pretty awful.

Banks are completely private businesses and they are the only organizations which issue paper money—them and some semi-public state corporations. The money's only as good as the issuin' organization is good. If the bank goes out of business—the money's no good at all.

In 1837 and 1838, when the banks failed people lost three ways. If you had money invested in the banks—you lost it. If you had money deposited in the banks—you lost it. If you had money that the bank issued—it was worthless. A lot of people lost just about everythin' they had.

To make it worse, the bank failures were caused by the drop in land prices. In the 1830s land in Michigan was really goin' up in price. People in the East bought land in Michigan, sight unseen, as investments. A lot of that land was worthless swampland, but they didn't care as long as they could sell it to someone else for a profit. The banks loaned money to buy that land and, suddenly, when President Jackson said that the government would no longer take paper money issued by banks as payment for land nor taxes, the banks began callin' in those loans. People tried to sell the worthless land to pay the loans. The prices dropped to hardly anythin' and folks lost all they had.

So, for the past few years, we've all been "careful" with money.

Anyway, one day Mister Wood came into the barroom and asked me to give him a dollar bill. I did and then he went outside with it. I was a bit curious about what he was up to, so I followed him.

Calvin went out to the outhouse and proceeded to drop the dollar down the hole!

"Mister Wood!" I said. "Why'd you do that."

Calvin smiled and rolled up a sleeve. "I dropped a half-dime down there and you don't expect me to reach down there just for five cents, do you?"

Anyone here like a good chicken diner?

Yes? Well, you just get yourselves back here when Misses Wood's cookin' her roasted chickens. She does a great job of it.

We got a new supplier for our chickens at the Tavern. Mister Wood provides some from his farm, but the other day I sent a boy out on his horse to scout for more. Well, he came upon a chicken that was settin' up side the road, and—boys being boys—you know he gave the chicken chase. Well, that chicken saw the horse acomin' and it took off like a shot. The boy said no matter how fast he galloped the horse, he couldn't catch that chicken. It was the fastest chicken he ever saw. He chased it for a mile and a half!

The chicken reached the farm and ran into the chicken coop and the boy had to ask the farmer about it.

The farmer smiled and said, "Well, I know a lot of your customers at the Tavern like to gnaw on a drumstick, so I bred these chickens—each one's got four legs on 'em."

"Wow!" the boy said. "How do they taste?"

"I don't know," the farmer replied. "We ain't caught one yet!"

I guess they snagged some and I understand they tasted pretty good.

I asked that farmer if it's proper to say a chicken is 'sitting" or "setting". He said, "It don't matter. What matters is if the chicken is "laying" or "lying".

Smart man, he.

Misses Wood brines her chickens before she roasts 'em and that makes the birds really juicy. You'll love it. She cooks with a variety of spices and loves rosemary in particular.

No, we've never had many complaints about our cookin'. Actually, the only person who ever came close to makin' a complaint this year was about the bread, or rather the lack thereof.

As you recall from your dinner, we give you plenty of bread. The bread bowl we give you with the entrees each have five pieces of bread in 'em. Usually we serve a couple of dinner rolls, a couple of muffins, and a small loaf of a specialty bread like pumpkin bread or apple bread. If you want, we'll even bring another bread bowl out to you at no extra charge.

Well, this one fellah came in and ate up his dinner and the entire contents of the bread bowl.

"How was your food?" I asked him when he was on his way out.

"Great, Silas," he answered, "But not enough bread."

"Oh! You know we coulda brought you five more pieces, if you had asked," I told him.

He didn't know that so he came back the next day and ate here, again. That time he ate up all his food and the contents of two bread bowls, too.

That's *ten pieces* of bread!

I asked him about the food and he said, "Not enough bread."

Well, by then I figured he was pullin' my leg, so I thought I'd show him. I told the fellah to come back the next day and I'd guarantee he's get enough bread. In the meantime I had Misses Wood bake a big, long loaf of French bread as long as from one fingertip to the other when your arms are outstretched. When the man came back the next day I gave him that whole loaf that I spit in two and slathered with two pounds of butter.

The man ate up all his food, and all that bread!

I smiled at him, "Did you get enough bread?"

"No," he said. "Only *two pieces*!"

Some people you just can't please.

Up there on the mantel? There are two tin containers. One has the ashes of Rob Harris. I told you about him and his cremation. In the other is cigars. If you want one, help yourself. Most of 'em have only been smoked once or twice. There's plenty of good smoke left in 'em.

We had a city fellah in here the other day. I was havin' a little fun with him. I pointed out through the window at a flock of geese that was flyin' by. I asked him, "You notice how those geese always fly in a Vee and, most of the time one of the arms of the Vee is longer than the other?"

"Yep," he said as he looked out at the geese.

"Know why?"

"No, why is one arm of the Vee longer than the other?" he asked me.

"'cause there's more geese on that side," I said.

He laughed.

I sent that fellah out to the chicken coop to help gather eggs and he came back with some in a basket. One of the eggs was somewhat smaller than the others. The city fellah held it up and said, "This must be a rooster egg."

I laughed.

He was here when another man came into the barroom. He asked if he could have a glass of water. I shrugged and pour him one.

"Can I take it outside?" he asked.

I figured he wanted to drink it as he was awaitin' a couch, so I said he could as long as he returned my glass.

The man left with the water and returned with the empty glass. He asked if he could have another and I gave it to him. He left, again, and returned for another.

You sure are a thirsty one, ain't you?" I asked as I pour him a third glass of water.

"No, it ain't that," he replied. "My wagon's on fire in front of the Tavern."

That's the same fellah who brought a ladder to the Tavern 'cause he heard that the drinks were on the house.

I know. I know. That's an old joke. But, not in my time, it ain't

I'm glad to see Doc Wilson here. Now, he ain't a drinkin' man, but he's a good doctor.

The other day a fellah went to see Doc Wilson and the fellah was pretty sick.

The doctor looked him over and said, "You're good and sick, all right, but I can save you. All you have to do is to give up drinkin', give up smokin', and give up runnin' around with women."

"But, I don't drink. I don't smoke. I don't run around with women," the man said.

"In that case, you're doomed," Doc said. "If you had a few bad habits, we coulda saved you."

That's why I keep a few bad habits in reserve. Just in case, right, Doc?

The other time Doc tried to help someone didn't work out as expected either. A man came to Doc Wilson fat and all tired out. Doc told him to go on a weight-loss diet.

"Eat nothin' but vegetables for two days, skip a day, then eat no meat again for two days. Keep doing that and you'll feel better."

The man did. A month later Doc saw him and asked how he felt.

"I'm losin' weight, all right." was the report. "But, I'm exhausted from all that skippin'!"

Some folks is just too literal, you know.

What's that, Doc? Oh, yes, let me tell you folks about the man who came to Doc with a bad cough. Doc listened to him and told him he knew of a man who died from a cough like that.

"He died?" the man gasped.

"Yep, he was under his neighbor's bed at the time," Doc smiled.

I saw a man come in the barroom, Scott, the rail-road worker, and he had his eyes all swollen up and dark. "What's wrong with you?" I asked him.

"Seen-us trouble," he said.

"You mean sinus trouble, don't you?" I ask

"No," he replied. "I was with this fellah's wife and he seen us."

Scott's wife, Addie, if she would have caught him, woulda closed both her husband's eyes, let me tell you.

We have another medical professional in town. That's Doc Taylor, the tooth-puller. He's a pretty busy man, too. He's a member of the American Dental Association that was founded a few years ago. In fact, the tooth-pullers got their own associated before the medical doctors did. The American Medican Association was just form three years ago in Philadelphia while the dentists got together a couple of years earilier.

There's a new idea in medicine that's called the Focal Theory. It says that most troubles in your body are caused by infections in your teeth. The dentist knows which tooth is connected to what part of your body and he pulls the bad tooth and clears up your illness. That's why they call the ones in front your "eye teeth" 'cause they're connected to your eyes. Other teeth are connected to your liver and what-not.

This idea works real well. Most of us are pretty healthy, but we ain't got no teeth left.

Doc Taylor will pull your tooth for two-bits, twenty-five cents. For an extra five cents he'll give you some chloroform so you can't feel him doin' it. That came up the other day. A man and wife came in to see Doc Taylor and the wife asked him how much it would be to pull a tooth.

"Twenty-five cents," Doc told her.

"And how much for the pain-killer?"

"Another five cents."

"Oh, that's too much. I don't need it. Go ahead and pull the tooth without it," she said.

"You're a pretty brave lady," Doc said. "What tooth is it?

The woman said, "Show him what tooth is botherin' you, dear."

The only problem with Doc Taylor is he is a real stickler for time. Never be late when you come to see him. One day a fellah showed up on a Wednesday when he told Doc Taylor he'd be there on Tuesday. The dentist didn't say nothin'. He just put the man out with chloroform and proceeded to do his work.

The man woke up and felt around with his tongue. "Doc!" he said. "You pulled the wrong tooth!"

"That's all right," Doc Taylor said. "You came on the wrong day."

Oh, if any of you folks know any youngin's who are lookin' for work—we're lookin' for children to work here. I need boys to muck out the barn, chop wood, and haul water. I need girls to wash dishes, do the laundry, sweep the floors, and do other women's work. I pay girls a penny an hour and boys two cents an hour.

Yes, ma'am, I pay boys more than girls. Of course. If women start gettin' men's wages, the next thing you know, they want to vote. That would be the end of civilization, as we know it.

We only work children twelve hours a day. That's fair. That's a half a day workin' and a half a day off. We also give 'em free food—mostly leftovers scrapped off the diners' plates so you know the food's good. And I'll let 'em sleep in the barn unless the animals complain. Most children who work for wages start workin' at about the age of seven. By twelve the boys are in an apprenticeship, if they're lucky. Boys work until they're men, then they work until they're dead. Girls work until they get married then they don't have to work ever, again. All the married women do is to cook, sew, darn, churn, milk cows, collect eggs, sweep, clean, scrub, scour, garden, rake, weed, and pull the plow for her husband if their horse dies. It's not like she's gotta work, or anythin'. If you put your children to work here, I'll send any money they make to you. After all, you supported 'em for seven or eight years. It's about time you start gettin' repaid, right? I'll deduct the cost of the postage from their pay before I send it. After all, we're givin' the youngin's free room and board. They don't have nothin' to spend money on.

Postage rates are five cents per ounce for anythin' up to three hundred miles and ten cents for anythin' beyond that distance. We have stamps. That's a rather new idea. It started with the English. They had a penny black with Queen Vickie's picture on it. Before stamps mail was mostly postage due. Now people aren't stupid. Let's say you're movin' to Michigan from New York and you want to let your folks back home know you got here all right. What you do it to write 'em a letter and seal it up. You give it to the Post Office and they deliver it to New York. That trip takes the Post Office three or four weeks by overland stage, steamboat, and canal. Your people get the letter and notice that secret mark you put on the outside that says to 'em, "Have arrived in Michigan safe—don't pay for the letter". They give the letter back and say they don't want it. Then the Post Office has to send it all the way back to you by overland stage, steamboat, and canal. You get the letter, tear it up and smile that you've notified your relatives of your arrival at no cost to you

But, now, you've got to pay for the delivery in advance by buyin' a postage stamp. They come on a big sheet and you cut 'em off with a knife or with scissors. There is glue already on the back of the stamp and all you have to do is it lick it and put in on the letter.

Mister Chandler is our postmaster here in Clinton. You may see his wife in the Tavern from time to time. She looks for folks who have letter a-waitin' em and likes to gosisp some, too, while she's here. Elisa Chandler's a real nice lady. I knew her Ma and she was nice, too.

The glue they put on them stamps is made from horses' hooves, so you can mail a letter and have a bit of a meal while you do it! Because the mail rates take into account weight, most letters are mailed on lightweight paper like tissue. That way you can say a lot for little money.

One of my regulars, a fellah named Chris, kissed Mrs. Chandler once. They was talkin' and Chris up and kissed the lady. That made Mister Chandler mad. I was surprised 'cause, according to her, he hadn't kissed his wife in a year and then got made when Cris did. Didn't seem just.

Was it a moment of weakness? No it was more like a half an hour of weakness by my count.

Chris was polite 'bout it 'though. He just didn't grab Mrs. Chandler and kiss her. He asked the lady, "If I was to kiss you, would you call for help?"

She said with a smile, "I don't know. Will you need any?"

Another beer, sir? Here you are. There's a good head on that one so once it settles some, I'll top it up. Just bring it back to me, all right?

My outlook on life? Yes, sir, I'm one of those fellahs who see a cloud in the sky and know the sun's a-shinin' behind it. I figure life's short and we gotta make the most of the days we have. Now, most people like that. I find that most folks like to be around someone who's positive and upliftin', don't you?

But, there is one of our regular customers, a man named Philip, who don't agreed. Phil's the kinda man who just comes in to tell me his woes. And he's got 'em, or he'll find 'em if he don't. The more I try to cheer him up, the madder Phil gets. "Phil, it could be worse," I often say and Phil hates that. I mean, I've seen troubles, being a barkeep and all. I've seen men in terrible straits and whatever Phil is goin' through, someone's had it worse. But Phil is one of those men who want everyone to believe that his is the worst kinda trouble. One day he thought he'd teach me a lesson so he came in with a made-up story for me. He was all shaky and looked terrible. He was a pretty good actor in it.

"Phil," I said to him, "what is the matter?"

"Silas," said he, "I just killed two people!"

"You did? What happened?" I asked.

"I came home from work today and I found my wife in the arms of another man. Well, I went crazy, grabbed my gun, and shot 'em both to death." He paused and looked at me to see what I was goin' to say.

"Phil," I said, "things could be worse."

"How could *that* be worse?" he asked.
I said, "If you came home early yesterday, *I'd* be dead."

It weren't true, but I thought I'd teach him a lesson, too.

Here, help me light more candles. It's good and dark out now. You lift the chimney and I'll light 'em.
Thank you.
Yes, we use only candles now. We have a couple of whale oil lamps, but the price of whale oil is too high for us to use 'em. I think it's a shame. Those fellahs in New Bedford, Massachusetts keep boostin' the price of whale oil. They say they're runnin' outta whales. That's ridiculous. There's plenty of whales in the sea. To say we could ever run out of 'em is like sayin' we could run outta buffalo or passenger pigeons. Never could occur.
There's two types of whale oil. The cheapest and most common comes from the blubber of the whale. A whaleboat has facilities to render the massive blubber of a sperm whale into oil that is stored in barrels in the hold of the ship. The blubber is the fat of the whale that protects the animal from the cold water it lives in. There's plenty of oil in it.
The other source of whale oil is what's called spermaceti oil. That oil is found in the head of the sperm whale and is a high-grade, pure oil that burns very well. It's kept in barrels, too, and sold at a high price. There are special lamps to burn it. We don't get much spermaceti oil out here in the West.
A lot of people still use grease lamps. They burn lard and the heat from the flame keeps the lard melted. The flame makes a poor light and it

smells like you're cookin' pork all day. Grease congeals on the walls. It's not the best.

Bees' wax and bayberry candles are nice, but they are not cheap, either. In some places they use camphene. That's a mixture of alcohol and turpentine. It gives a good light, but it's pretty dangerous. There are a lot of fires and explosions caused by its use.

At the National Hotel in Detroit they use coal gas for lightin'. The gas is pumped into the rooms in pipes and goes to what look like candle sconces on the walls. You turn a valve and light the gas. It's a pretty good light, but because people are not used to it, it can be dangerous. Sometimes people will blow out the flame before goin' to bed and the next day they wake up dead.

To keep that from happenin', the gas at the National Hotel is turned off to the rooms every night at bedtime. That was there can be no accidental deaths nor fires.

Now that the other candles are lit, you fellahs can read, if you want. There are some newspapers left behind by other travelers and you're welcome to read 'em. Just leave 'em for the next man, all right?

I told you about my daughter, Dorcas? She's the one who's livin' in Georgia now. Her husband, Randall, is a nice fellah for bein' a Southerner and a lawyer, too. Randall earns a good livin'. He's an associate of the new Speaker of the House of Representatives, Howell Cobb. Mr. Cobb was elected at the end of last year, 1849, after many ballots. He wasn't everyone's first choice but he sure is doin' a good job so far.

Randall's in private practice as well as helpin' Mr. Cobb. He had a case where his client sued an insurance company to make it pay for a fire at his client's business. When Randall gave the man his bill the man got mad.

"I did a lot of work on this case," Randall insisted.

The man said," You'd think *you* started the fire!"

My son-in-law was defendin' another fellah who was in jail accused of robbery.

"Don't worry," he told his client," I'll have no problem gettin' you off. First, I'll file for a writ. Then I'll demand a hearin'. Next, I'll file several briefs. Don't worry. You're in good hands."

"Is there anythin' I can do to help you?" the prisoner asked.

Randall looked over the case file he was holdin'. "You could escape," he said.

My daughter's husband went to law school at Transylvania College in Lexington, Kentucky. That's a good school but expensive. He had to borrow a thoussand dollars from his father to do it. Then his very first case as a lawyer was when his father sued him for a thousand dollars!

Well, well, well. Look who's here! Lady, and gentlemen, may I introduce Mister Daniel Brown. Dan'l's a sales agent for the McCormick Reapin' Machine Company of Chicago. He's quite the fellah—a good euchre player and a fine conversationalist.

What'll it be, Dan'l?

A lemonade? Certainly. Ain't drinkin' whiskey to-day, huh?

Here's your lemonade.

You're stayin' the night, then? Good. I can put you into Bed Number Three with those two other men over there.

Dan'l has a home in Springfield, Illinois and travels through Michigan sellin' the McCormick reaper. Durin' the summer he travels from Chicago to Detroit along the Chicago Road, doin' his sellin'. He is here in Clinton a lot.

The road is pretty good. It is planked from Detroit to Saline, ten miles shy of Clinton. From there it is a dirt road—mud road when it rains. Durin' the summer you could make New Buffalo on Lake Michigan in only six days from Detroit and then to Chicago by steamboat from there.

The steamer'll cut a whole day off your trip. When it's not runnin', like in the winter, you have to go by stagecoach around the bottom of Lake Michigan and that's all swamp, you know.

The only problem with the steamers is that they attract the more arrogant captains. When you get a steamer command, you're kinda on the top of your career, so you can't tell them fellahs nothin'. Eber Ward of Newport, Michigan owns quite a fleet of boats, both steam and sail. Oliver Newberry of Detroit has some, too. They're good men, but their captains are not.

I hear a story about a steamer that was crossin' Lake Michigan, by night, and they see a light up ahead. The captain took a sightin' and did all his calculations with his charts, and all. He figured he was on a collision course with another ship.

So the captain picked up his bows'n's lamp and signaled up ahead "CHANGE COUSE TEN DEGREES SOUTH."

A signal came back—"YOU CHANGE COURSE TEN DEGREES NORTH."

Well, the captain, bein' a steamship commander, ain't gonna do it. So he signaled ahead—"WE AIN'T CHANGIN' OUR COURSE. THIS IS A STEAMER!"

The captain received the signal—"HAVE IT YOUR OWN WAY— THIS IS A LIGHTHOUSE."

You can go, but you gotta be a bit careful about who your captain is.

Dan'l's a temperance fellah, but we let him in the barroom, anyway. He also haunts the Ladies' Parlor and is allowed in there.

In the Ladies' Parlor we don't allow no smokin', chewin', spitin', cussin', or talkin' politics. In the barroom we just about require them things.

Gentlemen like Dan'l who know how to behave themselves, are allowed to join the gentile folks in the Ladies' Parlor. I never get in there, myself.

Any of you fellahs from Ohio?

Yes, where?

Dayton? Yes, there's a new university there. Last year St. Mary's School changed its name to the University of Dayton. I have a friend who attends school there. He was real disappointed when he started. He thought the name of the school was the course of study, not the name if the town. He figured if he could get a degree in datin' he'd be able to get better women.

But he's gonna stick it out 'cause he figures education is a good way to get dates, too.

Oh, you've heard of that confusion before, have you.

Yes, do you know where Engagement, Ohio is? The way I understand it Engagement is somewhere between Dayton and Marion. (Datin' and Marryin')

I got a lot of respect for Ohio. You're way ahead of us in Michigan in transportation and such—what with all your rail-roads and canals and all. Michigan's never been much of a transportation center and, probably, never will be. We're kinda out of the beaten path, not like Ohio and the other states that have the National Road.

The National Road starts at Washington, D. C. and cuts through the Cumberland to the Ohio Valley. It is macadamized all the way to Ohio, then dirt beyond that. Macadam is a process of pavin' a road with crushed stone and that's the whole first half of the National Road. It's fifty feet wide and still brings in many settlers.

It was the National Road that populated the West before the openin' of the Erie Canal in New York in 1825. Before the canal people came by wagon to the Ohio River, then by barge and keelboat downriver. That was before steamboats so you floated west until you got where you wanted to go. There was no way to turn around and go back against the current.

In those days boats down the Ohio and Mississippi just went to their destinations where their cargoes were sold. The boats would then be scrapped, disassembled for their wood. The keel boatmen would have to travel overland back to their startin' points.

But now we have steamboats on the great rivers and they can go both ways. Crops and goods from the South now find markets in the North and the West. Our whole economy is changin' for it.

So you Ohioans have the river and the canals that connect it to the Great Lakes. You have rail-roads all criss-crossin' your state. And you have some great men servin' you in politics, too.

Senator Salmon Portland Chase is a Free-soiler elected to the Senate two years ago in 1848, and he has a wonderful reputation here. So do men like Thomas Ewing, Thomas Corwin, and the Lion of Ashtabula, Joshua Giddings. That one's quite the spokesman for the abolition cause in Washington.

Part of Ohio shoulda been Michigan, you know. We call that the Toledo Strip, a length of land that include the port city of Toledo. When we were about to become a state fourteen years ago in 1836, we claimed Toledo, Ohio as part of our state.

The dispute was over Michigan's southern border. It was originally defined as a line drawn due east from the southern tip of Lake Michigan. Well, when Indiana became a state they waved that requirement so Indiana would have access to Lake Michigan. When Michigan was to become a state we wanted the original line and Ohio wanted to extend the Indiana line.

We almost went to war over it. We sent down our militia to defend our claim. You Ohioans sent yours up to defend your claim. They passed each other. We arrested your sheriff in Toledo on the charge of impersonatin' a police office and put him in jail in Monroe.

No one really got hurt in the "Toledo War of 1836" except one fellah who got shot in his foot while crossin' a fence line and his comrade's weapon went off.

The compromise was Ohio got Toledo and we got the western part of the Upper Peninsula from the Wisconsin Territory.

At the time Michigan thought it was a terrible trade. The Upper Peninsula was nothin' but rocks and trees and Indians. Then we discovered copper and now iron ore and we began to feel a lot better about it.

I have a fellah from Ohio who comes here a lot. He met a Michigan man here in the bar and struck up a bit of a drinkers' friendship. They stayed here all evenin' and well into the night. Then it was time for the Michigan man to go home and he asked the Ohioan if he visits my bar often.

"Sure. A lot," the Ohioan smiled with a lift of his glass.

"How 'bout next Friday, next week. Will you be here then?"

"Yep, Friday I'll be here," he replied.

So the Michigan man left and returned on the appointed day. Sure enough he found the Ohio man sittin' in the same chair, drinkin'.

"I'm glad you could come back," the Michigan man said.

The Ohioan man said, "Come back? Who left?"

Folks, the beds are ready upstairs. You're welcome to go up there. You're welcome to stay here, too. A good-night to them who's off to bed.

Breakfast at six.

Recipes for Chapter Seven

ROASTED CHICKEN

Brine a whole cleaned chicken. Rinse the brined chicken in fresh water. Dry the chicken. Rub inside and out with pepper and other spices. Stuff with a bread stuffing or with cut herbs and roast in a covered roaster pan.

To brine a chicken—soak the cleaned chicken in heavily salted water for several hours or, better, overnight. This makes the bird incredibly juicy and will not make it too salty. Rinse the chicken well before cooking..

The spices to be used for roasting a chicken are rosemary, sage, paprika, and pepper. Also useful are garlic and marjoram.

Add a little white wine or hard cider to the roasting pan and baste during roasting.

Let the chicken rest on a rack for a little while before carving to let it set-up.

BREAD STUFFING FOR A ROASTED CHICKEN

Tear bread—stale bread is the best—into small pieces. Cut an onion into small pieces and sauté it in butter. Add the cooked onions to the bread and mix together. Add salt, pepper, sage, paprika, and marjoram.

You may also add minced and cooked giblets, minced nuts, or minced dried fruit.

Lightly stuff the chicken before roasting. Do not stuff tightly, as that will keep the chicken from cooking well on the inside. Sew the chicken shut before you put it into the pan.

To stuff with herbs simply cut fresh or dried herbs—parsley, sage, oregano, rosemary, etc.—and put them inside the bird.

SODA BISCUITS

Mix one quart of sifted white flour, one teaspoonful of baking soda, two teaspoonsful of cream of tartar, one teaspoonful of salt. Rub this mixture into two tablespoonsful of butter. Add one pint of milk.

Form the mixture into large pieces or put into a muffin pan and bake in a hot oven.

Serve these biscuits with plenty of freshly churned butter and jelly.

TARTS

Begin with a flaky crust mixture. Use flour, butter, lard or other shortenings, a pinch of salt and *very cold* water. Handle as little as possible. Roll out and chill before using, if you own an ice-box.

For the tart filling you may use fried fruit that has been stewed in water until thick. Add sugar to taste and bake in a tart pan or a pie pan without a crust on the top. You may criss-cross the top with crust strips, if you so desire.

BLANC MANGE

(Pronounced "Blah Mahghe"—it's French)

Dissolve one ounce of clarified isinglass, or gelatin, in one teaspoonful of boiling water. Stir constantly while boiling. Squeeze the juice of one lemon into one cupful of white sugar. Stir into the sugar a quart of cream and a pint of Madeira or Sherry wine. Add the dissolved gelatin or isinglass.

Stir well and pour into molds that you've wetted with water. Set the molds upon ice and let it gel until it is hard and cold. Once more, this can be done in an ice-box, if you have one.

Serve the Blanc Mange with sugar and cream or a custard sauce.

What is ISINGLASS? This isinglass is not the mineral mica that is used for the windows in coaches and in stoves when cut into sheets. This isinglass is gelatin obtained from fish, especially sturgeon. It can be used to thicken sauces, gravies and blanc manges. You may want to use another kind of gelatin, instead, in your cooking.

AFTERWORD

It has been my pleasure in servin' you folks.

I sincerely hope we will meet again as you travel along the Chicago Road. My wife, Sadie, and I look forward to servin' you in the future. On behalf of Mister and Misses Wood and the people of Clinton, Michigan, I invite you to return here to the Tavern.

Your beds will be a-waitin' you. The food will be hot and good. The barroom will be ready and I, God willin', will be here to pour drinks, tell stories, and throw out drunks.

As I tell folks that eat here—if you enjoyed what you ate here and you enjoyed what we did—please tell others. If you didn't—just keep your mouth shut!

Ladies and gentlemen—I remain, your faithful servant,

Silas H. Cully, Barkeep

BOOK TWO: NOVEMBER 1850

Introduction to Book Two

In my first presentation, "Book One of Silas Cully's Tavern Tales", I introduced the reader to the Eagle Tavern, the stagecoach stop in Clinton, Michigan where I keep bar. I talked about the drinks, the food, the customers and the times. I had a lot to say, but much was left unsaid. What follows is my attempt to continue what has already begun and to expand upon it.

The intent of this work is to present life in Nineteenth Century America to the reader in a way that will both entertain and inform. It is not a serious work of academic history, although I have striven to be accurate in what I say. "Silas Cully's Tavern Tales" is also not intended to be taken too lightly, either. It is MY story—the story of the most important person in the world—the common man.

The common man is the one for whom the wars have been fought. I am the one whom the politicians try to impress and the kings conquer. If a prince invades my country it is because of me. The rocks and trees may be nice, but it is the people who are the treasure of the land. When an inventor creates something, it is for me to use. When an artist paints or sculpts or writes, it is for my enjoyment.

I, the common man, am the audience, the market and the voter. I am at the very center of history. And so are you. Together, you and I, are the most important people in the world.

What follows is my story, but it is typical of many such stories. I am, perhaps, your great-grandfather or, a fellow your great-grandfather knew. I am Silas Hezikiah Cully, farmer in my youth, explorer of little note, soldier, wanderer, barkeeper, husband, father, grandfather and common man. I hope you enjoy my story.

Silas H. Cully

1850

Chapter Eight: The Barroom Where Mister Cully Begins His Story

Well, well, well! Look who's here! Welcome back. It's sure been a long time since I seen you. I suppose you've been on the road more than usual and just got to town, huh?

I though so. So what'll you have?

A Liberty cock-tail? Of course, I shoulda started pourin' applejack as soon as I saw you. Here you go, applejack…lemonade…ice… bitters…a sucker. Your Liberty Cock-tail. God bless the United States of America!

So, tell me, what have you been up to?

Not much, huh? Me, too. Just keepin' bar here at the Eagle Tavern pourin' drinks, tellin' stories, throwin' out drunks—the usual. Here, let me throw another log on the fire and we'll talk.

Hand me that medium-sized log there, will you?

Thanks. Here it goes, right on top.

You alone? Yeah, I remember the last time you were here you had a partner. He was a nice sorta fellow. Good tipper, too.

He's in Detroit, you say? Well, he'll do well there. Detroit's got 20,019 folks livin' in it. There'll be a lot of opportunity for your friend to do business. Cigar salesman, weren't he?

Yep, plenty of cigar rollin' in Detroit. I know two young men who just went into the business—J. J. Bagley and Danny Scotten. Them's two ambitious fellahs. They're both workin' for T. C. Miller and, I think, they'll make a livin' in the cigar business.

People just don't realize how important a business cigar rollin' is in Detroit. The tobacco comes up from the South and is made into the great Detroit Cigar by immigrant women and children. It good work, especially for the Irish.

No disrespect to the Irish. I never talk bad about the Irish. If it weren't for the Irish and the Germans I'd have no one in my barroom. They're my best customers.

I'm half Irish, myself, you know. Yes, my Pa came from Ireland. He was born Daniel Patrick McCully in County Roscommon. That's just about as Irish as you can get, ain't it?

You didn't know that? Well, it's true. My Pa told me some about his life in Ireland, but not much. He was rather tight-lipped about some things. I know his Pa came from Ulster and it was his Ma who originated in Roscommon

We'd better put another log on the fire. It looks like it's gonna be a cold night. You hold back the fire screen and I'll chuck in a log.

There. Thanks. Now set down and have a cigar. We'll talk some whilst you finish that drink.

More about my Pa? Sure, glad to tell you 'bout him. He was quite the fellah. Daniel Patrick McCully, born in County Roscommon, joined up the English Army in 1775. He took the King's shilling at a pub there.

"Takin' the King's Shilling"? That's what they call enlistment. The recruiter for the Crown offers you a shilling—that's your first pay—and if you take it, you've joined up. In the Irish pubs, the recruiters would drop a shilling into a beer mug and offer a young man a drink. The Irish fellah would drain the beer and as soon as the shilling touched his lips—he's in the army now!

That's how my Pa got recruited. Or, at least, that's how he told it. He told me now in Ireland a lot of beer mugs are made with glass bottoms so a young man can check for a shilling on the bottom.

Anyway, my Pa got recruited and sent to America to fight against the Boys of Freedom. A lot of the English Army was composed of Irishmen. Times were so bad in Ireland that a life in the army didn't sound bad to a young Irishman, you know. Well, at one of them battles, my Pa saw a lot of guns facin' his way and he decided to become a Colonial that night. He snuck over to Washington's side and we've been Americans ever since!

He changed his name from McCully to Cully, just in case the English won the war and the King was lookin' for 'im. Things worked out well, though. The English got whipped and my Pa married in Virginia.

My Ma was an English girl born in Kent. So I'm the product of a "mixed marriage". Both sides disowned my Pa and my Ma. Both sides thought their children was "marryin' down". Out of the shame of it all they moved to Kentucky where that sorta thing is allowed.

I was born just outside Danville, Kentucky, when Danville was the capital. My Pa farmed there and he and my Ma began a family. I was the fifth child born, the third son. I had three brothers and four sisters. My brothers were Calib, Sean, and Peter. My sisters were Margaret, Elizabeth, Mary, and Martha. We lived in Kentucky until 1800 when I was eight. Then we moved to Indiana for the Harrison Land Act of 1800.

We moved to Vincennes, Indiana, which was the territorial capitol, leavin' my sisters Margaret and Mary buried in our old farm. Margaret was taken as a child by cholera and Mary died just before we left of typhus, I think. She went quickly, without much pain as I recall.

When we got to Indiana my Pa found out that land was goin' for three dollars an acre and you had to buy a whole section. Well, no one could afford that, outside of land speculators, so we worked for others until 1805 when government land was offered at $1.20 an acre with ten years to pay the government for it. That's when we became official Hoosiers.

"Hoosiers?" That's what they call us folks from Indiana. No one knows really where that term came from, but it weren't no complement at first. Some say it was because so many newcomers were arrivin' in Indiana that you'd pull by some new farm and yell in "Who's here?" "Who's here" became "Hoosier", they say.

I don't know if that's true, but that's what we called ourselves after a while.

We farmed on land we cleared ourselves. It was all overgrown with trees and brush and although I was only eight-years-old, I was expected to help, too. My brothers, my Pa, and I felled trees, cleared brush—burnin' bushes and stumps as we went. We built a log home and expanded it when we settled in. At first the roof leaked bad. Every time it rained, we got wet.

You done with that drink? Let me get you another.

What's that? A mulled cider, instead? Sure, it's lookin' like a cold night. Hot cider with rum'll warm you, all right. Here, let me fix you one.

Here you are, sir—a mulled cider. If this don't warm you up—there's a mortuary two blocks down. Check yourself in there.

Yeah, we farmed in Indiana and did pretty well. Things were tough in those days, though. We didn't have no steel plows nor reapin' machines like now. My Pa fashioned a plow outta a heavy piece of wood with a frame he made himself. It weren't no good 'gainst hard dirt nor big rocks. I led the ox and my Pa cussed as he pushed on that homemade plow of his, but we got the job done. Seedin' was broadcast. We'd walk across the newly plowed field with a bag of seeds strapped to us and throw the seeds out in the best pattern we could. After a while we got good at it and not many seeds were wasted on bad ground.

Waterin' was by the rain and that was always by the Lord's schedule, not ours. Many a crop failed due to too little, or too much, rain. But, that's always been the farmer's lot, I suppose.

Harvestin' was by hand. I got real good at swingin' a scythe to harvest grains. Long, hard arcs would cut the grains down as I walked across the fields. We raised rye, corn, and wheat. My Ma and the girls tended a garden for pumpkins, squash, taters, and beets.

Of course, we raised animals, too. Horses and oxen for work. Chickens, hogs, goats, cattle, and sheep for food, eggs, milk, and fibers. My Ma made clothes, cooked the food, kept the house, laundered, cleaned and taught us to read and write. My Pa worked harder than any horse ever did and taught us to work hard, too. Twix the two of 'em I learned everythin' I needed to know.

One day my Pa came home with quite a story. He told us that he was out huntin' and came upon a huge bear—too big for him to shoot. So Pa ran with the bear right behind him. He knew he weren't gonna outrun that bear so Pa up and climbed a tree to save his life. And, you know what? The bear began climbin' too. All us youngin's were sittin' listenin' wide-eyed as he went on.

"Yep," Pa said "that old bear climbed right after me. But, he was too big and heavy to get as far up as I got. After a while he gave up. I climbed down and started back home but then I saw that bear comin' back and he had a smaller, skinny bear with him. I climbed up the tree again and, sure 'nough, that skinny bear got higher. But, once more, I could out climb the creature."

"And you escaped?" I asked.

"Not yet, Silas," Pa said. "I climbed down after the two bears left and started home. If it weren't for that tree, I'd be dead. That tree saved my life Then I froze in my tracts when I saw them two bears returnin'. I knew I was in trouble—'cause they had a beaver with 'em."

I started laughin' and so did everyone else. That's how I got my sense of humor, I guess, from listenin' to my Pa's stories.

Humor's important, you know. I find humor's the spice of conversation. When I'm tellin' people about my history or how things are goin' in 1850, sometimes I see their eyes gloss over and I know they're gettin' bored. But, then I throw in a joke or a humorous story, their eyes open up and they laugh. That gets their attention and lightens up things. I find people learn more by laughter than just about any way.

I saw Indiana grow all around us. We first got there in 1800 when the Ohio Country was divided in two. One part became the Northwest Territory and the rest was Indiana. General Harrison became the governor of the Indiana Territory at Vincennes. Chillicothe was the capital of the Northwest Territory.

In 1803 Ohio was organized as a state and there was enablin' legislation so the rest of the territories could become states, too. In 1803 General Harrison signed treaties with nine Indian tribes and we acquired lots more land along the Wabash. In 1805 the Indiana Territory was divided to form a new Michigan Territory and General William Hull was appointed its governor.

My Pa let me travel with him when he'd go to town for shoppin' and even a few times to St. Louis. Now that was quite the place!

You've been there? Yes, but now St. Louis is a huge town. There's 76 thousand people there in 1850. That makes St. Louis the third largest city West of the Appalachian Mountains. New Orleans is the biggest with over 200 thousand souls. Then there's Cincinnati, Ohio with 115 thousand.

St. Louis is mostly German. There are so many Germans there that they have their own synod of the German Lutheran Church in Missouri. But, when my Pa took me there, St. Louis was just startin' out. It was a small frontier town on the Mississippi River. I was there when Louis and Clark got back from their big trek West. I met Meriwether Louis. He was an impressive fellah. William Clark was exhausted and just wanted to take a warm bath, I think. Louis took me under his wing and treated me with a lot of respect. I liked him. That was in September of 1806 and Louis and Clark had just returned from their great exploration of the Louisiana Country all the way to the Pacific Ocean. Their work opened up the West and proved the overland route to the Oregon Country. Meriwether Louis told me much about his adventurers and I was wide-eyed as he talked.

I was glad that my Pa let me go with him to St. Louis.

Another explorer I met in St. Louis was one of the greatest Americans ever. That was Zebulon Pike, the explorer of the Southwest and soldier in the War of 1812. He spent a great deal of time with me. That was in 1806 after he and his party of explorers were released from captivity by the Spanish. In 1805 General James Wilkerson sent Lt. Pike to explore the Louisiana Country. In his first expedition Pike made it to the Minnesota Country lookin' for the source of the Mississippi River. In 1806 Pike's party explored the Southwest and he saw what we now call "Pike's Peak", the mountain. It was after that when he was captured by the Spanish and held by 'em for a while until released. I was about twelve when he met me.

Pike said he saw somethin' in me that was important. He wouldn't tell me what it was and I got mad.

"You've got to find it for yourself, son," the great explorer smiled. He slapped my back and laughed. "And I expect you will," he said. I've been lookin' ever since and I think I've found it.

Pike saw the common man in me. That's what impressed him. I weren't a great man like he was, but I was an important one, anyway. He knew it and, now, so do I.

Zebulon Pike died at the Battle of York, in the War of 1812. That was a great loss for the nation. I truly believe he would have gone on to be President. He was a great man.

The War? Yes, I fought in that one. We settlers in Indiana got into it before anyone else, you know. The English were busy stirrin' up the Indiana against us. They figured they'd be fightin' us soon and wanted to clear the West of Americans. The English promised the Shawnees all the lands we occupied to get 'em to join up with 'em. The great war chief Tecumseh took the English up on that offer and together with his brotrher, the Prophet, Tecumseh gathered near Vincenes. We got real nervous and gathered up a force to oppose the Shawnee. They came out to fight and we whipped 'em at the Tippicanoe River. That's the battle that gave our governor, William Henry Harrison, the name of "Old Tippicanoe". He kept it all the way to the White House, you know.

You sure you want me to go on? The rest of my story isn't all that inter-estin'—certainly not more so than yours. Yes, you're right, I'm the common man and that makes me an important fellah, but you're one, too.

Fine. I'll tell you my story and tomorrow you'll tell me yours.

So, I fought at Tippicanoe. That just got the Shawnees mad and they joined up with the English to fight us all over again beginnin' in 1812 when the war broke out. By then I was in the Indiana Militia and assigned to the garrison in Detroit in the Michigan Territory. That was the first time I was in Michigan and I wasn't impressed.

Michigan, in those days, wasn't much. Detroit was founded by the French way back in 1701. A fellah named Cadillac, Antoine de la Mothe de Cadillac, was the one who claimed the place for the King of France. He planted the French flag and called the place "Detroit" which means "The Straits" in the French language 'cause he spoke French, you know. The Detroit Rivers is a narrow passage between the upper Great Lakes and the lower ones. Old Cadillac saw it as a good place for a fort so he build one and brought his wife to Detroit to spend some time with him there.

LaSalle, another Frenchie explorer built a fort over on the other side of Michigan at what is now St. Joe. He called that Fort Miami 'cause of the Miami Indians that were nearby. Michigan was all part of what the French called "New France" that included Canada and a great deal of the West.

Then the English kicked 'em out after the French and Indian War and they took over. We kicked out the English after we won our independence durin' the Revolution and Detroit became an American town. It weren't much 'though. Just a fort and some homes. It burnt to the ground early on, but they rebuilt it. By 1812 Detroit was an important American fort in the West and General Harrison sent me there to deliver messages from him to General William Hull who was in charge of the Michigan Territory.

Hull decided to invade Canada and take it over for us. I was with him and his boys when they crossed the Detroit River in long canoes to capture what was then called Sandwich or South Detroit. That's Windsor, Canada now.

We crossed unopposed. Hull heard about the outbreak of the War before the English garrison in Sandwich or, South Detroit, as Windsor was called in those days, and I think those Canadians thought we was comin' over to gamble with 'en, or somethin'. Anyway, we held Sandwich for about five weeks durin' the summer of 1812. Then we heard there was a force of British troops comin' down to attack us from York—that became Toronto later on—and we looked around and decided we didn't want Canada after all and we went back to Detroit.

After that the English and the Shawnee, who were their allies, surrounded Detroit and demanded its surrender. By then I was on my way back to General Harrison and I missed the shame of givin' in without a fight. William Hull surrendered Detroit and for that act he was courtmartialed after the war. Only his record of bravery durin' the Revolution saved him from the gallows.

But, then what happen was that the English told Hull that they was a-leavin' and the siege would be carried on by the Shawnee. Hull and the men in Detroit knew what that meant. The Indians don't take no prisoners. They had a day to surrender to the English or to die under torture by the Shawnee. That's why they gave up they way they did.

Me? Yes, I went back to Indiana to fight there.

The War wasn't a pretty one, especially out here in the West. We was defendin' our homes and families, you know and most of the fightin' was between us and the Indians. Tecumseh was a great man, a fierce and brave war chief. You learn to respect your enemies after a while. But he weren't no gentleman. But, of course, neither were most of us. There was savagery on both sides and I was sure glad to see it end.

The Shawnee painted their faces, each one different. They sometimes had war paint all over their heads, or in stripes, or in some fightenin' pattern. The idea was to terrify their enemies and it did a good job on us. We fought then fellahs hard and long. There was no surrenderin' to 'em, 'cause they usually killed their prisoners. But, sometimes, they'd honor a particularly brave enemy by adoptin' him. That happen to Dan'l Boone in Kentucky, you know.

Back when I was very young Old Dan'l got hisself captured by the Shawnee and instead of killin' him they ran him through the gantlet. That's when the Indians line up in two lines and you're made to run down between those lines with the Indians hittin' you with clubs and such. Boone acquitted hisself so well in that gauntlet that the war chief Black Fish, adopted him to be his son.

A few of the men in the War of 1812 were treated that way, but most were just killed.

Boone? Yes, my Pa knew Boone well. Everyone in Kentucky in the 1790s knew Daniel Boone. He was one of the greatest Americans ever. Boone opened up the West by leadin' folks though the Wilderness Road and the Cumberland Gap from North Carolina. He founded Boonesbough as a fort to protect the settlers and fought the Shawnee to hold it. He was a brave man who lost his brother and two of his sons in the fightin', but he didn't quit.

My Pa said that Boone was the greatest man he'd ever met and my Pa met his share of great men.

What really put us on top out here in the War of 1812 was Commodore Perry's victory at Put-In-Bay in Lake Erie. His American squadron caught the British ships at anchor at Put-In-Bay, an island in the Lake, and he destroyed the English power on Lake Erie. That cut the English supply line West and they had to withdraw to York. A bunch of Kentuckians and Ohio fellahs caught the retreatin' English and Shawnees at the Thames River in Canada and we cut 'em to pieces.

That was after the horror of the defeat at the Raisin River in Michigan. A group of Kentuck fellahs came up to recapture Detroit and they was caught a-crossin' the River Raison near what is now Monroe, Michigan. The English and the Indians slaughtered them boys and tortured the captives after the battle, too.

At Thames, the battle cry was "Remember the Raisin!" and we sent in the Kentuckians first. Those Indians didn't stand a chance. That's where Tecumseh fell. The Shawnee dragged off his body and that ended their co-operation with the English and pretty much brought peace to the West.

After the War I didn't want to go back to the farm like my brothers did and I sure didn't want to be solder anymore. So I just traveled around some.

Ready for another drink? Sure. A mulled?

Here you are, good and hot. Let's throw another log on the fire. It's gettin' mighty cold outside now. Sun's down and there's already frost formin' on the windows.

There. That'll warm you. Be sure and get up to the bed first tonight and get the inside spot. On a night like this, you'll need it. There's a bed up there that's got two men assigned to it now. One's out on his rounds— he's a salesmen, you know. The other's a local man. I suspect they'll be here soon with it gettin' dark and all.

You may have time for a game of Euchre, after all.

Who are they?" It's Dan'l Brown, a hawker, and Latimer Booth, a cooper. I don't think you've met either one of 'em. They's both nice fellahs and, as far as I know, neither of 'em snore none.

If you need a fourth for your Euchre game, I'll sit in. But, you know, it is gettin' late. Dan'l and Latimer will most likely just be for bed when they get back. After a drink, of course.

Doc Douglass stopped by here the other day. He's rather new in town. I think he's related to young Doc Harris Tweed, but I ain't quite sure. There's a resemblance in their faces. Doc Douglass, his first name's Thaddeus, is a nice enough fellow but a bit arrogant by my way of thinkin'. That sometimes happens to men in his profession.

You know the old saw—what's the difference between God and a doctor? God don't think He's a doctor!

But, the docs have been doin' well by us. Life expectation is all the way up to fifty-two years! I guess they're doin' somethin' right.

Yes, I'm well beyond that, myself. That's why I'm havin' so much fun—it's bonus time for me now.

Well, Doc Douglass came by and told me a story about these two fellahs who were shipwrecked in the Pacific Ocean. One was in despair of anyone ever findin' 'em. The other seemed not to worry.

"Why are you so calm?" he asked relaxed fellah.

"Well sir, I go to church regularly," said he.

"So do I," the other man replied. "But that won't get us saved from this island.

"I'm a very wealthy man," the other offered.

"So? You money's no good here."

"Yes, but I tithe ten percent of everythin' I make. I suspect my pastor's on his way to rescue me right now!"

You liked that one, huh? Yeah, so did I. Doc Douglass is a Methodist, you know, and them Methodist know 'bout such things.

No, I don't fault no man for his religion. I got mine, 'though I don't tall about it much. I respect 'em who has some groundin' in a faith. It seems to me to make 'em better folks, you know.

Not that I have nothin' against the unbelievers, neither. I see 'em in my barroom a lot, too.

Doc Douglass was tellin' me about all the cures they have for ailments now in modern times. It seems, he claimed, that all illness is caused by an imbalance of your humors.

"Humors? Yes, I asked him 'bout that, too. Doc explained that you're filled with four types of humors—black bile, yellow bile, blood, and phlegm. You get sick went you've got too much of one kind, or not enough of another. The doctors cure you by gettin' things back into balance. There are four ways they do that—dependin' on which humor is affected. They have bleedin', blusterin', pukin', and purgin'. They all produce some pretty dramatic results and that's what we like to see. If a doctor just gives you some medicine and that's all, you feel cheated. But a good bleedin' or blisterin' will restore your confidence in his ability to heal you.

I got blistered and bled by Doc Douglass last week. I had a touch of the croup and he drew blood from me and passed a hot iron over one of my arms. The iron brought up blisters and that drew the poisons right outta me. That's what the doctor said.

If the blisterin' hadn't work he would have painted the inside of my mouth with mercury. That causes ulcers in your mouth and that draws the poison right out of your head. The doctors know that works 'cause no one comes back for a second treatment so they figure everyone's cured on the first attempt!

Leaches are used to draw out blood, too, and Doc Douglass knows just the right kind to use.

The other treatments, pukin' and purgin', you know about, I'm sure. They're pretty standard when it comes to medical practice.

How's the Mulled Cider? Still good and hot?

Speakin' of salesmen and hot, salesman Dan'l Brown told me one about salesman who died and he was given his choice of goin' either to Heaven or to Hell. A Spirit gave him a glimpse of each so he could make up his mind.

"This is Heaven," the Spirit said and the salesman was shown a beautiful lace where everyone was playin' harps.

"Nice, but borin'," the salesman said.

Then he was shown a glimpse of Hell and he saw men sittin' around in fine clothes, talkin', and sippin' wine.

"That's for me!" the salesman shouted and his choice was made. Instantly he was in fire and brimstone and bein' poked with hot pokers from the fire. "This isn't right," he protested. "I was cheated! This isn't what I was shown."

"Oh that?" the Spirit said. "That was the sales presentation. You know about 'em, don't you?"

Yeah, the salesmen don't sell the steak. They sell the sizzle. And sometimes the sizzle don't always represent the steak you'll be a-gettin'"

I bought a cockroach killer once. It was guaranteed to work. I opened the box and you know what I found inside? A block of wood and a small hammer. The instructions said, "Put the roach on the wood and hit it with the hammer." I was guaranteed to work, all right!

That's a true story—not that anythin' I say ain't true.

Look. Here comes Dan'l and Latimer. I'll introduce you to 'em and that way you don't gotta sleep with strangers tonight.

Recipes for Chapter Eight

Liberty Cock-Tail

This is a pleasant drink made applejack brandy, lemonade and bitters. It is a good drink with which to toast the freedom which makes our country strong..

Add one ounce of applejack to eight ounces of lemonade. Put over ice and add a splash of bitters. Serve with a sucker.

Applejack is a brandy distilled from hard cider. That makes it a apple brandy at somewhere around eighty proof, or so. It is an acceptable drink by itself or in a cock-tail like the Liberty..

Rye Whiskey Cobbler

Rye whiskey is the mainstay of Pennsylvania barrooms in 1850 and popular in the West, as well. It is distilled from the rye plant and had a distinctive somewhat sour flavor.

To make a Rye Whiskey Cobbler mix one ounce, or so, of straight rye whiskey with three ounces of simple syrup (sugar water). Add ice and four hard shakes of bitters. Serve in an eight ounce glass with a sucker.

Oyster Soup

Put into a large pot 3 quarts of drained oysters, 3 quarts of water, three chopped onions and two thick slices of ham chopped. Brin' this to a boil and cook until it is reduced by half. Strain and return the liquid to the pot. Add one quart of oysters and boil until they are cooked. Thicken flour dissolved in cream and the yokes of six eggs beaten. Season with salt and pepper

Note on oysters in Michigan. Since the openin' of the Erie Canal in 1845 oysters are available in Detroit in season. Advertisements in Detroit newspapers announce he arrival of live oysters from the East.

Chapter Nine: Silas's Story Continues

Dan'l…Latimer….I'd like you to meet your bed partner for tonight. He's in town after bein' on the road, too.

Dan'l Brown is a reapin' machine salesman. He represents the McCormick Reapin' Machine Company and is thinkin' 'bout openin' a sales office here in Clinton.

Now Dan'l, that introduction ain't leave for you to start sellin' your product to my customer. No business 'til tomorrow all agreed?

(These darn salesmen—they'll take your ear off, if you give 'em a chance. They're even worse than barkeeps in that regard– if that's possible.)

Latimer here is a local fellah—a cooper. He makes barrels, buckets, pails and the like with his son in the cooperage down the road. He stays here, from time to time, when his son puts him out. He's a widower, so he ain't got no wife to toss him out for bein' drunk. Now his son tends to that chore.

You two fellahs need a drink before goin' up to the bed? Sure. What'll it be?

A couple of cock-tails, huh? Sure one Gin Fix and one Appetizer. Comin' right up, gentlemen.

Here's the Gin Fix. It's a dandy drink made with a great Holland gin, lemonade, and simple syrup. It's just about the onliest way I'd be drinkin' gin.

Gin is now very much an English drink. I hear tell that before them English fellahs had to fight the French under Napoleon Boneparte, they had a taste for French brandies. Well, the war with Napoleon saw an end to that, so the English King encouraged his people to drink gin, instead. I guess them English are pretty patriotic 'cause they've been drinkin' boatloads of gin ever since!

Here you are—a Gin Fix

And an Appetizer Cocktail for you. This is a good strong drink. It's good before dinner to raise an appetite—hence the name—or before bed as a nightcap. It's made with Rye Whiskey and bitters. I put it over ice to calm it down some. Here you go—an Appetizer.

You remember my apprentice, John? I got a letter from him a while back and he's doin' good. Most of them boys I've trained up as barkeeps have gone on to good jobs. You remember Joe? Yes, Joe, my adopted son.

I bought Joe from some Indians for ten dollars and a jug of whiskey when he was young and brought the lad up as my own. He was a nice boy but I made the mistake of learnin' him out of the Bible too soon. He read that story 'bout the Prodigal Son and took off a-thinkin' it was good advice. Well, he learned his lesson just like the boy in the Bible and came back to work with me. He's doin' good, too.

I can't say that 'bout all my helpers, 'though. Some have been lazy. One would avoid work like it was catchin'. He was too lazy to sweat. I asked him once if it was a-rainin' outside and he said it was too much trouble to go see. So he just called the dog in to see if it was wet!

I told him the trouble with doin' nothin' is you never know when you're done.

The onlyest thing I ever seen that boy do fast was to get tired.

His sister was lazy, too. I hear when she was a girl she played step rope!

Before you fellahs came we was just sittin' and talkin' 'bout one thing and another. This fellah's been gettin'' me to tell 'em 'bout my life, like that were an interestin' topic.

You'd like to hear some of it? Well, all right.

You're all younger than me. You certainly weren't in that War, right?

I thought not. The wars that followed were bad to be in, but nothin' like he big one of 1812. You served in the Black Hawk War? That was a fight, too. But, you know what I mean, don't you?

Well, in that war we burned York—that's Toronto now—the capitol of Upper Canadain those days. That's where Zebulon Pike was killed. That was a tragic loss!

Later the English captured Washington, D.C. They burned down the White House and chased the President and the First Lady out of the place. With Millard Fillmore in the White House, I'd like to see 'em do it again!

No, he ain't my favorite politician. What with him signin' the Fugitive Slave Act into law and allowin' California to become a State—them's two grounds for impeachment right there!

Anyway, after the war I drifted a bit. I made it up to Wolf Point—that's part of Chicago now—and did some work there. I was in my twenties and sowin' some wild oats, as they say.

At Wolf Pointe I met a fellah named Gray Wilkerson. Gray was of African descent and one of the most honest and true men I've ever known. We drank together in a barroom there and, like so many friends in so many barrooms, we solved every problem of the world in one night.

Gray was a man of strikin' features. His hair was black and bushy-lookin'. It stuck out from under his hat like a thicket. His skin was dark and his eyes darker. Oh, how those dark eyes of his flashed when the man was upset or angered. Not that he was ever angry with me nor had occasion to be so. But, I saw Gray angered.

Like the time when a barkeeper wouldn't serve Gray no whiskey 'cause of Gray's color. The man was a large ugly white man with red hair He just wouldn't pour nothin' for my friend. Then, when he found out we was together, he wouldn't pour nothin' for me, neither.

I expected a fight, by Gray just turned way and walked slowly toward the door. The African swept back the blanket that was servin' as a door to that barroom and looked back at me. I was right behind him.

"Silas," said he, "let us repair to a more reputable barroom."

"Repair!" "More reputable!" That's he way Gray talked when he was angry. His dark eyes flashed and his mouth got all graceful.

We left and began drinkin' in another place. And, you know, that other place was where I met my wife—so I credit Gray and his reaction to ignorance to me findin' Sadie.

I often think of Gray Wilkerson when someone talks to be about slavery. I think of the slave in the South not as a faceless form laborin' in the fields, but, rather, as my friend Gray—a man of dignity and grace. That has given me an outlook on the institution of enslavement that makes it more personal it me. The very thought of my friend Gray in chains or bein' forced to work without compensation is abhorrent to me. The thought of this man of refinement and grace bein' whipped or otherwise abused by those who are his lessers is abhorrent, as well.

Sadie? Yes, I met Sadie at that barroom at Wolf Point. It was her Pa who owned the place and was the barkeeper. She and I began seein' each other and her Pa told me I couldn't marry his daughter 'til I had an honorable profession. So he taught me his.

I became the apprentice to Sadie's father and there he taught me barkeepin' and tavern-keepin'. It was a hard life, at first. Sadie's Pa wanted to see what I was made of and he worked me hard. I didn't mind. I remembered the Bible story 'bout Jacob who had to work for many years for Laban in order to marry Laban's daughter, Rachel. I just hoped, as I mucked out the barn, chopped wood, carried water and did other work at Sadie's Pa's tavern that I wouldn't be stuck with a substitute bride like Jacob did

It worked out good 'cause Sadie didn't have no older sister who needed to get married off first. When Sadie's Pa was convinced that I was an acceptable son-in-law he gave us his blessin' and we were married in his tavern with a Methodist preacher officiatin'.

You know, I wish more fellahs had to go through what I did to win his bride. It might make a few men appreciate more what they've got, you know.

Sadie was a MacAllister. He Pa was half Scot and half African. She had, and still has, the most beautiful dark eyes that's even been put in a woman's head. And how them eyes of hers flash when she's mad! Not that she's ever mad in my presence. (She ain't listen in, is she?)

I love my Sadie and I'm proud to say we'll be married thirty wonderful years this year. Thirty out of thirty-three ain't so bad!

And it's not like the three not wonderful ones were all together. They're been spread out pretty even over all the others.

We were married in Illinois and began our family there. Sadie and I have three children, one of each.

Just kiddin'.

We've got a son, Hezikiah, a daughter, Dorcas, and another daughter, Margaret. Hez lives in Ohio now where he's workin' as a harness salesman. Dorcus married a man from Georgia and she's down there with her family. Margaret's a widow and lives right here in Clinton. Hez has two youngin's, a boy named Michael and a girl named Ashley. Dorcas has three girls, Miranda, Hannah, and Karen and a boy, Devon. Margaret just has one daughter, Nettie. I see Nettie more than my other grandchildren 'cause she's right here in town with her mother and 'cause she helps me at the tavern a lot.

My youngest, Margaret—we call her Meg—has had a difficult life. She ain't even thirty yet and she's buried three husbands. Yes, she's a widow three times over.

Meg got married late in life—she was almost seventeen—so she took the first man who asked. She was that desperate. The fellah died of eatin' poison mushrooms. That ain't that unusual in Michigan, you know. With these morels and false morels, if you eat the wrong ones it could kill you.

Then Margaret remarried and, remarkably, her second husband died of eatin' poison mushrooms, too. That raised a few eyebrows in town, let me tell you. When her third husband died I had to ask. I said, "Meg, what killed this one?"

She answered, "Pa, it was a blow to the head—he wouldn't eat his mushrooms."

Well, she's done her time and now livin' with us—for the sake of her daughter, Nettie. But, I tell you one thing. I sure don't eat Meg's cookin' none. "specially her mushroom dishes!

Nettie washes dishes here and carries water for the bathin' on Saturdays. She's nine years old now and gettin' real big. She can sing, too, and sometimes sings for my customers here in the barroom.

Yes, that's right, the little girl who sung here the last time you were spendin' the night at the tavern. That's my Nettie. Ain't she an angel?

Gray? Yes, I lost track of Gray Wilkerson after we moved to Michigan. The last I heard he was doin' some fur trappin' in Illinois and got himself married to a beautiful Indian girl. I sure hope Gray 's doin' well.

Sadie and I moved to Michigan before Michigan was a state. It was the Michigan Territory in those days and we felt it was a good place to start a new life. There wasn't much here then. The roads were no more than trails the Indians had worn through the woods and most of the travel done was by canoe of by foot. When one was lucky enough to be located on what passed for a road, travel was still slow and difficult. The Chicago Road— the one the tavern's on now—was nothin' but the old Sauk Indian Trail, a foot path between Detroit and Lake Michigan. It was widened by cuttin' down trees on either side of the path and wagons bumped along over stumps and ruts for years until it was improved again. Logs were laid and covered with dirt but it was still a rough road.

Now, of course, that very same Chicago Road is a seventeen-foot wide plank road for the first forty miles out of Detroit. It's a fine, three-inch thick wood surface road that offers good travel from Detroit all the way to Saline which is only ten miles before you get here to Clinton. Beyond Saline, the road's dirt (mud if it rains) but it's still a lot better than it used to be.

The plank road is not to be confused with a corduroy road. A corduroy road is made up of logs, often different sizes, that are placed in swampy areas and filled in with stones or smaller logs. They can be dangerous with the logs rollin' and sinkin'. The plank roads are better. If they are properly maintained they'll provide us good transportation for years to come. The planks are put across sleepers or stringers and there are often ditches on either side of the road to give good drainage. Because they're now all toll roads, the owners will keep 'em up sos they'll get good income. Or that's the theory, anyway.

And the customers the road brings! People from all over the world come through here now. Well, just last summer I had a man from England, a man from Ireland, and a man from Scotland drinkin' in here at the same time. A funny thing happen, too. The windows were open and flies fell in those fellahs' drinks.

The Englishman looked at that fly in his drink and pushed his glass back at me. "Give me a clean drink, Silas. There's a fly in this one," he said.

The Irishman saw the fly in his glass and just flicked it out and kept drinkin'.

The Scotsman? What'd he do? Well, he picked out the fly from his drink, held it over his glass and said, "Spit it out. Spit it out!"

Yeah, I know that's an old joke—but not in my time.

Recipes from Chapter Nine

Gin Fix

Fill an eight-ounce glass with ice. Add one shot (or more) of a good Holland Gin. Add one ounce of simple syrup and fill with lemonade. Add a sucker (glass, silver, or macaroni drinking tube)

Appetizer Cock-tail

Fill an eight-ounce glass with ice. Add one and a half shots of Rye Whiskey and a splash of bitters.

Note on Rye Whiskey—rye is a grain from which this whiskey is made. It is widely served in the East in the middle of the Nineteenth Century and is available in the West, hut not as much as corn whiskey.

Lamb Stew

Cut up one and one-half pounds of lean lamb into 1½ inch cubes. Brown the lamb in hot oil in a large, iron pot. Cover with water and bring to a boil. Lower the heat to a simmer and cook until the meat is tender. Drain the meat and add two skinned and chopped tomatoes, 1 cup of diced potatoes, 2 ribs of celery, and four diced carrots. Season with salt and pepper to taste. Simmer for at least 20 minutes. Test to see if the vegetables are cooked. Serve with a crust bread or rolls.

To skin the tomatoes, drop them into boiling water for a minute, and then remove. Hold under cold water and skin with a knife. The skin should easily peal off.

Turtle Soup

Sauté 3 large, chopped onions in hot oil until they are well-browned. Add one tablespoonful of white flour and brown the flour. And 2 pounds of turtle meat and one large slice of ham chopped into small pieces or one chopped chicken breast. Fry until the meat is cooked. Add 4 quarts of water and bring to a boil. Lower the heat to simmer. Season with thyme, a bay leaf, garlic. Add two pealed, seeded, and chopped tomatoes. Add two chopped hard-boiled eggs and the juice of one lemon just before the soup is done.

Finely chopped beef may be substituted for the turtle meat. If this is done the soup is called "Mock Turtle Soup"

Chapter Ten: The Card Game

Would you three gentlemen like to play a few hands of euchre? I got a deck of cards back behind the bar if you're interested.

I thought so. No man's too tired to play euchre. It's the "national card game of Michigan" after all. No man can be in business without losin' a few hands of euchre to his clients. We'll throw a couple more logs on the fire and get goin'. Is everyone" drink full enough?

Here, another cider and another ale. And another mulled cider, too? Certainly.

Here you go. I'll sit in to make it four. We'll cut for partners and to see who deals the cards first.

Well, it's you and me, Dan'l, against the other two. I'll sit across from you here. High card deals.

King deals. Here you go, Latimer, you're dealer.

Around and around the cards go. Let's see. Hmmm…I think you two are in trouble. Here's a seven, see what you can do with that.

So, Latimer, I haven't seen you in a while. What have you been doin'?

Yes, I know of your plan for California. Now that California's a state Latimer wants to go there. He's a widower, you know, and he'll be turnin' over his cooper business to his son and it's "Ho! For California" for him. Latimer figures he'll take a group of mail-order brides out there for them miner fellahs. He wanted to go earlier in the year, but waited too long. Now he's got to wait here in Michigan for the Spring. He sure doesn't want to hit the mountains in the winter. That happened to the Donner party three years ago whilst they were bound for California. It weren't too much fun for 'em, let me tell you. If you go through the Donner Pass in the winter you want to take along some folks who have some meat on their bones, just in case. And a bottle of ketchup wouldn't hurt, neither.

No, Latimer will be stayin' here for the winter and set out for California in the spring. And he's got another great idea, too. He's goin' to introduce entertainment to California. He says them miners got nothin' to spend their money on, except whiskey and gamblin'—not that there's anythin' wrong with that. He figures to take musicians, dancers and the like, to the gold fields and make money off 'em, too.

What's that Latimer? Yep, I think it's a grand idea.

(Did he see me wink?)

Let's see. Hmmmm, I pass.

So do you?

Partner? All right, so hearts are trump. Let's see how this plays out.

Darn! All right, my deal. Here they come, gentlemen.

Now, don't get so caught up in the card game that you forget to reorder drinks. Mister Wood keeps me and my wife on here to make him some money. He's from New York, you know.

No, Calvin Wood ain't here today. He spends the night at his farm, anyway. But, today he's out of town. The tax collector arrived and he made himself scare, as he usually does when the taxman's around. Calvin bought the Eagle Tavern last year, in 1849, for three hundred dollars. He put a good fifty dollars into it, fixin' it up, and that raised his taxes. Was he mad when he learned about that. Calvin figured he was helpin' the local economy by reopenin' the tavern and improvin' it. Then he's punished for it! It ain't fair.

So, Latimer, where you been?

No, you really were drinkin' at Hiram Nimocks' place? Not, the Eagle Hotel. The Eagle Hotel, not to be confused with our Eagle Tavern, is another overnight place of accommodation here in Clinton, Michigan. It's owned by a 27-year-old fellah named Hiram Nimocks. It's our competition, you know.

I ain't got nothin' against Hiram and his establishment. The gentleman is just our competitor, that's all.

Besides, last year, when Michigan had its first State Agricultural Fair in Detroit, both Calvin Wood and Hiram Nimocks showed their best hogs. It was close, but Hiram won the blue ribbon for the swine competition and he had the nerve to come in right here to celebrate. He drank to his victory over Calvin right here in Calvin's own place! How rude!

Well, what happened is he got himself knee-walkin' drunk and went home without his blue ribbon prize. When Hiram got home his wife said, "Well, if you won the first place where is it?"

Hiram said, "I musta left it in the Eagle Tavern barroom. I'll go back and get it."

"No," his wife said. "You're too drunk. I'll sent the boy." So she sent their six-year-old son to my barroom to fetch the ribbon. He stepped up to my barroom and I looked over at him.

I asked him "What'll ya have?"

"Pap's blue ribbon," he answered.

Nine? Well, well, well. We got this hand, partner. They ain't gonna Euchre us this time.

So, Latimer, why are you drinkin' at the Eagle Hotel? Does Hiram pour any better than me?

I know—it's that Hiram's mother-in-law, Philomena Potts, is visitin', ain't it? She a handsome woman, I give you that but, she's a New Yorker, you know. I don't know if you're up to a New York woman, what with all their high manners, and all.

I ain't sayin' anythin' wrong 'bout you, Latimer. It's just I don't know if you're up to the task, that's all. It is perfectly acceptable for you to be spreadin' your business around as long as you know where your home is.

I suspect when Mrs. Potts heads back for her New York home, I'll be seein' more of you, right, Latimer?

Another mulled cider? Of course. Don't deal 'til I get back to the table.

Here you are, a mulled cider, good and hot. You two? Nothin' yet? All right, let's play cards, then.

Oh, Daniel, you'll be happy to hear that Elvira Wilcox was in here the other day, askin' 'bout you. Her husband's right pleased with that reapin' machine you sold him. I know you'd be glad to hear it.

Elvira Wilcox? She's a nice lady, ain't she, Dan'l? She was married to some fellah back East and one day he up and left for the West, takin' their sons with him. He never said a word of good-bye or nothin'. He just left. Well, old Elvira ain't the kind of lady to stand for that. She sold just about everythin' she owned, packed up what few things she kept and left, followin' her husband. She followed the fellah all the way out here to Michigan. She heard he and the boys might be in the Clinton area so she came here. That feisty woman supported herself along the way by workin' for folks and spendin' the meager amounts of money she had to.

You know Elvira never did find her family. She settled here in Clinton and met her new husband, Washington Wilcox. He's the one who bought the reapin' machine from Dan'l. She's a happy lady now, I hear. You can see it in her eyes, you know.

I suppose she still misses her sons, but I'm also sure that former husband of hers is real fortunate she never did catch up with him. She's a feisty one, as I said.

Whose deal?

You know you fellahs have me talkin' so much I'm losin' track of my card playin'.

Oh, that's your strategy, is it? Well, you'll be sad to hear that we barkeeps can talk and do several other things all at the same time. Our barroom duties require that skill.

Let's play Euchre.

Euchre? It's a great game, ain't it? It began in Alsace. That's a place in Europe that keeps goin' from French to German hands and has a little of each of them folks in it. The Bowers which are sorta wild cards are called that because of the German word of Bauer, which means farmer or Jack. That's why the Jack of Trump is always the highest card in Euchre and the Jack of the same color is the next highest. People who don't play Euchre find that confusin' but we Euchre players find it right simple.

Speakin' of the Right Bower, fellahs, here he is. That'll take that trick and give my partner and me four tricks this hand. That's one point for us.

My wife, Sadie? Where is she?

Well, let me tell you, Sadie's hard at work in the kitchen. She's cleanin' from supper and settin' out things for the morn's breakfast.

Yes, Daniel, I agree. She's an attractive woman. My Sadie's part African, you know. Like I said, her father was a MacAllister, part Scot and part African. Her mother was dead by the time I met Sadie. I don't know if Sadie's folks came over 'cause of them highland clearances the English have goin' over in Scotland or not.

The clearances? Well, that begun after the King of England defeated the highland clans in Scotland. The English began clearin' the highlands of Scots to replace 'em with sheep.

I used to tease my Sadie's Pa by sayin' the English replaced the Scots with sheep for three reasons—

Sheep are easier to control than Scots.

Sheep are loyaler to the English than the Scots.

And they smell a lot better, too.

That always made Mack MacAllister laugh.

Here's the Left Bower. That gives us this trick. Now the Ace and let's see.

Oh, Danl, Lizzie Donahue was askin' after you yesterday when she stopped by the Tavern. She wants to know if you're in the need of any more fruit. She's got a goodly crop of cherries comin' in, she says, and she's be pleased to sell you some of 'em.

Lizzie? Sure she's a nice lady who has a fruit plot just out of town. She'll make you fellahs a pie, if you want, too. She's a widow now what with her husband bein' killed two years ago in the Mexican War. If you could, buyin' a pair or two from Lizzie would help her out a lot.

I was tellin' you 'bout Sadie and me. Well Sadie and I got married a year after we met and moved to Michigan to give us a good start in a new place. That was a long time ago. Things sure have changed here since then. We weren't even a state back then—just a territory. In 1836 we applied for statehood with a population of about thirty thousand folks. Now, just fourteen years later we got almost three hundred thousand people in Michigan. And it ain't that we're all that prolific, neither. It's 'cause of all the people who came here from other places.

Well, look at this. You fellahs lost another one.

Drinks? Sure, I'll pour another round.

Here you are, gentlemen—drinks all around.

So, anyway, Sadie and I and the children moved to Michigan and I kept bar in a variety of places. I kept bar in Pontiac when we first got here, then Detroit. That was well after the fire of '05 and the town was growin' pretty good. Detroit had a big fire, you know, in 1805. I was there at the time, on business with my Pa.

No, I didn't start the Great Fire of Detroit in 1805, Dan'l. Yes, I know Father Gabriel Richard suggested it were me, but it weren't. I put that cigar out in a bucket of water. I swear!

But the town burned and the good Father and others helped rebuild it. Judge Woodward—Augustus Woodward—really did a lot. He helped lay out the lines for the new streets. He had 'em goin' out from the center of town like spokes on a wheel. Michigan Avenue, The Fort Gratiot Road, Woodward Avenue.

That's right—Woodward. Judge Woodward named the main street that. He was accused of namin' the best street after himself. He denied it. Woodward tried to tell folks that the road wasn't named for himself. It was named Woodward 'cause it went toward the woods. That's what the good judge said, anyway.

You know them politicians.

What's your bid, partner? And you? We'll I'm playin' alone. I hope I know what I'm doin'. These fellahs are slippery, you know.

So Sadie and I took up residence in Detroit in the back of the bar where I worked. We reared our youngin's there and made some money. She took in laundry for a bit, until I could get established. You gotta do what you gotta do, you know.

Yeah, that's one of my rules. I heard a fellah once say there are three rules to success in any endeavor, but nobody knows what they are. That's pretty clever, I thought.

But I figured out three rules. They are—

Rule One—Nothin's free.

You may not get everythin' you pay for in this life—but you're gonna pay for everythin' you get.

The ignorance of this rule has caused the world a lot of pain. Everyone's tryin' to get somethin' for nothin' and it just don't work that way. Beside, in my experience a meal you worked for tastes a whole lot better than one you didn't earn.

Anythin' you get for nothin' is worth the price.

Rule Two—You gotta do what you gotta do.

Sometimes you just gotta take what comes your way, buckle down and do it. Many things are negotiable, but them that isn't—isn't. If more people would stop tryin' to get out of their obligations and do what they should, I think we'd all be a lot better off.

Rule Three—All you can do is all you can do.

When my son Hez came home from school with an average grade on his math test—I praised him 'cause I knew math was hard for the boy. If he got an average mark that meant he tried his best. That's all I can expect from anyone—try your best. Don't hold back, but don't get discouraged when you're not as good at somethin' as someone else is. We all have our talents.

And mine is playin' Euchre! Here's the Ace and you gentlemen lose, again!

Want to call it a night? Fine. Finish up your drinks and I'll have Sadie pulled down the covers for you. I got you three in the best bed in the place. (Whatever bed's available is our best, of course).

I'll stay here and bank the fire for mornin'. No use in startin' it all over again tomorrow when a few live embers'll do the trick. I thank you fellows for your business, for your conversation, and for the game. I'll see you for breakfast. If you are expectin' any mail, I am sure Elisa Chandler, the postmaster's wife, will be by tomorrow. She's be glad to fetch any mail you might have a-waitin' you with her husband. It'll give Mrs. Chandler a chance to pry into your business some.

See you in the mornin', folks.

The Game of Euchre

Euchre is the most popular car games of mid-Nineteen Century in Michigan. It is a card game played taking tricks. It is played in fixed partnerships with four players, the partners sitting opposite from each other at the table. Five cards are dealt to each player.

The cards used are the Ace, King, Queen, Jack, Ten, and the Nine. The other cards are not used.

Once trump is chosen the highest ranking card becomes the Jack of the trump suit. This is called the Right Bower. (Bower comes from the German word—bauer—which means farmer, peasant, or jack)

The other cards are ranked as follows—

Left Bower—the jack of the same color as the trump suit

Ace

King

Queen

Ten

Nine

The other suits are ranked Ace, King, Queen, Jack, Ten and Nine.

The Left Bower becomes, in effect, the same suit as the trump suit. Thus if Spades are trump the Jack of clubs is the Left Bower and may be lead and follow as a Spade.

The winning score is ten. The first partnership to reach ten points wins.

The first dealer is selected at random by dealing the cards one at a time and the first Jack is the dealer. Then the deal rotates clockwise. Five cards are dealt to each player in two rounds. The dealer may give the players two cards then three, or three then two, at his choice.

The next card after the deal is turned up. This is used for selecting the trump suit. The remaining cards are not used.

Trump is selected beginning with the player to the dealer's left. He may pass or say "I take it up". The up-facing card then becomes trump. If the player passes, the next player may pass or say "I turn it down". If he does not pass he plays alone and the up card is trump. If he passes, the next player may pass or say "I order it up". If he does this the up card is trump. If he passes, the dealer may say "I take it up" and the up card becomes trump, or pass by saying "over" and turning the face card down. If this occurs the trump is selected trump is named beginning with the player to the dealer's left. If all pass then the cards are redealt and play is begun anew.

After trump is established any player may declare that he is playing alone. The partner of this player places his cards face down and sits out the hand.

Once the trump has been chosen the player doing so and his partner become the "makers" and the others the "defenders":

The play begins with the player to the dealer's left who leads in the first trick. If one player is playing alone the player to that player's left leads. If two players are playing alone the defender leads.

Any card may be led, and then suit must be followed, if possible. If suit cannot be followed, any card can be played. The highest card of the led suit wins the trick unless trumps are played. Then the highest trump played wins.

If the makers win three or four tricks, they score one point. If the makers win five tricks they score two points. If the makers take less than three tricks they are "euchred" and the defenders score two points. If a maker is playing alone and wins five tricks the makers score four points. If a defender is playing alone and wins at least three tricks, thus euchring the makers, the defenders score four points.

The first partnership to score a total of ten points wins.

Chapter Eleven—At Breakfast—Silas' California Adventures Recounted

I sure hope you're hungry—Sadie's got a goodly meal prepared for your breakfast.

The others? Well, Latimer went home. All sober and forgiven. Dan'l's on his way back from the privy. He'll be with you for breakfast.

Misses Wood's here, too. She's overseein' Sadie's cookin'—not that my wife needs any overseein' in that regard. But, Mister Wood owns the place and Harriet likes to see that things are done accordin' to her high standards

Breakfast? Bacon, sausages, pork chops, potatoes, toasted breads, gravy, and eggs. If that ain't enough, shame on you.

And for an eye-opener?

Corn whiskey, of course. I'll pour you a good one.

Here you are—corn whiskey—a great start to any day.

Dan'l said I should tell you 'bout my California adventures? What to hear?

Yes? Well, whilst Sadie is cookin' and Dan'l's findin' his way back from the back, let me bend your ear about it.

Back in '45, when I turned fifty-two, which as you know is the average life expectation in America now, I decided to throw all caution to the winds and Sadie and me went off to Spanish California. That was before gold was discovered there and before California became an American possession. I had heard about the place most of my life and for some reason it interested me.

Well, anyway, off we go, the two of us. We bid good-bye to our children, all of 'em grown by then. We sold what we had and put enough money together to go overland to Alta California—that's what them Mexicans called what is now the State of California.

Yes, overland. We shoulda sailed, but I didn't know that then. Besides, in '45 there weren't that many ships sailin' out of New York to California like there is now. So we made out way to St. Louis, crossin' the great Mississippi River by ferryboat. Five years ago St. Louis almost as big as it is now—76 thousand people. I had been in that town when I was young but it weren't nothin' like it was in 1845. When Sadie and I got there. St. Louis was huge—three times as big as Detroit and twice as big as Chicago—and it was filled with Germans and other European folks. I've always got along well with Germans. I am a barkeeper, after all.

So a nice German family, the Kochs, took in Sadie and me. Now them Kochs they called themselves "Cooks", pronouncin' their name like they was still in Westphalia where they originated. I said Koch. "You folks is Koch. My wife is a cook," I told 'em.

Ralf Koch was a real nice fellow whose family fed us well, gave us a bedroom to ourselves and let Sadie and me earn our keep whilst we was with 'em. She cooked and helped Ralf's wife with chores. I tended to the animals in the Koch's small barn. We stayed in St. Louis for a month until the weather broke and wagon trains were formin' in Western Missouri.

Well, Dan'l. I see you found your way back all right. Sadie's cookin' and I was just tellin' your new friend here 'bout our California adventures. How far did I get? To where we was leavin' St. Louis and Ralf Koch's family.

(He's heard this story a lot and Dan'l could probably tell it better than me).

So, anyway, Sadie and me was off to Independence, Missouri where we spend three hundred dollars to buy a Conestoga wagon.

Yes, three hundred dollars! But that was for everythin'—the wagon, a team of oxen, and all the provisions we would need to get us across the prairie and the mountains. Or so we was told. I had a large barrel of bacon and salt pork. Sadie made sure the bacon was properly cured, too. A lot of people headed for California now find their bacon turnin' green a month after they leave Independence or St. Joe and it's too late by then.

We also had a whole barrel of died beans, a barrel of flour and sufficient salt, sugar, and coffee to get us through. Also strapped to the wagon was two barrels for water. I figured water would be a precious commodity when we reached the desert. I sure was right 'bout that!

The oxen we got were big and strong. I knew they would pull the wagon slow and steady, just like we needed. I still tell folks who are considerin' a journey West to buy oxen and not horses to pull their wagons. There are good reasons for that. This ain't no horse race to California, you know. The wagon train will go no more than ten miles a day—less in the rough country—and you need an animal like an ox which will get you there. The oxen pull harder than horses, they pull longer than horses, and when they die—they taste a heck of a lot better, too!

No, we didn't have to eat our oxen. They got us there all the way.

Oh, the wagon train. Yes. We joined a train, of course. You must. There ain't no road west of Independence, you know. The only trails are those known to the wagon masters and guides. The members of a wagon train hire these men and your lives are turned over to 'em for the whole time you're on the trail. They hunt for food along the way—fresh meat like buffalo—lots of buffalo—rabbits, prairie dogs and the like. One of our guides had a taste for snake. That was a taste I never acquired, myself. He said it tastes just like chicken. Don't everythin'? It seems that every time someone's tryin' to get you to taste somethin' nasty he says, "It tastes just like chicken." I say, "So why don't you just eat chicken?"

So, anyway, we was on the trail. Some folks get the idea that you ride in them wagons the whole way. You don't. The wagon is for pullin' what you need to live on and, maybe, a stick of furniture, or two for when you get there. You walk the whole way, mostly, unless you're drivin' the oxen. Even then, most of the time you're walkin' along side the team, guidin' it. Sometimes, when she got tied, Sadie rode, and one time when I got snake bit and my leg swelled up, I rode. But, for the most part, we walked.

But, despite our advanced ages—52 for me and 50 for her—Sadie and me was in pretty good condition and a walk of a thousand miles seemed possible. So off we walked, a-guidin' our oxen-pulled wagon and lookin' at every day as a new chance to see new things.

And did we ever see new things! We saw Prairie Chickens dance—their feathers all puffed up and them birds dancin' around each other for hours. The wagon master told us that was the way the cocks impressed the hens. I don't know if they impressed the hens but they certainly impressed Sadie and me!

We saw buffalo. Of course there's still small buffalo herds in western Michigan and herds that roam across Illinois, but nothin' like out west. There's millions of them beasts! There were times when our wagon train had to encamp for two days just to let one buffalo herd cross the prairie in front of us. We'll never run out of buffalo. That'd be like runnin' out of Passenger Pigeons or whales. Never happen.

And whenever there's buffalo, there's Indians. The native people of the West look different than our Indians here in Michigan. To my eye they look more like the Shawnee I knew when I was young in Kentucky and Indiana. Their faces were painted like the Shawnee and they had faces that looked like the Shawnee. But these Indians rode horses like they was born on 'em and some of 'em had big clusters of eagle feathers like a bonnet.

Scared of 'em? Sure. Them Indians trailed us for the longest time. I didn't know what were their intentions and the wagon master seemed concerned, although he tried to hide it. But as soon as the buffalo turned from the trail the Indians were gone. Or, at least, I think they were gone.

Sadie and I crossed prairie with grass so high you can't see over it. We saw the prairie grass blow with wind and it looked just like waves on the

Great Lakes. Billows of waves flowed across the prairie and Sadie and I, high on a hill, watched.

There weren't many hills, 'though. It's mostly flat land for a long time. We followed the Platte River for the longest. Then we veered south to pull our wagons across land that didn't have a lot of grass on it—more barren it was—and after a while we saw the mountains.

Nowadays I tell folks they'll travel to Fort Laramie or Fort Bridger. Ever since the rush to the California gold fields started the government sent solders out West to protect the trails. You'll feel much more protected in 1850 than we did in 1845. Kit Carson and Jim Bridger will be there, too, to help guide your wagon trail west. Them's both good men. I met Bridger. Carson was off on some adventure of his own at the time. Both are explorers who found trails through the mountains. We're much indebted to 'em.

Back in '45 not that many folks was goin' to California so our wagon train was mostly on our own. We pressed on towards them mountains.

At first the Rocky Mountains were at a far distance, a dark blue line just at the horizon. Each day I expected that line to get bigger and each day it did not. That's when I knew how far away the mountains were and how big they must be. When we finally got to them I knew this was goin' to be the hardest part of our trip. I was right and I was wrong, too.

Yep, them mountains was fierce. The trails were narrow and steep and there certainly weren't no ridin' then. Sadie and me just about pulled them oxen up into the mountains and that's when I started to think that this wasn't just a good idea, after all. We was exhausted but there was no turnin' back and no restin'. We had to keep goin'. And we did. Sadie and I got our wagon to a safe place then we helped a family that was just behind us with their wagon. One by one the wagons of our group made it to a valley and we camped there.

In the mountains we saw goats which lived on the sides of the slopes like you and me live on the flatland. They jumped from crag to crag and never lost their footin'. I was amazed.

We ate one of them goats. The hunter our wagon master supplied got one at quite a distance. It was tough meat but a welcome change from salt pork and beans.

By the time we left the worst of the mountains we had been at it for almost three months. I knew the trip would take long but, when you talk about it and went you do it—it's different. The land began gettin' smoother. It weren't nothin' like the prairie, but compared to the mountains, it was comfortable. We crossed a river by makin' rafts for our wagons and floatin' across. We pressed on past big hills of solid rock with flat tops like someone scrapped off whatever was up there. We reached the desert and pressed on toward the western mountains—the Spanish named them the Sierras. It was while we was in that desert that I knew I did a good thing by bringin' those two water barrels.

It's funny how things are. Here in Michigan we don't even think about all the water we have here. We got rivers and lakes. We got heavy rains in the spring and summer. We take baths once a week, mostly, and when we bathe we sink neck deep in pure, clean water from the Rouge, Raisin, or Huron River. Out there water is more dear than gold. Out in that desert than goes on for weeks and weeks, water is rationed out by the cupful. Out there in the hot dessert sun water is life. I sure was glad I had two barrels of it.

The wagon master, a big, bewhiskered fellow named David Langer, led us to a waterin' place where we refilled our water barrels and watered the stock. We drank first then let the horses, mules and oxen wade in. I find that is a good schedule.

After the desert, more mountains, more rivers, more hardship. All through it Sadie was brave and strong. More than me, let me tell you.

Finally we reached the Western slope of that mountain range and we was in California for true. A bunch of us looked out over the valley of the Sacramento River and we prayed a prayer of thanksgivin'. We prayed for us who made it through and for the souls of the five we buried along the way. I held Sadie's hand and we sang "Now Thank We All Our God" and everybody cried. It was almost exactly six months from the time we left for California.

The wagon master led us down into the valley and we split up there. Some went north to farms they were to establish. Some went south. Sadie and me and some others went to Yerba Buena, as San Francisco was called then. That was where I wanted to settle. I figured a town like that—250 people, or so—would have need for a good barkeeper.

Oh, here's Sadie with your breakfast. I'll let you fellahs eat and tell you 'bout the rest of the trip later.

Yes, dear, I'm bendin' their ears 'bout our journey to California. But, I'll be quiet and let 'em eat now.

Let's tell 'em what you fixed and let 'em eat.

First—toasted breads. Sadie held this bread in front of the fire in a hand-held toastin' iron that gives the bread that pretty pattern of dark and light. With the bread—plenty of fresh churned butter.

Then we got eggs poached in milk and covered with a cream sauce that Sadie makes. Misses Wood don't like that much but we do.

The meats are sausage and Sadie's famous pork chops and potatoes. There's plenty of coffee and tea, too.

Recipes from Chapter Eleven

Milk Poached Eggs in Cream Sauce

Crack an egg into a shallow dish. In a shallow saucepan bring fresh milk almost to a boil. When bubbles begin to rise stir the milk to get it swirling in the pan in a clock-wise direction. While the milk is swirling, slide in the egg. Poach the egg to the degree of doneness you like. The eggs white may form pinwheels that will look good on the plate.

When the egg is done lift it out of the milk with a slotted spoon. Let excess milk drip off before you place it on a plate.

Serve the eggs with a cream sauce.

Cream Sauce for Eggs

Peal and slice an onion. Sauté' the sliced onion in butter until the onion is a golden brown. Add a tablespoonful of flour and cook it for two minutes. Do not brown the flour. Add milk—the milk in which you cooked the eggs is a good choice. Stir and cook until the sauce is thick but still creamy. Ladle this over the eggs and serve with toasted breads.

Sadie's Famous Pork Chops and Potatoes

Peal and slice medium thin several potatoes and an onion. Boil these in a pan with butter, salt, pepper, and rubbed sage.

Meanwhile, as the potatoes and onions cook, fry the pork chops—rib chops is what Sadie likes the best. Salt and heavily pepper the chops. Rub with ground sage leaves and a touch of marjoram and a sprinkle of oregano and dredge in white flour. My daughter, Meg, adds rosemary. Sadie does not.

Heat up a black skillet until water dances on it when dripped on the pan. Add enough grease to fry the chops. I like bacon grease. Sadie likes oils. Add the chops and cook until done. Drain on a rack and put on a platter for serving. Keep this warm on the stove.

Drain most of the fat from the skillet and add the cooked potatoes and onion. After you stir the bottom of the pan to bring up the cooked brown bits. Turn the potatoes in the sauce left in the pan. The potatoes should have absorbed the sauce and be just about breaking apart.

Put the potatoes on the platter with the chops—Sadie likes to serve the chops on top. You can put the potatoes on top, the bottom or around the chops. Sprinkle with salt and ground pepper.

This is a breakfast dish? In 1850 it is! It is also good for dinner.

Note on coffee and tea:

It is widely believed that coffee replaced tea in the tastes of Americans after the Revolution. This is not true. America was a tea-drinking nation until the Civil War when coffee was more convenient than tea for solders to take into their encampments. In 1850 coffee was drunk but not as heavily as it would be consumed later. Tea would always be on hand at taverns like the Eagle Tavern.

Chapter Twelve—After Breakfast—Silas' California Adventures Continues

So, breakfast was acceptable, was it? Sure, my Sadie's a great cook—not that Misses Wood nor her daughter ain't. It's just, after all these years, I have grown partial to my wife's cookery.

Yes, you want me to go on with my story 'bout us in California? Sure—as soon as I get you a drink. What will it be? A stonewall? Of course.

Here you are—a stonewall cocktail and let's see…where was I. Oh yes, Sadie and me just go to California. We made our way into the town of Yerba Buena that was to become San Francisco and we split up from the others and found a place to stay near the bay on Montgomery Street. That was before the sand dunes were leveled and filled in to bring the town farther out into the bay.

I got a job keepin' bar at the City Hotel that was the only decent place in town for food and drink. I worked there but Sadie and me lived in a warehouse on Montgomery that was owned by William Leidesdorff. Bill Liedsdorf's warehouse was just down from the Broadway cliffs where a small pond was formed by the surgin' surf at high tide. A makeshift bridge of planks formed San Francisco's first bridge over that tidal pool and Bill Leidesdorff's warehouse was often cut off from the bay beyond by high water.

Tides and their effects were all new to me. I was born in Kentucky, reared in Indiana and had spent my whole adult life in the Great Lakes area. I had never seen the awesome effect of the ocean tides. On the very first night of our arrival Sadie and me sat with Bill Leidesdorff on a small rise of San Francisco Bay and we watched he tide come in. We saw the water roll in toward us, fillin' the lagoon at the foot of the Broadway Cliffs until that tidal pool was swollen with dark seawater. We saw sea creatures, seals and the like, swim in with the tide to seek places to sleep on the rocky shore. We saw the moon, full and bright shine across the rollin' water. We stayed silent and watched.

Leidesdorff? William Alexander Leidesdorff was a great man. He was the first African in America ever to be worth a million dollars. He was born to a West Indian black mother and a Danish father who was a planter in the islands. Bill's father sent him off as a child to be reared by Bill's uncle in Louisiana. William Leidesdorff's uncle was a cotton merchant in New Orleans—a man of considerable means. He reared his brother's son in the wealthy white world in which he lived. By the time William Leidsedorff was a young man he was the social lion of the mon-eyed set in New Orleans and a very popular escort to the high born white young ladies of New Orleans society.

When I knew him in 1845 Leidesdorff was a handsome man. He had beautiful dark curly hair and dark eyes. His complexion was fair and I certainly could see how the half-black, half-white man could be taken to be fully white. And, knowin' him, I knew how he could be popular with both the men and women of New Orleans' high society. William Leidesdorff was a well-spoken, educated man who could easily talk on any subject of concern. He was well-versed in the classics and he knew the world of business. I could see him speakin' his fluent French to a lady as he escorted her to a ball or talkin' down to earth business with a Louisiana cotton broker.

In the 1830s in New Orleans William Leidesdorff fell in love. He courted the most beautiful blond-haired young woman of that southern city, a beauty named Hortense. After his father and his uncle died, leavin' him their fortunes, Leidesdorff became an even greater catch as a husband to Hortense. But there was one thing. It was impossible. There was no way that Hortense's proper and rich white father would allow such a union.

William Leidesdorff told his beloved his terrible secret and she, at once, knew their love would never be consummated in marriage. She returned the ring William Leidesdorff had given her and she clutched a tiny gold crucifix she always wore about her neck on a golden chain. "By this sacred symbol I swear never to love another," Hortense pledged to her love. She and Leidesdorff had a final embrace and she returned to her home and family.

William Leidesdorff sold all his holdin's in Louisiana and bought a ship, the *Julia Ann,* a one-hundred-six-ton schooner. He would sail for the Pacific Ocean to be a trader in foreign ports. The day before the sailin' of the *Julia Ann,* William Leidesdorff was on a final walk along Canal Street when he saw a funeral procession passin'. The hearse, a black and shiny horse-drawn caisson, displayed white plumes. Leidesdorff knew that announced the passin' of a young person. The beauty of the hearse and the large number of well-dressed mourners who walked behind the horse drawn ornate coffin announced that the dead one was of a rich family. As the young mixed blood man stood in growin' anxiety, he saw the first carriage contained Hortense's father, mother and sister.

A storekeeper stood beside Leidesdorff. "It is so sad," he said as the young man's fears grew. "She was a young society girl who fell in love with a mulatto. She died yesterday—of a broken heart or by her own hand. The priest accepted the former cause of death so the girl's body could rest in holy ground."

"Her name?" Leidesdorff demanded.

"Hortense," the man reported.

The next day the priest, a Frenchman, called upon William Leidesdorff. He stuck out his fingers and dropped into the grievin' mulatto's hand the tiny gold crucifix that Hortense had worn about her neck. The priest told Leidesdorff that Hortense had sent him this as a token of her undyin' love.

When I met William Leidesdorff in Yerba Buena he was wearin' that golden cross on a chain around his neck. He never took it off.

William Alexander Leidesdorff arrived in Yerba Buena in 1841. He had spent a few years tradin' across the Pacific and was now richer than he had been in Louisiana. By the time Bill Leidesdorff took in my wife and me he had built San Francisco's first hotel, the City Hotel, where he put me to work. He constructed his warehouse and was, most of the time, the sole importer of goods to the village that would become San Francisco. In 1845 when William Leidesdorff became American vice-consul he grew in importance in the affairs of Alta California. He built Yerba Buena's first flower garden and lived a good life there. But he never married and he never took off that cross he wore about his neck.

I kept bar for Bill Leidesdorff at his City Hotel on the plaza that was two blocks from Montgomery Street and the Bay. I found even as a well-experienced barkeep who had served drinks to the men of Michigan for years I had things to learn.

"Give me a steam, Silas," a Californian demanded with a slap on the City Hotel's bar.

I looked blankly back at the man.

"A steam," he repeated. "Beer?"

They called beer "steam" in Alta California. As beer is brewed it gives off vapors that look like steam. The Californians saw that process and began callin' beer "steam". So I poured steam to the men of Yerba Buena and learned other things as well.

"The whiskey we get out here, Silas," Bill Leidesdorff told me, "is what we can get. Sometimes it is rye or bourbon. I know you don't have much bourbon in the North but we get it shipped from New Orleans and other southern ports. We do not have much corn whiskey like you do back home but we do have tequila." He pronounced that like Tea-Key-Lah.

"Tequila?" I asked.

"It's made from cactus," I was told.

I tasted the stuff. I thought they left the cactus thorns in it. I couldn't come up with much of a cock-tail to use the stuff but most of my customers drank it straight, anyway.

However, one of them drinkers was a sailor who told me of his fear of scurvy. Scurvy is the bane of sailors. It causes your gums to turn black, your teeth to fall out and your skin to hang from your body. It'll kill a man. Scurvy is caused by not eatin' fresh fruits and vegetables. Those are rare things at sea, you know. I told the sailor how lemons and limes prevented that dread affliction. I proposed that I mix him a drink to prevent scurvy and he went along with it. I mixed lime juice with his tequila to keep him healthy. I added salt because it was hot and I was afraid the man was depleted of salt. It was an awful mixture but the man choked it down.

His name? I never knew it. But he was married to a Spanish girl— Margarita somethin'.

As I kept bar at the City Hotel, Sadie worked doing laundry for the town's single men. She set up tubs and lines in the back of the warehouse where Bill Leidesdorff allowed us to stay for free and she made us some extra money that way. Sometimes she's helped at the City Hotel too, cookin' and cleanin'. But Leidesdorff already had a number of Mexican girls doin' that sort of thing so Sadie did mostly laundry.

Montgomery Street was a narrow dirt, or mud, trail that was more imagined than real. There were dangers along it, but not from the relatively small population of Yerba Buena. When Sadie and I arrived the town had less than three hundred inhabitants, two hundred of them Mexicans or Indians. The Americanos, as the Mexicans called us, were outnumbered by three or four to one but there was no danger to us from our Mexican friends. Even when talk of a revolt against the rulin' Mexican authority became to circulate amongst us Americans, the Mexicans remained friendly. I think they had little friendly feelin's about those who ruled from far off Ciudad de Mexico and saw us newcomers as being closer to themselves than people like General Antonio Lopez de Santa Anna.

There were dangers along Montgomery Street and in the other narrow dirt, or mud, trails of the sleepy town of Yerba Buena. In 1843 a panther carried off an Indian boy from Jacob Leese's backyard on Dupont Street and two years later parents still scared their children into stayin' close with the recountin' of that occurrence.

Dupont in those days was called Calle de la Fundacion at it was there that Ohio trader Jacob Leese built his house and it was from there that the Indian boy was taken by that panther. Or so the story was told. Church services were held there, in that area, later to become Portsmouth Square. The Presbyterians and the Congregationalists offered their services there. These were the first Protestant churches formed in what was later San Francisco. The Catholics, of course, had a grand mission up on the river Delores. This mission, San Francisco de Assis, would lend its name to he city of Yerba Buena.

The Russians had a church there, too. Located on Russian Hill, the Russian Orthodox mission to northern California was the reason the Spaniards established their presence in San Francisco Bay. When the Russians moved South from Alaska, Russian North America, the King of Spain feared the Russians would establish a claim to his California possession. To stop the Russian fur traders from takin' California for their Tsar, the Viceroy of Mexico, then under Spanish rule, sent a mission to Yerba Buena and they built a fort. Their fort, or presidio, is still there. The earthworks fort was built in 1776 and controls access to the bay.

The Russians stayed and their church is still there.

Many a night Sadie and I would walk along Montgomery at low tide and look out at the moonlit bay where great seals and an occasional shark could be seen.

Sharks? Sure we saw 'em. Never close up, 'though. We saw their fins in the water, cuttin' through whilst they chased a seal or some other unlucky creature. They got fish like that out there that you Great Lakes fishmen would not believe. We seen 'em jump outta the water and some of them's enormous. That's why I never went swimin' out there. I got a rule—I don't do no swimin' in water when the fish is bigger than me.

But the water, the ocean, is beautiful and Sadie and me, often joined by our friend and benefactor, Bill Leidesdorff

We walked along Montgomery Street at night and watched the moon dance across the small waves of the bay. Those were great nights. Sometimes, when Sadie was busy with her laundry Leidesdorff and me'd sit on a rock and smoke cigars. We'd talk about one thing and another. That's how I learned about him and his Hortense.

Cigars? Sure them Californians smoke cigars. Why a meal at the City Hotel was never complete without smokin' a fine cigar imported by sea from the Caribbean or America. Or a pipe. I can't imagine Californian men not smokin' in a place like the City Hotel's restaurant. It wouldn't be natural.

Say, you need another drink, don't you? Another stone-wall? Sure. I'll get it.

Here you are, fresh ice and everythin'. I didn't give you no clean glass—I didn't give you a clean glass the first time.

So, where was I? Oh yes, sittin' along Montgomery Street and the bay—watchin' the tide roll away.

We stayed at Leidesdorff's warehouse 'cause it was free to us and because it was better than any other place. For instance just down Montgomery from us was a boardin' house owned and operated by one A. J. Ellis. Ellis had a grogshop attached to his place to serve the sailors who rushed off their ships after comin' into port. One day one of the customers complained that Ellis' whiskey tasted bad and Ellis told him, "go drink water, then. The well's in the back."

The customer and his friends took Ellis up on his challenge and trooped out back to pull a dead sailor up from the well.

No, the warehouse was fine for Sadie and me. We lived there and Sadie did laundry there. It seemed we'd stay there.

Yep, them was good times.

Then things began to change. I met a friend of Leidesdorff's who would help change everythin'.

Bill came into the City Hotel once with a tall, well-dressed man who had a mustache and goatee and an honest lookin' face. "This here is my friend, Captain John C. Fremont," said Leidesdorff and I shook the hand of the explorer and army officer.

Fremont was the son-in-law to Senator Thomas Hart Benton of Missouri. He had opened trails to the West and had quite a bit of respect in Alta California. John Fremont was a good-lookin' fellah with a long, straight and thin nose and long dark hair. His eyes were dark and piecin'. As he stood before me at the bar of the City Hotel, I immediately perceived him to be a man with which to be reckoned. I later learned he was in town to enlist William Leidesdorff in the plot to free California of Mexican rule and make it into an independent country as Texas had done in '36. With war almost certain between the United States and Mexico, Fremont and others argued this was an opportune time to rise up.

I didn't care one way or the other. I just wanted to be left alone to keep bar and live out the rest of my life in California. I really did not care to whom my employer paid his taxes nor whose flag flew over the acalde's home.

But there were plenty who did care and I met some of 'em. Why I was there at one of them missions—they got missions all up and down the Pacific coast about forty miles, or one day's journey apart—and William Todd, an American who was for Californian independence got people all worked up to revolt against Mexico City. He grabbed a piece of cloth and was to make a flag for the new Republic of California. I helped.

Will Todd wrote the words CALIFORNIA REPUBLIC across the bottom of the flag and then he cut out a star, like he star of Texas, and put it on one side of the top, over the writin'. Then he cut out a silhouette of a rabbit and wanted to put that on the other side. I told him, "Bill, ain't no Mexican soldiers gonna be afraid of no rabbit". I cut the rabbit's ears more pointy and gave it a bit more heft and made him look more like a bear. That's what we stuck on that flag. So, if it weren't for me they'd be the "Rabbit Republic of California."

No, that's true.

Things started gettin' excitin' after that, let me tell you. The war with Mexico started and California became a prize. Commodore Stockton sailed into Yerba Buena to claim California for the United States. He found that General Montgomery had thought he had already done that and a big fight started twix them two. When the American flag was hoisted up over Yerba Buena my friend Leidesdorff was rewarded for his part in the revolt by becomin' a member of the town council and city treasurer. By then the African blood man was worth over a million dollars and he had become the first of his race to achieve that distinction in North America. I knew then that California would never forget him.

By 1847 Leidesdorff and others worked to open San Francisco's first public school. It was built on the plaza and in April of 1848 and Thomas Douglas, a Yale graduate, became its first teacher.

I really liked Thomas Douglass. He drank only eastern drinks like cognac and brandies, shunnin' steam and cactus juice. I kept a bottle of fine brandy under a shelf just for him.

In late '47 Leidesdorff organized the first formal horse race in California. After buyin' a beautiful horse from professional guide Langford Hastings, Bill cleared a flat meadow up near Mission Delores and men gathered there to race their horses and to watch others race as well. The few American ladies in town and many of the high-born

Mexican ladies all gathered at those races to show off their dresses. The mud that was splattered on those gowns gave more work to Sadie who still took in laundry.

It was 1847 when J. C. Christian Russ arrived. He was a jeweler from New York who came to California with his three sons to start a jewelry business in Yerba Buena. He and the boys dragged a ship's cabin to Montgomery Street and set up shop in it.

Bill Leidesdorff also introduced the first steam ship to California water. In 1847 he bought the *Sika,* a thirty-seven food steam powered launch that had been built as a pleasure craft for some Russians in Alaska. He was so proud of his side paddle ship and often had it sailed up and down in front Montgomery Street to show it off to the population.

William Alexander Leidesdorff died in May of 1848, just after gold was discovered along the American River. He had the brain fever and there was nothin' that could be done for him. He died in my arms. I held his fevered head in my arms as Sadie lovin'ly blotted sweat from his brow. He called her Hortense at he end and she did not correct him.

Pardon me. There seems to be somethin' in my eyes. Let me wipe 'em.

There.

The gold? Sure I was there when it was found. You know, I hate to say I was responsible for the gold rush, but I think I was.

Among the men whom Bill Leidesdorff introduced me to was Captain John Sutter. Sutter, a Swiss fellah, had a settlement up on the Sacramento River, up from San Francisco Bay. Bill hired a young fellah, Jerry Thomas, to keep bar at his hotel so I could work for Sutter for a while. I left Sadie in town 'cause the place Sutter's place weren't no proper place for a lady. John Sutter was a little touched, you know. He had built a fort in the Sacramento and pretty soon he had me and a bunch of other men marchin' around his fort like we were soldiers or somethin'. I got sick of that real quick. I was in the army in the War of 1812, you know, so I got my belly full of solderin' a long time ago. So when Sutter asked if anyone would like to go up to the American River to built a mill for him there, I volunteered. So did my friend, Jimmy Marshall and a Mormon fellah named Sam Brannan.

We worked hard, even in the constant rain of January 1848. Then, on one clear day when the mill was almost done I saw a creature come out of the woods to take a drink from the water. It looked just like a possum to me and, being from Michigan and all, I thought—there's dinner.

I looked over at Jimmy Marshal who was astandin' near the river. "Hand me one of them rocks over there," I said to him, "and I'll chuck it over here and hit that possum on the head and we'll have ourselves a fine stew tonight."

"Sure, Silas. Which rock?" James Marshall asked back.

"Give me that real shinny one in the water," I told him and the rest is history.

Sam Brannan got that rock, you know. He was a feisty fellah. He knew a good thing when he saw it. He grabbed the rock from Jim and began a-runnin'. It was a few minutes 'for any of us knew why. Then it hit us like that rock shoulda hit that possum. It was gold!

"Gold! Gold along the American River!" Sam Brannan screamed as he ran through the muddy streets of San Francisco. "It's gold, boys!"

The place was never the same after that.

I had actually seen, but not met, both Brannan and Sutter before 1848. Just after Sadie and me got there a fellow named Pickett, Charles Edward Pickett, was arrested for murder at Sutter's fort. Pickett had a tradin' post at Fort Sutter and killed a man in obvious self-defense. A trial was held and Sutter was there as an observer, as was Leidesdorff and I. Sam

Brannan served as judge and prior to the trial he, the jury, the defendant and we spectators were treated to an enormous amount of brandy by Captain Sutter. Then the trial began and after the defense stated its case Brannan climbed unsteadily down from the bench to argue the prosecution's case.

"How can he do that?" I asked William Leidesdorff who was sittin' with me watchin' the trial. "He's the judge."

"He is also the prosecutin' attorney," my new friend told me. I looked at him in disbelief. "This is California," he shrugged.

A hung jury led to a new trial at which Pickett was found not guilty. He went on to found a hand-written newspaper he called the *Flumgudgeon Gazette and Bumble Bee Budget.* I never could decipher the man's long hand.

By the end of 1848 William Leidesdorff was dead and buried under a stone slab in Mission Delores and thousands and thousands of men were pourin' into San Francisco. The word had reached the East and ships were sailin' around the Horn in what we call the Gold Rush. Wagon trains would be formed for California no longer by pioneers and settlers but by gold seekers. A wharf was built into the bay from Leidesdorff's warehouse and the street there was named for my friend. The wharf was called the Long Wharf and joined Clark's Wharf juttin' out into the bay.

The first Wharf in San Francisco was built by William Squire Clark, late of Maryland, in 1848. As the Gold Rush pumped more and more people into the place more wharves were constructed. Soon the sand dunes were leveled and the area between the wharves was filled and the city moved out into the bay. More land was filled along the beach we called North Beach and the city expanded in that direction, too.

With Leidesdorff dead and young Jerry Thomas doin' a good job keepin' bar at the City Hotel, I took a job on Telegraph Hill. That did not last long.

Telegraph Hill was so named, not because of any electronic telegraph, but because of a tall pole we put up with a series of ropes and levers on it. I could see with a spy-glass ships a-comin' through the Golden Gate passage from the hill and with a pull on the ropes I could signal the city below what ship was arrivin'. The only problem was that the Muldoons were readin' my signals and rushin' to the wharves to attack newly arrived immigrants to rob 'em of their goods.

The Muldoons? They were an Irish gang that controlled the shanty-town that grew up at the foot of Telegraph Hill. They were cut-throats and thieves of the worst sort. The other gang was the Sidney Ducks, a bunch of Australian thugs. As long as here was plenty of pickin's in town, them fellahs left each other alone.

Last year, in 1849, a newspaper in San Francisco ran a series of stories about the evil work of the Muldoon gang. The paper was so afraid to say things direct that they spelt Muldoon backwards. A missettin' of type gave us the new word *Hoodlum*.

Anyways, I quit my job on Telegraph Hill, figurin' I didn't want to be part of such a bad affair. I was hired by my apprentice, Jerry Thomas, who had gained the appellation of Professor by his drink mixin' ability to work with him at the El Dorado saloon. The El Dorado was no more than four wooden walls and a canvas top but it became the most popular barroom in San Francisco. It was there that the ""Professor" and me invented the Blue Blazer Cock-tail.

I've told this story before but I think I need to tell it, again.

It was the winter of '49 and a grizzled old prospector came into the El Dorado half frozen from workin' in the water of some claim. He stepped up to the bar and said, "Give me somethin' that'll warm me right down to me gizzard."

Jerry and I conferred and we came up with a drink for him. The Professor got two silver tumblers. Into one he put whiskey and into the other boilin' water. I muddled up some sugar and a slice of lemon peal in a class and Jerry lit the whiskey afire. He proceeded to pour the burnin' whiskey and the boilin' water back and forth twix the two tumblers and a beautiful blue flame arched over the bar. Then Jerry poured the drink into the glass and the prospector drank it down.

The old man gasped for air and his eyes bulged out. His face fell, hittin' the bar. I thought he was dead but he raised his head and smiled a toothless smile. "Right down to me gizzard," he reported.

The man didn't have to have another drink for a week and a half.

After workin' at the El Dorado for a while I took a job with a local baker, a French fellah named Boudin. He was doin' well. You know the only things you have to take to the gold fields is bread, salt pork and tea. You can hunt and trade for other meats, but you can live on bread, pork and tea. So Boudin was makin' a lot of bread. One summer day in '49 last year, just before Sadie and I decided to come back home—it was a hot day as I recall—Boudin had a whole bunch of bread dough he left out and it went sour. The baker was gonna throw it all out and start fresh. I told him, "Boudin, waste not, want not. These Californians will eat sour dough bread and not even know the difference." I understand the man's still in business.

By then there were thirty-thousand people livin' in San Francisco. The streets had to be redrawn to accommodate the new construction. There are no trees there—only chaparral—so wood had to come from where ever one could get it. It was imported from China and stripped from the hundreds of abandoned ships in the harbor. A half a thousand sailin' vessels lay in San Francisco Bay, abandoned by their crews for the gold fields. Their wood provided buildin' materials for those who got to 'em before someone else did. There were plenty of shacks along Dupont and Montgomery with little round windows bein' the former cabins of sailin' ships.

Jasper O'Farrell and I were hired to lay out a proper plot for the growin' town. O'Farrell was a burly Irishman who had worked as a civil engineer in his native Dublin. He had bushy hair and a large, bushy beard through which his teeth were forever smilin'. I liked O'Farrell, drinkin' and smokin' cigars with him as we planned our work. John Bush, another itinerant surveyor, also drank with us at the El Dorado. We surveyed as best we could and O'Farrell got a bit ambitious. The first plot of Yerba Buena was done by a fellah named Jean Vioget in 1839. The angles were wrong and O'Farrell's first job was to right 'em. He laid out streets so far into the countryside where no one will ever live—one he called Market Street—that them who owned the land there tried to hang us for takin' their land for no good purpose. Jasper fled and I began packin' for home. Market was to be a wide road cuttin' at an angle through established streets and virgin land to Los Pechos de la Choca, twin peaks that in English were called The Breasts of the Indian Maiden.

When the plot that included Market Street was announced a meetin' of landowners declared O'Farrell, Bush and me to be thieves for stealin' their land to build a road where no one will ever live. Besides the land that would be Market Street was the very best bear huntin' land in the area.

By then Sadie was sick of the place, anyway. Her friends had all married gold miners or had fled to civilized places. Thugs and criminals ruled the streets so much that a decent person could no longer sit and watch the tide move in the bay. And if a panther ever ventured into town again, he'd be killed and his hide used for clothin' and his meat sold as pork.

Just before I left town John Bush, my drinkin' friend and an assistant to Jasper O'Farrell, and I talked to a nice Italian fellah named Domingo Girardelli. It seemed this Girardelli fellah was workin' the gold fiends but had been in the chocolate importation business in his earlier years. John Bush and I told him to go back into that occupation. "When these gold miners get some money in their kick, they'll spend it on foolish things like chocolate," I told him. "You could make money off 'em." He was thinkin' 'bout it when we left.

I don't know how things out there will work out. The teacher Leidesdorff hired for the first school, Thomas Douglass, ran off to the gold fields and the school lies abandoned. Sam Brannan, the fellah whose big mouth started the gold rush, has founded the *California Star*, the town's first newspaper. A fellah named Geary had just become the first American alcalde of San Francisco before we left and he seemed like a good man. If him and some of the good men of the town take charge and hang a few of them Muldoons and Sidney Ducks, things just might work out for 'em.

John White Geary was quite the fellah when I met him. He was born in Pennsylvania and served in the Mexican War with a Keystone State regiment. After the war he was appointed Postmaster of San Francisco and it was him who handed Sadie and me our mail, if we had any comin'. Geary was elected to the State Constitutional Convention at Monterey and was elected alcalde of San Francisco in 1849. I hear now he's the major, still.

When I left the town had some glimmers of hope. The St. Francis Hotel was open for business. It was no more than three cottages built atop one another at Dupont and Clay but it was a start. And Mammie Pleasant Williams was still there. The fiery woman, a friend and confidant of Sadie, ran a boardin'house at Dupont and Washington, throwin' out unruly guests with the best of 'em.

Don't you have some business to attend? I don't want to keep you from your day's work with my stories. Tell you what. You go about your business and come back. I'll be here and I'll tell you 'bout our trip back from California. And I'll tell you what "seein' the elephant" means, too.

Songs from the California Adventure

A Ripping Trip (to the tune of "Pop! Goes the Weasel")

You go aboard a leaky boat,
And sail for San Francisco;
You've got to pump to keep her afloat,
You have that, by jingo!
The engine room soon begins to squeak,
But nary a think to oil her;
Impossible to stop the leak—
Rig goes the boiler.

The captain on the promenade,
Looking very savage;
Steward and the cabin maid
Fighting 'bout a cabbage;
All about the cabin floor,
Passengers lie seasick;
Steamer's bound to go ashore—
Rig goes the physic!

Pork and beans they can't afford
To second cabin passengers;
The cook has tumbled overboard
With forty pounds of "sassengers";
The engineer, a little tight,
Bragging on the Main Line,
Finally gets into a fight—
Rig goes the en-gine!

Now cholera begins to rage,
A few have got the scurvy!
Chickens dying in their cage,
Steerage topsy-turvy.
When you get to Panama,
Greasers want a back-load;
Officers begin to chaw,
Rip goes the rail-road.

When home, you'll tell an awful tale,
And always will be thinking
How long you had to pump and bail
To keep the tub from sinking.
Of course you'll take a glass of gin,
'Twill make you fell so funny!
Some city sharp will rope you in,
Rip goes the money!

Old Rosin, The Beau

I live for the good of my nation,
My sons are all growing low,
I hope that my next generation
Will resemble old Rosin, the Beau.
I've travel'd this country all over,
And now to the next I will go:
For I know that the good quarters await me,
To welcome old Rosin, the Beau.

When I'm dead and laid out on the counter,
The people all making a show,

Just sprinkle plain whiskey and water
On the corpse of old Rosin, the Beau.
I'll have to be buried, I reckon,
And the ladies will all want to know,
And they'll lift up the lid of my coffin,
Saying, "Here lies old Rosin, the Beau."

Then shape me out two little dough-nuts
Place one at my head and my toe,
And do not forget to scratch on it
The name of old Rosin, the Beau.
Then let those six trusty good fellows,
Oh! let them all stand in a row,
And take down that big-bellied bottle,
And drink to old Rosin, the Beau.

Sacramento

When formed our band,
We were all well-manned
To journey afar to the promised land.
The golden ore is rich in store
On the banks of the Sacramento.

CHORUS
The Ho, boys, Ho to Californy-o;
There's plenty of gold so I've been told,
On the banks of the Sacramento.

As oft we roam o'er the dark sea's foam
We'll never forget kind friends at home.

But memory kind still brings to mind,
The love of friends we left behind

(CHORUS)

We'll expect our share of the coarsest fare,
And sometimes sleep in the open air,
On the cold damp grounds, we'll all sleep sound,
Except when wolves go howlin' around.

(CHORUS)

As we explore the distant shore,
Filling our pockets with the shining ore,
How it will sound as the shout goes 'round,
Filling our pockets with dozens of pounds.

(CHORUS)

The gold is there most everywhere,
We dig it out rich with an iron bar,
But there it is thick, with spade or pick,
We take out chunks as big as a brick.

(CHORUS)

CHAPTER THIRTEEN—LATER THAT DAY—SILAS FINISHES HIS CALIFORNIA STORY

Well, I am glad to see you back. Had a good day of business, did you? Drink?

Here you are—a rye whiskey cobbler.

So, how was business? Good? I am happy to hear it. The more money my customers make, the more money they have to spend here.

What? Oh, you remembered. "Seein' the elephant"? That's an expression they use in California that means findin' gold. In a bar someone will announce "I saw the elephant!" and he's treat the whole house with the money he got from the bag of gold dust he sold that day. Or someone would ask a fellow drinker, "Have you seen the elephant?" and the other fellah would look down into his drink all sad 'cause he hadn't.

I suppose it got started 'cause findin' gold became as rare and as enormous as seein' an elephant.

But, of course, you didn't have to find gold to make money in San Francisco. That's what John Bush and me was tryin' to tell that Girardelli fellah. All you have to do is to find somethin' the miners need or want and sell it to 'em. For instance eggs. They sell for a dollar each.

Yes, that's right—a dollar for an egg! Out here in civilization a dollar is a day's wages for a workin' man, but things are different out there. One man I met made a thousand dollars in one day by rowin' out to one of them islands in San Francisco Bay to collect gull eggs. He brought back a thousand eggs and sold 'em all that same day for a dollar each.

You can make fifteen or twenty dollars a day just be siftin' the dirt from the streets of San Francisco. As the gold miners walk to the assay office to weigh and sell their bags of gold dust some of that heavy dust comes out of their bags and gathers on the roadways. People pick up handsful of dirt, blow gently over it and, there it is—gold on the palms of their hands! You pick up the flecks of gold with a wet finger or a wet stick and collect it. By the end of the day you have fifteen or twenty dollars!

Twenty dollars back here is just about a month's pay for a lot of workin' men. The problem is, in San Francisco, twenty dollars will get you, maybe, one night's lodgin'.

Yes, things are that expensive out there.

Remember I mentioned my wife's friend, Mammie Williams? Well Mammie—here real name is Mary but everyone called her Mammie—made five hundred dollars a month cookin' for rich men in San Francisco. Five hundred a month! That's almost two years wages for a workin' man in Michigan. And that was just for a month's cookery service.

Mammie is quite a woman. She has an ebony black complexion and was married to a white man, an abolitionist from the East. He died soon after the couple arrived in California in 1849. She cooked for folks and opened her boardin' house. It seemed she had a lot of young women friends 'cause there were a lot of 'em stayin' at Mammie Pleasant Williams' boardin' house and they had a lot of gentlemen callers—it you get my drift.

Everythin''s expensive in San Francisco. Shacks that in 1847 could be bought for a drink or two now rent for thousands of dollars a month. A meal that costs two bits here could cost ten dollars there. It is crazy.

How'd we get home? Well, let me tell you, there was no way we was goin' to come back the way we came—overland. Neither Sadie nor I would have survived another thousand mile walk. No, we sailed.

We met a man named George Gordon of New York who was in the business of bringin' emigrants to California. He had made two sailin's and had a good ship bound back for New York. Most of the ships that get to San Francisco lay abandoned in the harbor, many burned or stripped for wood plankin'. But Gordon protected his ship 'cause he was to sail back for more passengers. Sadie and me were among the few who signed on for that return trip.

On board was a crew of old men and boys who had failed to see the elephant. There were passengers who had. Several men on board had tens of thousands of dollars and they were bound for home and family to spend their fortunes. One man, an Irishman, sat on the deck all day, smokin' cigars and drinkin' good Irish whiskey as he watched the crew at work.

"Silas, me boy," he said to me as we sat on the deck together. "I shall be the richest man in Dublin." He took a long pull on his cigar and tossed his stogie overboard to promptly light another. He offered me a smoke which I accepted. The two of us, one rich in money and one rich in spirit sat on the rollin' deck of that ship and smoked fine cigars.

Sadie was leanin' over a rail. She and the rollin' sea did not get along well. My poor wife spend days lookin' down at the water—if you know what I mean.

The journey by sea took as long as had the journey by land. It was a full six months before the *Caroline* rested at anchor in New York Harbor. Durin' that journey I saw men buried at sea, some dyin' of illness, others by injury. We sailed South along the California coast, stoppin' briefly at the sleepy little pueblo precidio of Los Angeles. In 1849 there were about three hundred people livin' there. We stopped to pick up fresh water, somethin' we found not common in Los Angeles.

From there we sailed south along the Mexican coast and on to South America. We were becalmed off of Peru and for two weeks the ship had to be pulled by the crew in long boats, those men rowin' to haul the ship to wind. When the wind finally came we were a-sail, again. We made the bottom of South America three months from the time we left San Francisco. There we ran into the most terrible gale I've ever seen.

Our ship was heeled over for weeks, makin' runs and broad reaches before a strong wind. Poor Sadie, who had enjoyed the calm of no wind, was below deck all the time with her friend, a bucket.

Went he finally broke out into the Atlantic things got better. The wind was a fair one and we made good time without the storm. Gordon was to have us put to port in Montevideo but the English and French navies were blockadin' that port in some sort of dispute. Instead we put into Rio De Janeiro where the Brazilians resupplied us. The country of Brazil is a huge place under the control of an Emperor—Dom Pedro II. That fellah is the son of the former Emperor of Brazil, Dom Pedro I, who resigned to make his son the boss. Dom Pedro II's sister is the new Queen of Portugal, so the family's in the royalty business. There is still a little unrest in Brazil because of royal politics and we saw lots of soldiers in the streets. George Gordon got nervous about bein' in that harbor too long and as soon as we had taken on fresh water and food, we were at sea, again.

That disappointed Sadie who was happy to get her feet on dry land.

By fall we were in New York—safe and sound.

Ever been to New York? That was my first time there. What a city! The population of New York City is over a half a million people! That's 500,000 folks all livin' together in the same town. And that is just on Manhattan Island. There's two hundred thousand more in Brooklyn and others scattered all around the place.

New York City is fifty times bigger than Detroit. Ain't that somethin'?

Well, Sadie and I just had to see New York City before we came back to Michigan—not that we weren't anxious to get home. When we left our daughter Meg had a three-year-old. In 1849 that little girl, Nettie, was livin' with Margaret in Clinton, a-waitin' our return. We wanted to see her. Our other grandchildren were in Georgia and Ohio so there weren't much chance of us seein' 'em.

So we stayed in New York for a little while. I took a job as a barkeep, of course, at a New York hotel that was owned by the family of John Jacob Astor, the fur millionaire. Astor had died but before he did he sold his American Fur Company and bought most of the top half of Manhattan Island. Right now New York City is developed up to 40th Street. Astor figured that people would be movin' north of that line soon and he bought the land they'd be a-wantin'.

He also built he Astoria Hotel in the north part of the town about 35th Street. There I kept bar with a few other fellahs and Sadie and I lived in a roomin' house nearby.

The town of New York City is a cluster of neighborhoods, like Detroit, with each area bein' settled by a different people from a different part of the world. What they call "Five Points" down near the pointy end of the island is all Irish. There are several Irish gangs which control things from the five Points to the Washington Market. The Plug Uglies and the Dead Rabbit Gang are among 'em.

The Plug Uglies—that's what they call themselves—are bad but not as bad as the Dead Rabbit Gang. What them folks do is if you are a businessman and you don't pay 'em money every month, they hang a dead rabbit on your shop door as a warnin'. If you don't pay after that—you replace the rabbit.

Most men pay.

There's a lot of Irish in New York now—about a quarter of he population. That's 125,000 Irish. Most are good hard workin' men and women who escaped the terrible famine in their homeland to find a new start in a new place. Some, a few, are thugs.

The Irish are buildin' a new church in New York, you know. Yes, they call it St. Patrick's. It's up on Fifth Avenue beyond where the homes are. It's mostly woods up that way and a nice settin' for a big church building. The cornerstone was just laid this year, in January of 1850 and they've been workin' at it all year. Slow. Irish labor. You know—lay a brick, have a drink. Lay a brick, have a drink.

Just jokin'. My Pa was Irish, you know.

But New York is better for all them Irish. Unfortunately, the New Yorkers don't know it. They keep us Irish livin' in what they call tenements which are filthy little apartments—no more than a room or two—for which the Irish are charged high rents. And they're doin' everythin' to keep the Irish from becomin' citizens and votin', too.

While I was keepin' bar at the Astoria one of my customers was a fellah who belongs to a club called the Tamany. This club wanted to keep the Irish down and they elected men to do just that. This fellah, William Tweed, was one that saw the Irish as a danger. Without tellin' him about where my Pa came from I talked to him. I told Tweed that, in my opinion, the Irish could make good allies to an ambitious politician. "Think about it, Boss," I smiled, "if you are the only one who helps the Irish you'll get all their votes. While the others are tryin' to keep 'em down, you'll be rakin' in Irish support."

I don't know if I got to him. He still was talkin' bad 'bout the Irish when I left.

Another fellah I met in New York owns a museum. He was born in Connecticut and now lives in New York. Phineus T. Barnam is he.

Yes, the same P. T. Barnum who's sponsorin' Jenny Lind's tour this year. That's the one. Quite a fellah, he. I visited his American Museum just to see the Siamese Twins. I was disappointed. The Siamese Twins had retired from show business, but I understand they're still together.

Bad joke, I know.

The museum was somethin' to see, 'though. Six stories of the most astoundin' oddities in the world. Barnum had the Fiji Mermaid on display. I thought it was goin' to be alive, but it weren't. What it was what looked like a big fish in a huge jar of alcohol and it had what looked like a monkey's head on it. We were told it was caught off Fiji in the Pacific Ocean. I just sailed over that ocean and I never saw nothin' like that Fiji Mermaid. But, maybe it lives in another part of the Pacific from where we were.

A fellah near us suggested it was a fish with a monkey's head stuck on it. You know—a humbug. Maybe it was but it sure looked real to me.

The "Six Foot Man Eatin' Chicken"? Sure we saw that show. I had heard 'bout it before but we went anyway. They have a big poster out front of the American Museum announcin' the "Six Foot Man Eatin' Chicken" inside. It had a drawin' of a big bird with fangs and blood drippin' from those fangs. Inside they put us in chairs in front of a curtain. Barnun stepped up and said, "Ladies and Gentlemen—behold! A six foot man eatin' chicken!" He pulled back the curtain and there sat a six-foot man, eatin' a chicken dinner!

We all roared and many brought back their friends to see that joke.

Others I met? Well, let's see. I served drinks to Commodore Vanderbuilt. Commodore? That is what they've called Cornelius Vanderbuilt ever since he was a young boy takin' passengers out to ships in New York Harbor in his small boat. When he was young he beat out the other small boats to get the priority passengers from incomin' ships. See, in New York, like most ports, the big sailin' ships have to be taken into the docks by pilots who know the harbor. The pilots are taken to the ships in cutters that are faster than the other boasts. Then those cutters pick up passengers who do not want to wait until the ship gets to the dock. Young Cornelius Vanderbuilt had the fastest cutter and, more than that, as he made his money he began hirin' the other boys to work for him. Pretty soon he had lots of money.

Now he's a millionaire buildin' a big mansion on Fifth Avenue south of that new Catholic Church I was tellin' you about. Vanderbuilt's place will have a ballroom just that much larger than Lady Astor's ballroom. You see, the Vanderbuilts ain't on Misses Astor's guest list. New money, you know. That's funny 'cause the Astor money is from old John Jacob who began by trappin' fur animals. But that was a long time ago and, I guess, his family is allowed to keep heir noses up in he air if they want.

So Vanderbuilt drank at the Astors' hotel and I served him. He was talkin' 'bout buyin' more rail-roads, but I don't pass on information I get as a barkeep. Ain't right.

I can tell you what everyone knows in New York. Vanderbuilt made a whole pile of money in the shippin' business and, recently made more by not doin' what he coulda done well. By that I mean he wanted to build a canal down in Central America to get ships to California faster. The English own the rights to build such a canal in Nicaragua and they paid the Commodore a whole bunch of money not to be their competitor. Ain't that somethin'? He made money by not doin' what he coulda done well.

Now he's buyin' rail-roads and my guess is if he owns 'em all he could have his customers pay him not to transport the goods of their competitors. Once more, Vanderbuilt would make money by not doin' what he coulda done well.

But, he's a New Yorker, after all.

I did see the new Astoria Place Opera House. It is a beautiful place where they have musicals and plays. There was a big riot there when an English actor claimed to be the greatest actor in the world and the supporters of American actors took offense. Then the English fellah called New Yorkers a bunch of uncivilized beasts and they rioted. Several men died in the riot. That showed him.

Well, we stayed in New York for a while then headed back home. We sailed up the Hudson River on a steamer, reachin' the New York state capitol of Albany.

No, we did not meet Governor Hamilton Fish. Why do you ask?

Yes, I know it seems we've meet most every famous person wherever we went but that's the way things worked out. That' s all.

From Albany we boarded a packet boat on the Erie Canal and nine days later we was in Buffalo. From Buffalo it was only a five-day steamer trip to Detroit. In Detroit we met some folks we knew from before and soon we were back in Lenawee County. The first ones we saw in Clinton were our daughter, Margaret, and her daughter, Nettie.

How Nettie had grown. When Sadie and me left for California little Nettie was only three. Now she's nine. She all grown out, lanky and beautiful. And she's in school, too. Her mother saw to that. Nettie attends school durin' the mornin' and works right here in the Tavern afternoons and evenin's. The family's together, again.

So, tell me—how's your family?

One of the things I learned when I was away in California was that families is important. I met and loved a lot of people while Sadie and me was away, but it's not the same as havin' family. I know families can be challengin'. They get on your nerves and make you mad. They never seem to do what you want, but they're all you got. Protect what you have. That's what I say.

Where you headed from here? Novi? That's a good town. Novi, Michigan was founded a few years ago, in 1832, as Novi Corners. There are them that'll tell you that Novi got its name 'cause it was the NO. VI stage coach stop from Detroit, but that ain't true. Mrs. Doctor J. C. Emery, one of the town's founders, named it for the Latin word for "new" meanin' a new start for the folks who settled there. If you think about it you know that Number Six story is humbug. 1832, when the place was named, was long before the plank road was built to go from Detroit to Howell through Novi so it wasn't the number six toll boothon that road. It was long before Lansing was founded so it wasn't the number six stop from Lansing. There ain't no rail-road there so it ain't no No. VI rail-road station. Besides, no one numbers stage coach stops and if they did they wouldn't do it in Roman Numbers.. But, it makes a nice story, I suppose.

To get to Novi the best way is to take the stagecoach east from Clinton to Saline. You'll pick up the plank road there. It's ten miles to Saline from here so that's only two hours by coach. From Saline to Ypsilanti is another ten miles—two hours—then an hour to the Canton Cutoff. Take the Cutoff north through Canton, Sheldon then Plymouth. When you're in

Plymouth please look up the schoolteacher, William Starkweather. He owes me two dollars. There's a commission in it for you if you can collect that debt for me.

Never lend money to a schoolteacher. They never have any cash money, you know.

From Plymouth continue north through Mead's Mills, Waterford Bend, Northville. Novi is only two hours—ten miles—beyond Northville. This time of year you can't make it in a day. It's fifty miles and that'll be about ten hours. There ain't ten hours of daylight in November. You'll probably spend the night in Plymouth or Northville to be in Novi the next day.

Unless it rains or snows hard. Then I ain't promisin' nothin'.

Leavin' right after breakfast tomorrow? I'll make sure Sadie and Misses Wood has your food ready for you early. Drink up and we'll have a game of draughts before you go to bed.

A Chronology of Significant Events in California When Silas and Sadie Were There

1846

February

4—A large band of Mormons leave Navoo, Illinois. They are driven out by locals over polygamy. At the same time the ship, *Brooklyn,* leaves New York bound for San Francisco with a contingent of Mormons with 26-year-old Prophet Samuel Brannan is charge. They are to establish a Mormon presence in Yerba Buena.

March

13—Mexican Col. Castro declares John C. Fremont a bandit.

April

18—Col. Castro becomes Commandente-General and Pio Pico become the Governor of Alta California.

May

23—The war between the United State and Mexico begins. Commodore John Drake Shoat is sent to California to establish American control.

June

14—The "Bear Flag Revolt" is begun by John Fremont and others. The California Republic is established with William B. Ide as president. Governor Vallejo was captured and sent to Fort Sutter. William Todd creates the Bear Flag a Mission Sonoma.

24—Col. Castro's troops from Monterey fight the Battle of Olompali north of San Rafael. The Mexicans under Joaquin de la Torre lose five dead. Two of Fremont's men are killed.

July

1—The Presidio at Yerba Buena (San Francisco) is taken by Fremont's men. John C. Fremont names the passage there the "Golden Gate".

2—Commodore Sloat arrives in Monterey bay. He stays on his ship, the *Savannah,* at anchor.

7—Commodore Shoat goes ashore and raises the American flag at Monterey. He promises the people of Monterey greater political freedom as they become part of the United States.

8—Capt. James B. Montgomery, United States Navy, takes possession of Yerba Buena for the United States. He appoints Lt. Washington Allen Bartlett to be the first American Alcalde because the lieutenant speaks Spanish.

9—Captain Montgomery with 70 sailors and marines take down the Mexican flag at the plaza to replace it with the American flag. Their ship is the *Portsmouth,* giving that name to the plaza square.

11—The American flag is raised over Fort Sutter.

12—Capt. Montgomery conducts the first public Protestant worship service in what becomes San Francisco.

23—Robert F. Stockton replaces the ailing Commodore Shoat at Monterey.

31—The sailing ship *Brooklyn* arrives in Yerba Buena with 230 Mormons under Sam Brannan after a five and a half-month voyage.

August

2—General Vallejo is released from his confinement at Fort Sutter.

10—The frigate *Congress* with Commodore Stockton arrives in San Francisco Bay.

14—Sam Brannan delivers the first Mormon sermon in Yerba Buena.

15—The first issue of the *Monterey Californian* is published using the old press of Augustine V. Zamorano that had been used to print books and Mexican proclamations. It is half in Spanish and half in English.

October
8—Mexican loyalists, the Californios, are routed by United States Marines in southern California.

November
2—a party of immigrants from the East led by the Donner family and the Reeds stops for the night in a high pass in the Sierra Mountains on the way to California. They are trapped by a snowstorm and are snowbound until February of 1847. 40 of the 87 in the Donner party died. Many survived by eating the dead.

16—American and Mexican militia units fight at the Battle of Natividad near Salinas.

18—A Day of Thanksgiving is declared in San Francisco.

December
6—In the battle of San Pascual in southern California Californio rebels kill 22 Americans serving under General Stephen Watts Kearney. Martial law is declared in Ciudad Los Angeles by Capt. Gillespie and it is captured by the rebels.

1847

January
9—*The California Star*, Yerba Buena's first newspaper is published by Sam Brannan and Dr. E.B. Jones.

10—General Kearny and Commodore Stockton recapture Los Angeles.

13—All organized resistance to American rule in California is ended. General Kearney pardons all rebels in the Capitulation of Cahuenga.

16—The Russian ship *Constantine* from Sitka arrives in San Francisco Bay.

23—Charges are made against Alcalde Bartlett of misappropriated of funds. Jos. B. Hull of the Northern California Naval District supports Bartlett.

24—A law is enacted to control stray hogs in Yerba Buena. A five dollar fine will be assessed against ownersof such animals.

28—American Army Lieutenant William Tecumseh Sherman arrives in Monterey.

30 Yerba Buena officially becomes the Town of San Francisco by order of Alcalde Bartlett. It is named for its patron saint, San Francisco de Assiss, Saint Frances of Assisi

February
22—Edwin Bryant replaces Bartlett as Alcade of San Francisco.

March
1—Brigadier General Kearney becomes the civil governor of California. Kearney's capitol is at Monterey.

10—Jasper O'Farrell begins his survey of San Francisco to provide a proper plot for the town.

15—The 7th Regiment of New York Volunteers arrive in San Francisco aboard the ship *Brutus*. They are commanded by Col. Jonathan D. Stevenson.

26—Captain John L. Folsom is appointed quartermaster of Stevenson's regiment.

—12 members of the family of Adolphus G. and Frederick Russ' arrive to join the Russes who came with Stevenson's volunteers.

27—Vera Cruz, Mexico is invaded by 12,000 American Troops under General Winfield Scott.

April
19—Twice a week mail service is established between San Francisco and San Diego by two soldiers on horseback.

May
2—The Rev. Thaddeus M. Leavenworth, a Connecticut man, holds the first Protestant Episcopal worship service in San Francisco.

31—Gov. Kearney is replaced by Col. Richard B. Mason.

June

1—Alcalde Bryant resigns.

The *Monterey Californian* newspaper is published in San Francisco as the California.

2—George Hyde is appointed Alcalde to replace Bryant.

August

19—Captain Sutter and John Marshall begin the construction of a sawmill on the American River. This will be at a place the Indians call "Culloomah".

September

13—The first Town Council of San Francisco is formed. Its members are William Glover, William D.M. Harwood, William A. Leidesdorff, E.P. Jones, Robert A. Parker and William S. Clark.

14—American troops under General Zachary Taylor and Gereral Winfield Scott capture Mexico City, Mexico.

November

2—Lt. Col John C. Fremont is charged with mutiny by General Kearny for siding with Commodore Stockton in a dispute between the Army and the Navy over authority in California. He is court-marshaled on these charges.

1848

January

11—The Town Council of San Francisco bans gambling in the town.

24—James Marshall and Peter Wimmer discover gold at the construction site of Sutter's Mill on the American River

31—John C. Fremont is found guilty of mutiny in his court-marshal. He is offered a full pardon by President Polk which he refuses, saying that would be an admission of guilt.

February
2—The Brig *Eagle* brings the first Chinese workers to San Francisco.
The Treaty of Guadalupe Hidalgo ends the Mexican War. California is ceded to the United States as is New Mexico, Utah, Arizona, Colorado and Nevada.

March
25—An article in the *California Star* announces the discovery of gold at Sutter's Mill.

April
3—The first American school is opened in San Francisco with Thomas Douglas as its teacher.

May
12—Sam Brannan sets off gold fever as he runs through the streets of San Francisco waving a bottle of gold dust. "Gold! Gold! Gold from the American River" he shouts.
27—The crews of American ships in the San Francisco harbor desert for the gold fields.
30—Col Mason is promoted to brigadier-general.

June
14—The *California Star* ceases publications. Its entire staff has gone to the gold fields.
18—Captain Charles Welsh arrives in San Francisco. He will build the first brick house in the town.

July
11—Governor Mason and General Sherman tour the gold fields.

August
19—*The New York Herald* announces the gold find in California.

September
10—The price of gold dust is officially set at $16 per ounce.

October
18—The United States Navy offers $40,000 reward for sailors who deserted for the gold fields.

November
1—Capt. Sutter's son, John A. Sutter, Jr. announces a plan to build a new city on the Sacramento River.

The Rev. Timothy Dwight Hunt begins weekly Presbyterian services in San Francisco.

9—The United States Post Office is opened in San Francisco at Clay and Pike Streets.

18—Edward C. Kemble resumes publishing a combined *California Star* and *Californian* as the *Star and Californian.*

28—The *U.S.S. Lexington* leaves San Francisco with a half a million dollars in gold bound for the East.

December
5—President Polk in a message to Congress confirms the gold find in California.

31—A cold spell hits the bay area. 37 degrees is recorded and snow covers the hills.

1849

January
4—The name of the *Star and Californian* is changed to the *Alta California.*

9—Henry M. Naglee and Richard H. Sinton opens a bank on Kearny Street facing Portsmouth Square. It is the Exchange and Deposit Office.

22—John White Geary is appointed Postmaster of San Francisco.

The *Alta California* becomes a daily newspaper.

February
15—Harbormaster Edwards A. King buys Goat Island, also known as Sea Bird Island, for one dollar from Nathan Spear.

28—The steamer *California* arrives in San Francisco to begin the first regularly scheduled steam ship service in California.

March
22—The ship the *Julia* runs aground at the Presidio.

April
12—Brig. Gen. Bennett Riley arrives with an army brigade at Monterey aboard the *Iowa*.

19—The first meeting to propose a rail-road to California is held in San Francisco.

May
12—An auction is held to action the estate of William Leidesdorff.

AFTERWORD

Well, here you are—done with breakfast and ready to leave for Novi. I certainly hope you enjoyed your stay here at the Eagle Tavern and come back to stay with us the next time your business brings you this way. And I hope I did not bore you with my foolish stories.

I'm gonna give this paper upon which I've written some things that may make your journey more tolerable. I posted these suggestions when I was a-workin' at the El Dorado in San Francuisco and they were well-appreciated there. I hope you find 'em to your benefit.

Once more, it has been my pleasure to serve you.

Tips For Stage-Coach Travelers in 1850

The best seat inside the stage is at the front, even if you have a tendency for sea-sickness when riding back-wards. You will be jolted and jostled less there.

In cold weather wear no tight-fitting boots, shoes, nor gloves. When the driver asks you to get off and walk, do so without protest; he will not make such a request unless it be absolutely necessary.

Do not keep the stage-coach waiting. Do not smoke a strong pipe inside the coach. Spit on the leeward side only. If you have anything to drink in a bottle or flask, pass it around.

Do not cuss nor lop over your fellow passengers while sleeping. Take small change for expenses. Do not point out where murders have occurred especially if there are women passengers aboard.

Do not talk too much to other passengers who may wish to sleep, nor appear bored by the conversations of others.

Engage in no political discussion with ladies, nor embarrass such female travelers with ribald stories or jokes.

Do not lag at the wash-basin. Do not grease your hair because traveling is dusty. Expect annoyances, discomfort, and some hardships. This will make the pleasant times more welcome.

Silas H. Cully

Barkeeper

Eagle Tavern

Clinton, Michigan

November 1850

A CHRONOLOGY OF 1850

(with Mister Cully's Comments)

January

There are 6306 children in Detroit. 4000 of them are enrolled in the public school. Of these only 1743 attend classes. There are 19 small "unitary" school (all grades) and one new union school (graded 1—6). The union school is named for Education Board member Barstow and is housed in the former State Capitol Building in Detroit. A separate school is held for Detroit's children of African descent. This school is called "The Colored School" and meets at the Methodist Church on East Fort Street. The Reverend Mister J.M. Brown is the teacher there.

John Ladue takes office this year as Detroit's mayor. *Ladue recently moved from New York to Detroit. He was elected mayor although a relative newcomer. I guess the devil you don't know is sometimes better than the devils you do.*

Ira Bidwell, originally from Rochester, New York, has several successful businesses in Adrian, Michigan. His business and personal slogan is "Honesty, Perseverance, Economy".

The Michigan Central Railroad now connects Detroit with New Buffalo, Michigan. That journey takes twenty hours which is quite the improvement over the five or six days it takes by overland stage coach. From New Buffalo there are steamship connections to Chicago and Milwaukee. The track of the Michigan Central is heavy rail except for 44 miles from Jackson to Kalamazoo where it is still light rail. There are 6000 miles of railroad track now laid in America.

The war between Denmark and its breakaway provinces of Scheleswig and Holstein enters its second year.

1—New Year's Day.

The cornerstone to St. Patrick's Cathedral in New York City is laid. *This is an Irish project that is doomed to fail. The Irish have the talent and the will but not the money to build such a big church.*

The one and only issue of the American Gleaner is published in Detroit.

The Monthly Hesperian and Odd Fellows' Literary Magazine is first published in Detroit. Henry Barnes is the publisher. *The Oddfellows is a men's service and civic organization. You really don't have to be odd to join. I know Henry Barnes and he ain't odd—much.*

St. Clair, Michigan in St. Clair County is organized as a village.

2—The women's Medical College of Pennsylvania opens. It is the first medical school entirely reserved for women. *An abomination!*

Representatives of the United States and El Salvador sign a treaty of amity, navigation, and commerce.

3—King Frederick William (Freidrich Wilhelm) IV signs the new Prussian Constitution that guarantees autocratic rule. Popular vote is severely restricted and royal appointees are installed in place of the national assembly. *Them Europeans is always up to something. If it ain't a revolution, it's a king cracking the whip. That's a good thing, 'though. It brings more hard-working immigrants here.*

4—The Celestial Jon-Ling opens in San Francisco as that city's first Chinese restaurant. It is located on Jackson Street. Many Chinese are coming to California for the Gold Rush. They face fierce discrimination and violence but many work hard to succeed.

5—William Marcy Tweed is sworn in as an alderman in New York City. It is the first public office he had held. *This is a fellow to watch. He's part of that Tamany crowd which wants to keep the Irish down. Tweed's an up-and-comer, I think.*

7—Vice President Millard Fillmore's birthday. He turns fifty years of age today. *The only good thing that Vice President Fillmore has brought to*

America is a return to prayer. As long as he's our Vice President, we're all praying real hard for the health of the President.

9—British and French naval forces have ended their two year long blockade of Montevideo harbor in support of Argentina's claim on Uruguay. *These folks always seem to have their noses stuck where they don't belong, don't they?*

10—George Henry Boker's play, The Betrothal, a comedy, opens in London and in New York. Actor Edwin Booth is appearing in Boston in *Richard III* with his famous father, Junius Brutus Booth. Actress Lola Montez, the former mistress of Ludwig of Bavaria, has her American debut in *Betty the Tyrolean* at the Broadway Theater in New York. *I ain't real big on stage plays, although I've seen some. I've never seen Booth perform, but I hear he's good. His son Edwin seems to be taking to the stage, too. He's got a young son, John Wilkes Booth, who is a brat, I hear. This Lola Montez woman is quite the sandal. She dances a "Snake Dance" that ladies can't abide. I hear she's thinking of going out to California. That makes sense. She left her paramour, the King of Bavaria, when he got kicked off his throne. She likes to go where the gold is.*

11—Boston author, Frances Parkman's book, California and the Oregon Trail, is published in Michigan. *Interest in the Far West is really increasing. Good land in Oregon and gold in California. Every spring now scores of wagon trains form in St. Joseph and Independence, Missouri. From there it's "Ho! For California!"*

15—San Francisco and Los Angeles, California are incorporated as cities. San Francisco has formed a "Citizens Vigilance Committee (Vigilantes)" to keep order. In two years San Francisco has grown from a sleepy village of a few hundred to over 25 thousand. This is due to the Gold Rush. *The "get-rich-quickly" folks from Michigan have all gone out to California. Good riddance to 'em, I say. My brother went out there and we ain't heard from him. I figure that means one of two things—either he died along the way or he got rich. Those are the only two reasons he wouldn't have written home. If he had gone bust we woulda heard from him by now.*

They call finding gold "Seeing the Elephant" in California. People ask, "Have you seen the elephant?" and every one knows what they're asking.

The Medium, a semi-monthly magazine moves to Detroit. It is of interest to the New Jerusalem and Swedenborgian Churches. *These are churches that are organized around the beliefs of a fellow named Swendenborg.*

16—John S. Bagg has bought the Detroit Democratic Free Press. He will continue it as an instrument of the Democratic Party. *Each political party has a newspaper of its own. The Detroit Free Press is the one of the Democrats'—too conservative for my tastes. It was founded in 1831 by a fellah named Sheldon McKight as the Democratic Free Press and Michigan Intelligencer. That's a lot of ink just for the masthead.*

17—Detroit Sheriff E.V. Cicotte has organized a volunteer "Night Watch" of citizens to stem crime. He reports a growing number of disorderly persons inhabiting the city. *Don't blame only the Irish for this. Other folks act up, too. Cicotte's got his hands full.*

William P. Laing opens a store in the Shiawassee County town of Perry Center. He is the first Postmaster there and the founder of the town. *A lot of Michigan towns are named for the founders. Someone builds a mill on a river and then the farmers bring their grains to be milled. Someone puts up a tavern so the farmers have a place to wait whilst their grain's being milled. Then some ladies put up a church because of the tavern and, just like that, you've got yourself a town.*

Hall's Corners in Branch County becomes California, Michigan with Israel R. Hall as its first Postmaster. *See?*

19—American playwright, George Henry Boker, publishes a new play, Ann Boleyn, in Boston. *Ann Boleyn was the second wife of King Henry VIII of England. She lasted 100 days before he had her head chopped off her. I'm told she had six fingers on one of her hands. Maybe the king shoulda chopped one of them off instead of the lady's head.*

20—Charles Dickens' book, David Copperfield, is published in London. *I met this Dickens fellah and wasn't impressed. He was rude and did nothing but complain. Nothing in America was good enough for him. I told*

Dickens he was acting as if there weren't no Christmas. "Bah, Humbug!" he said to me.

22—Russian author, Feodor Mikhailovitch Dostolievski, is deported to Siberia for his part in Communist plots against Tsar Nicholas Romanov in 1849. *Siberia is a really cold place where the Tsar sends folks he don't like. With the way this Nicholas fellah behaves it looks like Siberia will be the most heavily populated province of the Russian Empire soon.*

23—Price B. Webster becomes the first Postmaster of Metamora, Michigan in Lapeer County. *Metamora has a new tavern. It's called the White Horse, built a couple of years ago. Good food and it's not really horsemeat, neither.*

28—Phelpstown in Ingham County becomes LeRoy with Perry Henderson as its Postmaster. *Leroy is on the way from Detroit to the new state capitol of Lansing, Michigan. The overnight is Howell. Then the next day you go through Cedar, then Leroy. From there it's on to Lansing through Williamstown and Hamilton.*

29—Senator Henry Clay of Kentucky proposes a series of eight resolutions to settle controversies between the North and the South over slavery and other issues. This effort will be called the "Compromise of 1850". It includes the admission of California as a free state, the establishment of territorial governments in Utah and New Mexico without reference to slavery, the adjustment of the boundaries of Texas and New Mexico with the assumption of the Texan debt by the Federal Government, no interference with slavery in the District of Columbia, the abolition of the D.C. slave trade, and a more effective fugitive slave law. *I hope and pray that this Compromise of Clay's will really save the Union. As much as I am opposed to slavery, I can't see no way to end it right now. We can stop the abomination from spreading out of the fifteen states that currently hold human beings in bondage, but what with a Southern-leanin' Supreme Court and Congress divided on the issue the hope of abolition is remote. We must hold the Union together or all is lost!*

31—Stephan Batchelden becomes the first Postmaster of Manistee, Michigan. The town was founded in 1841 when John, Joseph, and Adam Stronach built a sawmill there. *They are cutting timber along the Manistee River and shipping the logs across Lake Michigan to Chicago. The Mears brothers and others have sawmills there to cut the logs into lumber to build Chicago It's good Michigan wood that's being used to build Chicago. I hope they take good care of it and watch their cows and lanterns.*

February

T.C. Miller owns a tobacco manufacturing facility in Detroit. The tobacco is stored on the second floor of his shop and is cut on the first floor next to a stable. This produces cigars that have a "horsy smell" that has become popular and prized among cigar smokers. *And you ladies think the cigars stink in your time?*

Jenny Lind, the "Swedish Nightingale" will be touring America. New York showman, P.T. Barnum, will produce a multi-city tour. Barnum expects to profit $100,000 by the Lind tour. He is paying his star $1000 a performance at a time when the average worker in America makes $300 a year. *Jenny Lind came to America with her own valet, cook, and maid. Barnum even shipped her personal coach over so she'll feel comfortable riding around. She's European, you know.*

The excavation of the ancient Assyrian capitol of Nineveh in Mesopotamia is proceeding under the direction of Turkish Assyriologist, Hormuzd Rassam. *There is grown interest in ancient ruins ever since the uncovering of Pompeii in Italy. Folks decorate their homes with things that look like old stuff. I tried to convince my wife of that but she said my old comfortable chair don't qualify.*

Several farmers in Marshall, Michigan are forced to sell their farms in order to pay fines imposed upon them in 1848 for their help to Adam Crosswhite, an escaped slave. In 1847, Crosswhite and his family were protected from slave catchers by his neighbors and a Detroit court ruled against the neighbors at trail. The Crosswhites escaped to Canada. *The struggle against the slavecatchers will go on, especially if the new Fugitive Slave Bill is passed. Even those who don't want to end slavery in the South hate the slavecatchers coming into their towns to kidnap their neighbors.*

Tavern owner, Rufus R. Cook, has opened a general store in Cook's Corner's, a town named for him in Ionia County, Michigan.

1—Seymour Finney purchases land in Detroit upon which he will build the Temperance House Hotel and barn. He will use both in his work in the Underground Railroad. *Finney's an associate of George deBaptist and William Webb, two men of African decent who work in the Underground Rail-road in Detroit.*

Edward Baker Lincoln, the second son of Abraham and Mary Lincoln of Springfield, Illinois dies in Springfield. He is four years of age at his passing. *I hope this is the last tragedy these nice people have to endure.*

2—Norman Little, agent for Alfred M. Hoyt of New York City, begins building East Saginaw on the East side of the Saginaw River across from the existing town of Saginaw, Michigan. *They're clear-cutting the Saginaw valley now for those fine pine trees. Sawmills are going up all along the Saginaw River. It's a real growth area of Michigan, only 100 miles, or three or four days from Detroit.*

3—A Quaker school opens in Birdsall, Michigan in Lenawee County. *The Quakers are thusly called because they "Quake in fear of the Lord" They seem to be nice folks but I don't see too many of 'em in my barroom.*

5—The great debate begins in Congress on the Compromise of 1850. Henry Clay of Kentucky, John C. Calhoun of South Carolina, and Daniel Webster of Massachusetts who form the great senatorial triumvirate give speeches. *Imagine these three great orators in the Senate at the same time. I'd sure like to hear 'em debate the Compromise bills if I could leave my duties at the Tavern for the three week trip from Michigan to Washington.*

German composer, Robert Schumann, publishes music from his latest work, Faust.

French composer, Charles Louis Ambroise Thomas' new opera, A Midsummer's Night Dream, opens in Paris.

6—Hiram College in Hiram, Ohio is founded.

7—Stephen Foster publishes his new song, De Camptown Races. *Stephen Foster writes music in Pittsburgh, Pennsylvania. This year he'll be married and move to New York.*

William S. Mead opens an inn in Meadville in Ingham County, Michigan.

An escaped slave named Noel Johnson from Missouri sells his copper claim to the Mass Mining Company. This becomes Mass, Michigan. *Men and women, of African descent once given the opportunity to succeed in freedom do well. One founded what is now Chicago. An African woman gave her fortune to build a beautiful church on Gross Isle, Michigan, and others have already made their mark in business and the arts. Imagine what how America would benefit from the liberation of the three million Africans now held in bondage in the South.*

East St. Joseph, Michigan on the St. Joseph River is declared vacant by a special act of the Michigan Legislature. *Towns come and towns go.*

10—William Makepeace Thackeray's novel, History of Pendennis, is published in England. It follows his popular Vanity Fair. *I read Vanity Fair. It's about the time of Napoleon and folks who lived then. Not bad.*

12—The United State Congress agrees to purchase the manuscript of George Washington's Farewell Speech. *The government is collecting historic documents now that we have the Smithsonian Institution in Washington and a greater sense of the importance of such things.*

13—Benjamin Peirce, the American scientist who discovered the planet Neptune in 1848, has announced his preliminary report on the constitution of the rings of Saturn. *We now know there are eight planets. Peirce discovered the Neptune by studying the irregular orbit of Uranus.*

—M. Allen and O.S. Goiley become the publishers of Detroit's Michigan Christian Herald newspaper.

15—The Boston Music School opens in Boston, Massachusetts.

William A, Burt of Detroit patents his "solar compass". This is a surveying instrument that finds a true north-south line using the sun's position in the sky. *Burt's a surveyor and has a lake named for him in Michigan. He may go to London next year for the big exposition they'll be holding there.*

17—The second volume of Washington Irving's Mahomet and His Successors is published.

19—W.D. Cochrane opens the Detroit Business University to meet at the banking house of David Preston & Co. in Detroit. This bank is located on the southeast corner of Woodward and Larned.

20—Cyrus McCormick's company opens a sales office on Larned in Detroit. It sells the McCormick reaper that is manufactured in Chicago. *The McCormick reaper was first developed by Cyrus' father back east. Cyrus perfected it and now manufacturers the machine in Chicago. We get some of his salesmen at the Tavern, Dan'l Brown amongst 'em.*

Father M.E.E. Shawn is installed as pastor of SS Peter and Paul Roman Catholic Church in Detroit. *This is in a French area of Detroit.*

21—Handy, Michigan in Livingston County receives its first Post Office. John T. Watson is Postmaster.

Fort Pleasant in St. Joseph County, Michigan is renamed Leoadias after the ancient Spartan king. *Leoadias was commanding three hundred Spartan warriors and a few thousand other Greeks to hold off a million invading Persians. The Persians said they'd "blacken the sky with their arrows" Leoadias replied, "Then we'll fight you in the shade". A brave man, him.*

22—The American Painter, John Thomas Peele, completes and shows his latest work, Sunny Days of Childhood. He specializes in studies of child life.

24—Poplar French dramatist, Augutin Eugene Scribe, presents his latest play, The Queen of Navarre, in Paris.

25—Lynn, Michigan in St. Clair County is organized by lumberman Alfred A. Dwight and named for his foreman, Edward J. Lynn.

27—Isaac LaGrange becomes the first Postmaster of Cedar Creek, Michigan in Barry County. The town is so named because of a nearby stream that has its source in a cedar swamp.

28—The Post Office at Medina, Michigan in Lenawee County is moved to Canandaigua.

March

Steamships, the Mayflower and the Atlantic, ply the Great Lakes, each carrying 300 passengers with 85 staterooms. These ships are side-wheelers.

It takes about 45 days to sail from New York City to Liverpool, England and about three months to sail from New York to San Francisco, California. The Cunard and the Collins lines offer steamships across the Atlantic, cutting the time of passage to a few weeks.

Izambard Kingdom Brunnel, a famed English civil engineer, has designed and launched great sail/steam ships. His latest, the mammoth Great Britain, is launched this year. It is the world's first all iron ship and has a screw propeller, unlike Brunnel's earlier ship, the Great Western, which is a side-wheeler. The Great Britain routinely makes the transatlantic crossing in less than 12 days. *Brunnel was a bridge designer who discovered that later ships were more efficient in their use of fuel. Instead of needing twice as much fuel as a 50-foot long ship, a 100-footer needs only fifty percent more. That has led to his huge ships and better travel across the ocean.*

The usual working week for a factory or shop hand is 12 hours a day, six days a week. A dollar a day is a good wage. *A barkeep can make up to $1.50 a day, but we ain't the average workers, are we?*

David and Soloman Johnson of New York City run a steam sawmill in Zilwaukie, Michigan, a town they so named to confuse German immigrants bound for Milwaukee, Wisconsin.

Levi M. Comstock opens a mill at Mill Grove in Allegan County, Michigan.

3—George B. Truax and Sophia Slocum have registered their plats for Trenton, Michigan. The area had been previously known as Truaxton, Monguuago, and Truago. It borders Solomon Sibley's limestone quarry. *This is a town across from Grosse Isle, an island in the Detroit River which you can cross by ferryboat from Trenton.*

French novelist, Madam Armatine Lucile Aurore Dupin Dedevant, writing under the name of George Sand, has published her latest book, The Devil's Pool. *A woman using a man's name to publish books. Only in France, huh?*

4—A speech by Senator John C. Calhoun of South Carolina in support of the Compromise is read to the Senate by Senator James M. Mason of Virginia. Calhoun is too ill to deliver the speech himself.

A mob destroys the home of Senator John B. Smith of Wisconsin in Milwaukee in retaliation of his tax legislation on whiskey and beer. *This was a great act of civil pride. You don't stand between the Germans and their beer, you know.*

E.G. Salisbury buys a mill site in Orangeville in Barry County, Michigan. He will build a water-powered mill there.

5—Nathaniel Hawthorne's The Scarlet Letter is published. It is 1850's most popular book. *This is a racy novel about a woman who has to wear a scarlet letter on her blouse everywhere so goes because of something she did. It's not for the ladies' eyes!*

6—The Mississippi legislature calls for a convention of slave-holding states. The convention is set for June 3rd in Nashville, Tennessee.

7—Senator Daniel Webster of Massachusetts delivers a stirring speech in the Senate in support of the Compromise. In this speech Webster declares, "I wish to speak today, not as a Massachusetts man, nor as a Northern man, but as an American…I speak today for the preservation of the Union. Hear me for my cause." *This may end any hope of Webster becoming president.*

Lyman Lawrence records his plat of Mattawn, Michigan in Van Buren County.

8—A settlement begins at Norwich Mine in Ontonagon, Michigan.

10—English poet Alfred Tennyson publishes his In Memoriam in honor of his deceased friend, Arthur Hallam.

11—Senator William H. Seward of New York speaks against the provisions of the Clay Compromise.

Sir Robert Peel, the late Prime Minister of England, dies in London. He was 72 years of age.

Sanilac Mills in Sanilac County, Michigan is given its first Post Office. Isaac Lenty, co-founder of the town, becomes the first Postmaster.

12—California formally requests admission to the Union as a state. *Sign the petition in the barroom to stop California statehood! All men may sign.*

13—Senator Jefferson Davis of Mississippi speaks against the Compromise. He says is doesn't go far enough in preserving and extending slavery. *Jeff Davis was a hero in the Mexican War. He's a Senator now and quite the patriot, I hear.*

14—The closed Post Office at Exeter, Michigan in Monroe County is restored.

15—The Chicago Philharmonic Society is established.

17—American author and traveler, Bayard Taylor, publishes a book recounting his recent travels. The book is called El Dorado. Taylor writes for the New York Tribune.

19—Fort Wilkins in Keneenaw County, Michigan has its Post Office closed. The Fort was built in 1844 to protect government interests in the copper mining community. *Huge amounts of money were made in Michigan's Upper Peninsula from copper. A huge boulder of copper was taken to Washington for display in the new Smithsonian Institution.*

21—Joseph Oliver organizes Frankfort, Michigan in Benzie County.

22—The settlement in Genesse County formally called Mt. Pleasant is renamed Long Lake, Michigan.

26—Ohio Senator Salmon Portland Chase speaks against the Compromise.

27—Senator Louis Cass of Michigan sides with Clay and the Southerners opposing the Wilmont Proviso and supporting the Compromise. The Wilmont Proviso would prohibit slavery in he recently acquired territories in the West. *Cass ran in 1848 as the Democratic Party's nominee for president. He lost. His support of "squatters' sovereignty" cost him votes. I didn't vote for him, but I still admire the fellah. He's done a lot for our state.*

31—John C. Calhoun, Senator from South Carolina and a leader of the Southern cause in Congress, dies in Washington, D.C. He served as Secretary of State under Monroe and was Vice President under John Quincy Adams and Andrew Johnson. While Taylor's Secretary of State Calhoun secured the annexation of Texas. He was also the only person to resign the Vice Presidency. In the Senate once more (1845—1850) Calhoun led the opposition to the admission of California as a state opposed the Wilmont Proviso to stop the expansion of slavery in the West, and led the Southern faction in the debate on the Compromise of 1850. In his Discourse on the Constitution that was published after his death, Senator Calhoun proposed a duel presidency with one president from the South and one from the North, each with the veto power. *This is a great loss to the Southern cause. Calhoun has been their champion for many years. He was a great debater and quite the orator.*

April

A change in the legal age in Michigan for marriage is proposed as part of the new state constitution. It will be 18 for males and 16 for females. This is a change from the 1838 law that was 17 for males and 14 for females. *There's going to be a big rush of fifteen-year-old girls getting married this year to beat the deadline.*

The Democrats outnumber the Whigs in the United States House of Representatives 112 to 109 with 9 of other parties. The Democrats hold the Senate over the Whigs by 35 to 25 with two of other parties. The White House is in Whigs hands. Roger B. Taney of Maryland is the Chief Justice of the United States. The Speaker of the House of Representatives is Howell Cobb of Georgia.

A tavern west of Clinton on the Chicago Road is the Davenport House. This is a tavern in the Irish Hills at Evan Lake. It was built in 1834 by Henry Sisson and in 1850 is owned and operated by John Davenport.

Beyond the Davenport House is the Walker Tavern at Cambridge Junction. It is owned and operated by State Senator Walker. This is about 18 miles from Clinton and, because of the hills, is a day's journey by stagecoach.

Battle Creek, Michigan spiritualists, Reynolds and Debrorah Cornell, have founded the town of Harmonia, Michigan in Bedford Township of Calhoun County. They hope to establish a spiritualist community there.

The Reverend Mister Albertus C. van Raalte and others have petitioned to have the name of the Black River Post Office changed to Holland, like their 3-year-old town of Holland, Michigan. Dutch immigration into that area of the state continues. *Dutch men are good customers although the members of the Dutch Reformed Church don't come in much.*

2—Ralph Waldo Emerson publishes his Representative Men, continuing his expounding of Transcendentalism.

Pierre Joseph Proudhon is arrested in France after the government of President Louis Napoleon seizes Proudhon's People's Bank and closes his newspaper, The People, under the newly enacted Press Laws. *This will bring more French to America, I hope. They're good barroom customers, too.*

3—The British Meteorological Society is founded in London, England.

5—Commodore Cornilius Vanderbilt in New York has announced the formation of a new steamship line, the Vanderbuilt Line, to compete with the Collins Line and the Cunard Line for transatlantic traffic. Also beginning regular service will be the New York and Havre Steamship Company, which is also American, owned. *Cornilius Vanderbilt started his career in modest means as a young man who owned a small boat. He sailed out to the ships coming into New York harbor to pick up priority passengers and the mail. He always beat the other boys and soon bought their boats. By 1850 Vanderbilt owns his own shipping company and is buying rail-roads. He has a huge home on Fifth Avenue in New York City. Another American success story.*

6—Queen Victoria of England gives birth to a son, Arthur. He is her seventh child and is created the Duke of Connaught. *From what I hear about Victoria, she seems like a nice lady. She's been Queen of England for 13 years now and still going strong. Queen Vickie, I call her.*

Captain Arthur Edward's ships, the Southerner and The Baltimore, inaugurate regular steamship service between Detroit, Michigan and Cleveland, Ohio. *Steamer service from Across Lake Erie has been ongoing but not regular. These ships will improve the trip. It's one day from Detroit to Port Clinton and one more to Cleveland, unless a storm makes the steamer stay in port.*

7—Susan B. Anthony attends an anti-slavery meeting in Rochester, New York, meeting there for the first time Frederick Douglass and Elizabeth Cady Stanton. *This is a dangerous combination. I heard Fred Douglass speak and was highly impressed. He brought tears to my eyes when he talked about his days in slavery and his brave escape. I am proud to have been in his presence. But, if he hooks up with Susan Anthony and Mrs. Stanton, who knows what will happen. I'd hate to see Douglass' talents turned from abolition to women's rights.*

The Second Presbyterian Church in Detroit moves from the old State House Building where it had been holding services to its new building located at Lafayette and Wayne Streets. *I don't see too many Presbyterians in the barroom but they do stay at the Tavern while on the road. Nice folks.*

8—English philosopher, Herbert Spence, publishes his first important work, Social Statistics, in London.

9—Heavy rains overtax the new private stone and brick sewer system that was installed in Detroit in 1849. Because of bad engineering many of these sewers are flowing the wrong way and drain waste away from the Detroit River and into occupied neighborhoods. *Ain't that something? You'd think these fellahs could figure out that water don't run uphill!*

Steam Mill in Oakland County, Michigan is renamed Mahopac.

James Kenny is appointed Postmaster of the new Post Office in Kenny's, Michigan in Shiawassee County, Michigan. The town is named for him.

10—The University of Michigan at Ann Arbor opens its new medical school. This is the third building in the university, joining the South and North Buildings, both built in 1849. *This is quite the new idea—educating doctors in a formal way. But, they say there's a lot to learn now to practice medicine. The University will have a year-long course to become a medical doctor. Then the fellah still has to apprentice with a doctor to hone his skills.*

George Palmer Putnam, American author and owner of the Putnan Publishing House and Putnam's Magazine, has published his latest work, The World's Progress.

11—The Michigan Secretary of State, George Redfield, resigns. Charles H. Taylor replaces him. *Both Democrats, of course.*

12—Anna Jameson, noted Irish author and critic, publishes her latest book, Legends of the Madonna.

13—The Michigan Southern Railroad places a contract to lay tracks from Hillsdale, Michigan to Coldwater, Michigan. The track presently begins in Monroe and ends in Hillsdale. *This extension of the Southern may pose a problem for us. The Michigan Southern will more or less parallel the Chicago Road and this extension may take more business from the stagecoach companies that supply us with customers. Mister Wood's hoping the deal falls through.*

John Norvell dies of apoplexy in Detroit. He was a United States Senator from Michigan and former Michigan State's Attorney. He had served on the Board of Regents of the University since 1837.

14—Bill Perry, the Tipton Slasher, wins the world bare-knuckle boxing championship in England, beating Paddock in the 29th round. *I lost ten dollars betting on the outcome of this fight! I had Paddock 'cause he's so much bigger than Perry and can outreach the Slasher. How was I to know that Paddock would turn coward after only 28 rounds?*

15—Harper's New Monthly Magazine is first published in New York.

—Kansas City, Missouri is incorporated as a city. *So civilization is spreading to that part of the State of Missouri—if you can call Kansas City civilized.*

16—Madame Tussaud (born Marie Grosholtz) dies in London at the age of 90. She established the famous wax museum in London. *She made wax figures of the European heads of state and other famous people. It is quite the popular attraction in London.*

18—Senator Clay's proposed Compromise bills are referred to a Select Committee of 13 United States Senators to be chaired by Clay himself. *Ain't that grand? The author of the bills chairs the committee set up to judge 'em. But, that's politics, I suppose.*

19—The Clayton-Bulwer Treaty is ratified by the U.S. Senate. It provides cooperation between the United States and England in any venture to build a canal across the isthmus of Nicaragua. The treaty is unpopular among American expansionists who distrust the British intentions in the region. *And some of the fellahs my age fought the English in the War of 1812 and still look askance at any idea of letting 'em have more influence in "our" hemisphere.*

Goodenough Townsend becomes the first Postmaster of Davison Centre in Genesee Counrty, Michigan. *This fellah's name is really "Goodenough". I suppose that's better than his Ma looking at him and naming him "Nogood" or something. In fact, there are plenty of times I wished someone told me I was "Goodenough".*

23—English Poet Laureate William Wordsworth dies. Alfred Lord Tennyson succeeds him as Poet Laureate of England. *Tennyson's got a nice little poem about an Eagle I like a lot. I wish him well in his new job*

26—Grand Traverse, Michigan in Grand Traverse County opens its first Post Office. Robert Campbell is postmaster. *This settlement began as a mission to the Indians. It was founded by the Rev. Peter Doughtery of the Presbyterian Church in 1837.*

27—The Atlantic sails from New York for Liverpool, inaugurating regularly scheduled steamship service between those two cities. It sails for the Collins Line, an American-owned company in competition with the British-owned Cunard Line. *The crossing by sail can take two or three months. By streamer, 45 days! There's gonna be some money made there.*

May
The population of Michigan is 341,591. The population of Detroit is 21,019. The population of Clinton, Michigan is 978. *At statehood in 1837*

Detroit's number was about 8,000 and the population of Michigan was 30,000. We are growing, ain't we?

Cincinnati, Ohio has gained the nickname of "Porkopolis" for its many meat-packing facilities. *About a third of Cincinnati's people are German speakers. Milwaukee and St. Louis are other largely German towns. Because of the pork production soap-making from pork fat is also a growing industry. There are two fellahs in Cincinnati in that business by the names of Gamble and Proctor.*

The postal rates in America are 5 cents per once for letters sent under 300 miles and ten cents per ounce for letters beyond that distance. *That's about an hour's wage to mail a letter. But, with all the Post Office goes through to get the letter to the recipient, I suppose that's a bargain.*

Both Russia and France claim the right to protect holy places in the Turkish realm. This leads to more tensions in Europe. *As the Turkish Ottoman Empire weakens, its neighbors, especially Russia find ways to gain influence in the area. Russia would like a way to get its Black Sea fleet into the Mediterranean Sea and the French and the English want to stop 'em. The English just about think the Mediterranean is an English lake, you know. Tsar Nicholas is using the protection of Christian holy sites in Anatolia as a reason to extend his control.*

1—George Ripley becomes literary editor of the New York Tribune. He worked on the Dial with Ralph Waldo Emerson and Margaret Fuller. *The Transcendentalist influence spreads.*

Cutler's Corners in Hillsdale County, Michigan is renamed North Adams.

Eureka Township in Montcalm County, Michigan is organized by State Representative A.L. Root and named for the Greek word meaning, "I have found it."

2—American Naval hero, Robert Field Stockton, has resigned his commission and plans to enter politics. He fought in the war with Tripoli in 1814, secured the territory that became Liberia in 1821, found against the slave trade in the West Indies, and commanded our Pacific forces in the recent Mexican war. In 1848 Stockton took position of California in the name of the United States. *He should do well in politics, having survived the muddle of political activity that followed the seizure of Alta California from Mexico. He, Kearney, and Fremont had it out.*

3—Henry David Thoreau's A Week in the Concord and Merrimack Rivers and essay Civil Disobedience are first published in Michigan. Both were written in 1849.

6—Ground is broken for the building of the Elton & Crawford Park in Detroit on land donated by Crane & Wesson Co. Other existing parks are to be cleared after being used as dumps for years. *Detroit is coming to age. The people no longer think of themselves as backwoodsmen. They see a real future for their town and want to dress it up some.*

8—The Senate select committee reports three of Clay's bills to the floor. It is an omnibus bill including California statehood, the two territorial governments, and the abolition of the slave trade in the District of Columbia. *Those were the easy ones. We're waiting to see how the new Fugitive Slave Bill will be prepared.*

10—The Weekly Oregonian begins publishing in Portland. *The Oregon Territory has almost three thousand people in it now. Abraham Lincoln of Illinois just turned down an appointment as its territorial governor. He almost took it but found out that a political rival turned it down and he didn't want to take the man's leavings. Besides, there ain't enough people out there for Mary Lincoln to lord over.*

11—Le Citoyer, a French literary paper is offered in Detroit on Saturdays. It costs $2.00 a year by subscription. *There continue to be a lot of French folks in Michigan, especially in the Detroit area. It was a Frenchman, Cadillac, who founded the place in 1701, after all, and Michigan was part of New France until the French and Indian War.*

The Naglee Building is begun in San Francisco. It is San Francisco's first brick building. *Will this be the Three Little Pigs' solid brick house or Matthew 7:24's house built on a poor foundation. Only time will tell.*

15—Joseph Henry, the first secretary and director of the Smithonian Institution in Washington, transmits the first telegraph weather reports and uses them to forecast weather conditions. *The Smithonian was started with money from an Englishman named Smith who never came to America but left money in his will for this purpose. Mr. Henry says if we study weather patterns, as he is, someday, we'll be able to predict weather a day or two in advance. I doubt that will ever be accurate, though.*

16—The two week-long Presbyterian General assembly opens in Detroit. It will draw many distinguished persons. *More business for our Tavern, little for the barroom.*

18—Roswell Curtis is appointed the first Postmaster of Gravel Run, Michigan in Washtinaw County. He was the founder of the town in 1842. *Gravel Run is on the road between Ann Arbor and Brighton just before Hamburg, or Livingston.*

19—The second expedition led by General Narcisco Lopez lands in Cuba at Cardeenas. Manned mostly by Americans, this invasion of Spansh-held Cuba was led by the Venezuelan-born former Spanish army officer Lopez in an attempt to free the island of Spanish rule. *Gen. Lopez is getting support from Southerners. He has many in the South convinced that Cuba is ripe for revolution and the island could be added to the United States as a new slave-holding territory. To punish the United States for our support for this invasion Queen Isabelle II of Spain cut off our rum supply from her lands in the Caribbean. I wish she had shelled a couple of U.S. cities, instead.*

20—The Lutheran School of St. Matthew in Detroit opens its new building at East Congress and Russell Streets. *This is in Detroit's Third Ward where a lot of Germans live. The Northern Germans, mostly Lutheran, live North of the Fort Gratiot Road while the Southern Germans, mostly Roman Catholic, live on the South side. Just like at home.*

21—The Richmond and Backus paper warehouse in Detroit is opened. *While some manufacturing is now done in Detroit, most of the business there is warehousing and mercantile supply houses. Goods are brought in by boat from the East and warehoused in Detroit before being transported into Michigan and the rest of the West. The pay for working in a warehouse is good—up to 75 cents a day!*

22—An expedition financed by New York merchant Henry Grinnell and led by Lieutenant Jesse De Haven sails from New York for the Arctic to search for Sir John Franklin who disappeared while exploring the polar region in 1845. *I hold little hold for finding Sir John alive. A month lost in the Arctic is fatal and he's been missing for five years.*

25—A convention in New Mexico adopts a constitution that establishes boundaries for the proposed state and prohibits slavery. *This is a good result of "squatter sovereignty". These folks voted down slavery. But, what was voted down could be voted in someday, you know.*

The Detroit Democratic Free Press runs an advertisement offering for sale or exchange a house located on Fort Street, between Rivard and Russell Streets. Lt. U.S. Grant of the United States Army currently occupies it. *Hiram Ulysses Simpson Grant is stationed in Detroit and in 1850 he is moving to another house. The barracks where he works are located near the Fort Gratiot Road and Russell Street. When Grant's in town he's one of my best customers.*

20—The closed Post Office in Cotterellville, Michigan in St. Clair County, is reopened with Stephan B. Grummond as its Postmaster.

June

H.R. Johnson in Detroit offers gas lighting in his hotel located at the foot of Third Avenue. The gas is distilled from coal and is shut off at 10 PM each night to prevent accidents It will be another year before coal gas is commercially produced in Detroit and nine years before the first producing oil well in Pennsylvania allows for the production of kerosene. *The gas at Johnson's hotel is shut off because people, used to oil lamps or candles, would blow out the flame before retiring for the night and the next day they'd wake up dead.*

Camp meetings are regularly held just outside Clinton, Michigan under the direction of the Methodist and Presbyterian Churches. Circuit preachers routinely preach at these outdoor rallies, converting many. *We often rent out the barroom to preachers on Sundays. We don't get a lot of drinkers on Sunday morning anyway. Most are still too sick from Saturday night's drinking to be out of bed. Mister Wood and I put away all the liquor and the preacher holds forth right behind the bar. Then we clear out the church folks and let in the drinkers and, sometimes a few of the church folk slip back in, too.*

The Manchester Mill in Manchester, Michigan (North of Clinton) is being run by Emmanuel Chase and Harry Gilbert. It was built on the River Raisin in 1832. *Emmanuel Chase owes me ten dollars. If you run into him, I'd appreciate you reminding him of it.*

The Michigan Constitutional Convention in Lansing begins. A new Constitution for the state is proposed. If adopted it will be the first constitution change since statehood in 1837. *Them politicians are kicking around some good ideas and some bad ones. Some want to make Michigan a dry state—bad idea. Some want to let the ladies inherit property along with their brothers when parents die—a good idea. There are other suggestions being made. We'll see what happens.*

English Christian Socialist, Charles Kingsley, publishes his novel, Alton Locke, and his tract, Cheap Clothes and Nasty, which is a biter diatribe against labor exploitation, exposing "Show-shops" and "slop-shops" where tailors and seamstresses work long hours for meager pay in appalling conditions. *Bad working conditions are not only in England. These kinds of things go on in America, too, mostly in New York where immigrants are packed into tenements and forced to work for low wages in dangerous conditions. There's a fellah in London, a German named Karl Marx, who wrote about this sorta stuff. But his idea of change doesn't appeal to me. He thinks the workers should own the means of production. From the work I see from some of the men I've worked with, I don't think they would have made good partners.*

1—C.B. James & Co. opens a hardware warehouse in Detroit.

—Moses Pitts, founder of Pittsburg in Shiawassee County, Michigan dies. His son, Safford, now runs the family farm on the Grand River Turnpike.

—Lot Whitcomb begins publishing his newspaper, *the Western Star*, in the Oregon Territory.

2—Herman Melville's White-Jacket, is published. *This fellah writes good books, mostly about the sea. He's working on a new one—about a big whale and a whale hunt—while staying with his mentor, Nathaniel Hawthorne, in Massachusetts*

3—The Freeman Bros of Detroit open a millinery warehouse.

—In Oregon City, Oregon Territory five Cayuse Indians are hanged for their participation in the Whitman Massacre. This ends the so-called Cayuse War. *I'll be telling anyone going to the Oregon territory that's it's safe to make the trip now.*

4—Oregonian Peter Hatch begins the construction of a road around the Falls from Canemah to Oregon City. This will replace the back-pack and hand-cart trail that is presently used.

5—American historian, William Hickling Prescott, arrives in Europe for a short tour. He is received with the highest distinction among European academics.

6—The Aztec copper mine opens in Houghton County, Michigan.

9—Joseph B. Sturgis, foreman for Marvin Hannahs, finishes building a sawmill in South Haven, Michigan. *This is not the same Sturgis for whom Sturgis, Michigan was named. The town of Sturgis was named for Judge Joseph Sturgis and first called Sturgis Prairie. It was later called Sherman for Colonel Benj Sherman, then Ivanhoe for the Sir Walter Scott novel. It was renamed Sturgis in 1845.*

10—A convention of slave-holding states being held in Nashville, Tennessee, supports the extension of the Missouri Compromise line westward to the Pacific. This would include the Southwest and California and open those areas to slavery. *This is the great issue of the day. We won Utah, New Mexico, and California from Mexico two years ago (1848) and both the slavery states and the non-slavery states claim this area for their side. If the Missouri line is extended, it's slave. If the Wilmont Proviso is adopted, it's not. That's one of the points of Clay's Compromise—to leave slavery up to the locals.*

Sounds good, but it could lead to the spread of violence like that already beginning in Kansas.

Rowland, Michigan in Hillsdale County is renamed Bird. Rowland Bird was its founder. *First name—last name, the town's still named for him. John R. Williams was the first mayor of Detroit and he's got two streets named for him—John R and Williams Streets.*

12—A contract is let to continue the laying of track on the Michigan Southern Railroad. The new contract covers the route from Coldwater to Sturgis. The section for Hillsdale to Coldwater is already under construction. *This is scary. The completion of this rail-road will really affect us on the Chicago Road and Sturgis is mighty close to the Michigan-Indiana border. It's not much longer to Chicago from there. We'll have a petition in the barroom to stop this construction. Come in and sign it.*

14—The Trinity Lutheran School in Detroit opens at Rivard and Russell Streets. *More Germans!*

The Third Great Fire of San Francisco destroys 300 buildings and does $5 million worth of damage. *Just so the El Dorado Saloon is untouched.*

15—Nathan Holmes opens his new gristmill on Seeley Creek at Wolf Lake. This is located in the newly organized town of Grattan, Michigan.

16—The trial of Professor John W. Webster for the murder of Doctor George Parkman begins in Boston, Massachusetts. Judge Lemuel Shaw is presiding. It draws national attention. *This is the "Trial of the Century". Everyone knows about the case and follows it. The telegraph lines are buzzing with the latest from the Boston courtroom. Parkman and Webster were society men and Shaw is one of the most respected jurists in America. I wish I could be in that courtroom to hear the case. But, I'll just have to read the details in the newspapers.*

17—Warren Isham becomes editor of Detroit's Michigan Farmer and Western Agriculturist newspaper.

—Pine Plains in Allegan County, Michigan is organized. It is a lumber town named for its most common trees.

19—John B. Gough delivers his first lecture in temperance at the Presbyterian Church in Detroit. This begins the formation of the "Sons of Temperance" and the "Cadets of Temperance". Together they form the Temperance League of Michigan. *This is scarier than the extension of the rail-road! I had hoped that Michigan men had more sense than to be caught up in this notion, but I was wrong. I got nothin' against temperance fellahs. It's just they don't drink enough to keep my barroom in business.*

—The Methodist Episcopal Church begins the Kaw Mission at Council Grove in Kansas.

20—The Reverend William Blades is appointed supply minister for the Saginaw, Michigan Mission of the Methodist Episcopal Church's Michigan Conference. Saginaw is a logging center with a growing farming community. *Now that they got their own preacher, the folks in Saginaw don't have to travel down to Flint to get married or buried no more.*

—Queen Victoria of England, Scotland, Ireland, and Wales marks the beginning of her 14th year as British monarch. *Nice lady, Queen Vickie.*

21—Nathan Barlow is appointed first Postmaster in Gun Lake, Michigan in Berry County.

—David LaBlanc becomes the Postmaster at the reopened Post Office in Ecorse, Michigan.

22—Sara Jane Lippincott, using the pseudonym Grace Greenwood, publishes her Greenwood Leaves, a collection of her poetry. She lives in New York.

27—Actor Edwin Booth, 16, makes his New York debut in *The Iron Chest.*

The Town Council of San Francisco, California Territory organized a fire company. *Not a bad idea, considering.*

30—The Reverend Charles F. Stockton, late the head of Albion Michigan's Wesleyan Seminary, dies on his way to preach in the gold fields of California. He is buried at sea. *This is a tragic loss. Mr. Stockton was a fine man who may have made California a civilized place for decent folks. He was a temperance man, but I forgave him for it. I figured with him being a preacher and all, that's an occupational hazard.*

July

Doctor Louis Cavalli has opened a museum in Detroit, Michigan. It is located on Franklin Street, East of St. Antoine. The museum displays a large selection of stones, shells, minerals, and insects from all over the world. He also has paintings as well as items from Herculanium. *I visited the Cavalli Museum. It was nice but all them rocks and shells looked like just rocks and shells to me. They coulda come from out back of the Tavern, as far as I could tell. The paintings and other stuff were impressive, 'though. It was worth the ten cent cost of admission.*

Widespread mourning marks the passing of President Taylor. Funeral services are held in churches, townhalls, and in other public places as America's interest in funerals continues at a high level.

There are 18 church buildings in Detroit with 2562 members. That represents 12% of the city's population.

There are 626 ships in San Francisco's harbor. Most are abandoned with their crews rushing to the gold fields. *Free building materials and firewood. All you have to do is to strip the abandoned ships.*

There is one dentist in Detroit who performs "painless dentistry" by employing the use of ether. *If you live in Detroit this is the fellah you may want to see.*

1—The first overland mail service west of the Missouri River is established on a monthly basis between Independence, Missouri and Salt Lake City, Utah Territory. *It's still 10 cents an ounce—quite the bargain.*

—Emmett Township in St. Clair County, Michigan is organized by Irishmen Patrick Kennedy, Dennis Gleason, Patrick Fitzgerald, James Cogley, Henry McCabe, and David Donahue. It is named for the Irish patriot Robert Emmett.

3—The citizens of Astoria, Oregon Territory celebrate the launching of the Columbia River's first home-built steamboat. Named the Columbia, this steamer will run more of less regularly between Astoria and Oregon City. *Lot Whitcomb of the Oregon Territory is building a steamboat of his own. If completed it will be bigger than the Columbia. There are other steamers working the Columbia but they were built elsewhere and sailed to Oregon.*

4—Independence Day—the Nation is celebrating our 74th anniversary of Independence. *We'll be shooting the anvil and doing a lot of drinking to-day.*

—The new public library in Wayland, Massachusetts is established by a gift of President Francis Wayland of Brown University and is to be supported by regular tax funds.

6—Professor Benjamin Cocker arrives in Detroit from England. He is on his way to Ann Arbor where he will teach at the University of Michigan. *Professor Cocker will teach Medical Ethics—if that ain't an oxymoron.*

7—Casper Butz buys the German language newspaper, *Der Allgemeine Zeitung* in Detroit, Michigan. *This is one of a few German language newspapers in Michigan. I love Germans. They're good folks and the men and good customers in my barroom.*

8—With great ceremony James J. Strang, a Mormon leader in Michigan, becomes King Strang at his "capitol" of St. James on Beaver Island, Michigan. A religious community was established there. *The "king" said that God, himself, told him to become king of the Mormons. I don't know if that's true, or not. I wasn't there to hear the voice of thunder. Strang's a respected man, 'though. He'll go on to serve in the Michigan Legislature.*

—Theron J. Wilcox is appointed the first Postmaster of Vandalia, Michigan. Asa Kingsbury is the first merchant there.

—Whigville, in Lapeer County, Michigan is named for the Whig Party. Stephan Grinnell becomes its Postmaster. *The Whigs are still powerful is many towns in Michigan, although the state is controlled by the Democrats. Here in Lenawee County we call the town of Addison "Coon Town" because in the election of 1840 the coonskin was a symbol of the Whig Party. So many people in Addison nailed a coonskin on their doors the place got that appellation.*

9—President Zachary Taylor dies in Washington, D.C. Vice President Millard Fillmore of New York becomes our thirteenth president. *This was* *quite a shock. We learn about this in Clinton on the 12th and got right to mourning. There are mock funerals with flag-draped coffins, eulogies, and the wearing of black armbands. Taylor was a fine man and a great leader. He would have vetoed the Compromise bills (except for the California statehood which he supported). I don't know how Fillmore will jump. At the Tavern we sing "My Country 'Tis of Thee" to honor the passing of the president.*

—Jean Pierre Boyer, former president of Haiti, dies in Paris to where he fled following his ouster in 1843. *Haiti is a republic on Hispasnola Island in the Caribbean Sea. It broke from France in a bloody revolt some time ago. The killing of the former slaver holders in Haiti by their enslaved is held out by American slaver holders as a reason against abolition. The real reason for the slaughter in Haiti was the cruel treatment of the enslaved there and that there was no orderly transfer to freedom. This does not have to be the case in America.*

19—Margaret Fuller dies in a shipwreck off Fire Island, New York. She had worked with Emerson and George Ripley and had been a critic for Horace Greeley's New York Tribune. Her writings had been published under the title *Literature and Art* in 1846. Her 1845 publication *Woman in the Nineteenth Century* remains a powerful work of feminism. In 1848-49 Fuller, then married to Marquis Angelo Ossoli, participated in the Roman Revolution. She died with her family while returning to America. *Fuller was one of the most influential women of our times. It was her writings that really started all this women's-rights notions. But I don't want to speak harshly of the dead.*

—The town of Kedron becomes Chelsea by a vote of its men. *This is a town on the Michigan Central Rail-road between Ann Arbor and Grass Lake.*

20—Grand Ledge, Michigan in Eaton County has its first Post Office with Henry A. Trench as postmaster. Mrs. Edward L. Lamson named the town after a great ledge of rocks near the town past which runs the Grand River.

21—Doctor Herman Kiefer, popular German-born physician in Detroit marries Francesca Kehle who came to America as traveling companion to Dr. Kiefer's mother. *Although "kiefer' is the German word for "jaw" I understand Dr. Kiefer also works on other parts of the body.*

22—President Fillmore appoints Massachusetts Senator Daniel Webster Secretary of State. Charles Winthrop replaces Webster in the Senate. *Was this a political pay-off for Webster's recent support of the Compromise? I would hate to think that such a renowned person as Webster would sellout so cheaply. I hope he got some money, too.*

—Congregation Emmanu-el is founded in San Francisco, California Territory.

26—Ichabod by John Greenleaf Whittier is published as is his *Songs of Labor*. Icabod attacks Daniel Webster for Webster's March 7th speech in support5 of the Compromise.

31—The Senate passes, 32 to 18, a bill establishing a territorial government for Utah with no restriction on slavery. *Squatters' sovereignty, again. If you leave an issue like slavery to the locals, each side sends in settlers like they are doing in Kansas and you end up with raids and bloodshed. There must be a better way.*

August

The National Hotel in Detroit has expanded to four floors. *Imagine a building that high? I suppose you could see all of Canada across the Detroit River from the top floor, but you might get a nose bleed being that high up.*

Clinton is abuzz about the new plank road extension. It consists of three-inch thick oak planks and now covers the distance from Detroit to Saline, which is a town just ten miles east of Clinton. Other plank roads lead from Detroit to Mt. Clemens, to Birmingham, and to Howell. *These are toll roads and, I hope will put the rail-roads out of business.*

1—The Beth El Jewish Society is formed in Detroit. They meet in private homes, hoping to build Michigan's first Temple soon. *They needed ten Jewish men to form the temple and they got 'em. They have to live near one another 'cause they can't drive their carriages on the Sabbath.*

—The Evening Picayune newspaper is founded in San Francisco.

4—Richard Wagner's new opera, Lohengrin, is first performed. *I saw this one. It's too long, but it's got some nice tunes in it. I liked the costumes.*

5—Bengal, Michigan in Clinton County receives its Post Office with Cortland Hill as Postmaster.

—Tom Hyer, famed pugilist, is fined $50 for riding a horse through a barroom while drunk. *That's a bit harsh of a punishment, ain't it?*

8—Fort Akinson is built by Lt. Col. Edwin V. Sumner of the First U.S. Dragoons in order to protect the Santa Fe Trail.

9—The U.S. Senate approves, 30 to 20, a bill adjusting the boundary between Texas and New Mexico and provides a payment to Texas of $10 million. *This is quite the deal for Texas. The $10 million is the former Texan national debt when they were a republic. Texas gives up about half of what becomes the New Mexico Territory and gets all that money. There ain't nothin' in New Mexico worth $10 million!*

13—The California Statehood Bill passes the United States Senate by a margin of 34 to 18. *That's 18 patriots to 34 traitors. We'll have a petition to President Fillmore to veto any California Statehood Bill coming to his desk. Maybe he'll pay attention to our petition—if he can get someone to read it to him.*

14—A new 150 horsepower pump begins operation in Detroit, pumping water through wooden water mains from the Detroit River. There are 4000 customers of the private water company in Detroit. There is not one plumber working in the city and repairs to the water system are difficult to make. *Most of the twenty thousand people in Detroit still get their water from well and cisterns. There is, however, the beginning of a fire protection system that uses the pumped water from tamarack log mains. You've got to be a customer of the private fire company to have 'em put out a fire at your house. If you're not a member, or your fees aren't paid up to date, they let the fire burn!*

15—The United States Senate approves, 27 to 10, a bill that establishes the Territory of New Mexico with no restriction as to slavery. *Another Compromise bill. Notice that there are 60 members of the Senate and only 37 voted. Some folks are sitting out this one, I guess.*

16—The Second Baptist Church in Detroit, Michigan hosts the 9th meeting of the Amherstburg Baptist Association. The church meets in an old school building on Fort Street near Hastings. It had 80 members and the Reverend S.H. Davis is the pastor. This is one of Detroit's two African-American churches. *The convention will being more people along the Chicago Road, but them being Baptists, no business for the barroom.*

20—French writer, Honore' de Balzac dies in Paris. He was a leading voice of the Romantic Age. *I never read any of Balzac's stuff—he wrote in French. I speak every language in the world except Greek, you know. But, French is Greek to me!*

21—The steamer Pacific of the Collin's Line sets a new transatlantic record. It arrives in London from New York in 10 days, 4 ½ hours! *That's faster than the sharks can swim, I'm told.*

—Worcester, Michigan is renamed Marquette in honor of Father Marquette an early Michigan missionary.

23—The Fugitive Slave Bill passes the Senate 27 to 12. *All flags should be at half-staff. What a disgrace! The work of the Underground Rail-road will be more important now.*

28—The plank road from Detroit to Saline, Michigan is dedicated. *This will put the Michigan Southern Rail-road out of business and save the Tavern. I went to the dedication and heard Governor Berry speak. They were giving out free beer, so it was worth the trip.*

September

For the past five years McGuffy's Eclectic Readers have been used in the Detroit School System. *I learned to read from the Bible, taught by my Ma, like most people in those days. Now formal schooling for common folks is more common. That, by the way, is why some many people of my age have Bible names like Silas Hezekiah. The Bible was the onlyest book we had in our homes.*

Due to the ongoing "Potato Famine" in Ireland that started with the "Black Harvest of 1845" one quarter of the populations of New York,

Philadelphia, Boston, and Baltimore are Irish. In the past five years over two million Irish have arrived in America and now represent 10% of our population. Most arrive in "coffin ships", converted slave ships and many die before reaching what they call "North Amer-i-kay." The crossing can cost as little as $10. *In Detroit, in Clinton, and in many American cities and towns there are "Corktowns", Irish populations set apart for the rest of the community. In 1840 Ireland had a population of 8 million people. From 1845 to 1850 one million died and two million left. Others are still preparing to leave. That's over a third of the population already gone and more going. What a tragedy for the Old Sod!*

The second annual Michigan State Agricultural Fair opens in Detroit this month. It was first held there last year, 1849, and was the first such fair held in the nation. *Calvin's gonna take his prize pig to Detroit this year for the Fair. He hopes to win a prize there. It's quite a pig, let me tell you. The Fair will be held in different cities over the coming years to make it "fair" for every part of the state. I love puns, don't you?*

1—The Western Evangelist is first published in Detroit by Jabez Fox. It will cost $1 per year by subscription.

2—The Reverend Oren Whitmore is appointed in charge of the Lansing Circuit for the Methodist Episcopal Church. Lansing, three years ago just a clearing and a swamp, has been Michigan's capitol since 1848. There are 70 members of the Methodist Church worshipping in Lansing. *You'd think with all them politicians in Lansing there would be more need for prayer.*

6—The Tabernacle Baptist Church in Detroit begins meeting at the Young Men's Hall.

7—The California Statehood Bill passes the United States House of Representatives. *Another day of mourning.*

—German scientist Alexander von Humboldt publishes the 3rd volume of his masterwork, *Cosmos*, a work of scientific theory.

—A run on the banks in San Francisco occurs.

8—James M. Holden becomes the first Postmaster of Oak Plains, Michigan in Livingston County.

—The Southwestern Plank Road is completed from Chicago to Fullersburg, Illinois, just beyond Doty's Tavern. The Northwestern Plank Road connects Chicago with Oak Ridge and the Western Plank Road goes from Chicago to Elgin.

9—California joins the Union as our 31st state! *September 9, 1850—a date that will live in infamy!*

—New Mexico is organized as a territory with a payment to Texas of $10 million for its abandonment of all Texas claims on New Mexico.

William S, Miner becomes the first Postmaster of Proctor, Michigan in Allegan County. In 1836 Miner built the first log cabin there.

—The Green Oak Center Post Office opens in Livingston County, Michigan. Ambrose Warner is Postmaster.

10—Mead's Mills in Wayne County, Michigan opens a Post Office with Jabash M. Mead as Postmaster. He and his brother, Amos Mead, have a sawmill there.

11—Jenny Lind, the Swedish Nightingale, debuts at Castle Gardens in New York City. It is a sensation. 40,000 people showed up to greet her boat upon arrival from Europe. At the concert Lind sang songs and arias by Bellini, Rossini, Weber, Meyerbeer, and others. As an encore she sang Stephen Foster songs. *Jenny Lind will tour America under the direction P.T. Barnum. I'd sure like to hear her sing but the closest she'll get to Michigan is, maybe, St. Louis.*

12—The Fugitive Slave Act is passed by the House of Representatives 109 to 76.

16—Danby, Michigan in Ionia County, opens its first Post Office with John Compton as postmaster. Danby is named for Danby, Connecticut, the home of its early settlers.

17—The Fourth Great Fire of San Francisco, California destroys 150 buildings and does $500 thousand worth of damage. The newly formed fire department has no water to fight the fire.

18—The fugitive Slave Act is signed by President Fillmore. An amendment to the 1793 Fugitive Slave Act, it removes fugitive slave cases from state courts to federal courts. Special commissioners will be appointed to hear cases and issue warrants. A mere affidavit from a slave-holder is accepted as proof and those accused of being runaways from enslavement are denied jury trials and are not allowed to testify on their own behalf. The commissioners hearing the cases are to earn $10 for granting a certificate of return and $5 for denying one. Those evading or obstructing this law are subject to fines and other penalties. *Well, that's it. Fillmore has signed the Fugitive Slave Law and the California Statehood Bill. What more do we need to impeach the man?*

19—In the New York State Whig Convention a walk-out is led by Francis Granger, a Fillmore man, after Senator Seward's radical positions is approved. Because Granger has gray hair and led the walk-out, these Fillmore men are called the "Silver Grays." *The Whig Party may be in serious trouble. It's already broken up along regional lines. Now the New Yorkers are split. Folks are talking about starting up a new party to challenge the Democrats. Maybe it'll work out.*

20—The slave trade is outlawed in the District of Columbia as of January 1, 1851. *Slavery will still be allowed there, but the buying and selling of people will be banned in the nation's capitol.*

—The United States Congress authorizes land grants in Illinois, Mississippi, and Alabama for railroad construction between Mobile and Chicago. This will be America's first North-South railroad and is the result of efforts in Washington by Senator Stephen A. Douglass of Illinois. *This rail-road land grant will cost the government nothing, Douglass argues. The government will give alternating sections of land to the rail-road, then sell the rest. The value of the land not granted will go up because it will be near a rail-road and the government will break even on the deal. That'll be the day when the government does something and it don't cost us no money!*

23—A thousand people for 11 states gather to discuss women's rights in Worcester, Massachusetts. Mrs. Elizabeth Cady Stanton of Seneca Falls,

New York Falls provides the written opening remarks. She regrets she could not attend the Worcester Convention but she is at home expecting her fourth child. Delegates include Miss Lucy Stone, a graduate of Oberlin College in Ohio, and Dr. Harriet Hunt, a self-educated physician. *This conspiracy began two years ago in Seneca Falls when Mrs. Stanton and her friend, Lucrecia Mott, sponsored a meeting. My wife and I discuss this topic, but not when she's holding any weapons. This town of Worcester where the meeting's being held is pronounced as if it were "Whister" or even "Whistah". That's 'cause them New Englanders don't know how to speak English no good.*

—A barn fire behind the Michigan Railroad Hotel, located at Griswold and Michigan in Detroit, spreads to the main building. The hotel is completely destroyed. *If you're looking for a bargain while staying in Detroit, I think the Michigan Rail-road Hotel may be discounting their rooms. Non-smoking rooms are NOT available.*

25—William Boughton becomes the first Postmaster of Pipestone in Berrien County, Michigan. This name comes from the fact that the Indians found the clay in that area the best for making smoking pipes. The settlement is also called Shanghai for the bred of chickens Dr. Joab Enos imported there. *A good chicken dinner and a smoke—it don't get no better than that.*

—Croton, Michigan in Newago County is organized. It is named for the Croton Water Works of New York.

27—The Oregon Donation Act is signed by President Fillmore. It allows any white male American to claim 320 acres of land in the Oregon Territory. It also allows addition claims of 420 acres for a wife and 160 for each child. *Now that the Cayuse have been defeated their land is up for grabs. Other Indian lands are given to white settlers, too.*

28—President Fillmore appoints Brigham Young governor of the Utah Territory. Before the Mexican War, when the area was still a part of Mexico, it was known as the "State of Deseret" with Young as governor. *The Mormons have suffered greatly in the East and I hope they'll be safe out in*

Utah. One thing for sure, this time no one will try to take their land away from 'em—no one wants it!

—Congress outlaws flogging in the United States Navy and in the American merchant Marine. *Good news for the sailors.*

October

Shubael Conant, Edward Brooks, and others form the Detroit Anti-Slavery Society to oppose the Fugitive Slave Act and the other Compromise measures recently passed by Congress. The work of the Underground Railroad begins in earnest as slave-catchers come North to seek their prey under the protection of the Federal government. Clinton, Michigan is one of the towns on the route to freedom. The formerly enslaved come up through Ohio to Adrian and to Tecumseh to go to Detroit through Clinton. From Detroit they are smuggled across the Detroit River to Canada where both slavery and slave-catching is illegal.

The Michigan Supreme Court is lead by Charles W. Whipple, Chief Justice. Warner Wing, George Miles, S.M. Green, and E. Mundy are the Associate Justices. The Court continues to meet in Detroit.

Theodore Newell is selling home plots in the newly plated Muskegon, Michigan. *A mission was established a mission here near a river the French called "Masquignon" for an Indian word that means "swampy river". So, if you buy land in Muskegon, be forewarned. See the land first!*

Jonathan Lee and George Mitchell have settled in Sanalac County. They are the second residents there.

There are 57,000 miners working the gold fields of the new State of California. *And none of 'em you want your women to be around.*

2—Benj Vernor, a prominent real estate agent in Detroit, has begun the construction of a beautiful home in that city. It will be completed next year and is located on West Fort Street near the large home of Senator Louis Cass. *Ben is thirty years of age and already making a name for himself. There's another Vernor in Detroit you may know of, James Vernor, the drug-gist. If you have an upset stomach, James'll make you a ginger drink to settle it.*

3—The Philadelphia College of Surgery (dental) is opened. *The tooth-pullers got their own organization before the medical doctors. The American Dental Society pre-dates the American Medical association by a few years. They are also using painkillers like ether before the docs.*

4—William Horton becomes the first Postmaster of Oakland, Michigan in Kent County.

6—The Congregational Unitarian Church is organized in Detroit. It meets occasionally in various homes.

8—The arrest of a colored man named Rose in Detroit as a fugitive slave had caused so much excitement that Mayor John Ladue called out Army troops under General Schwartz to keep the peace. *Anti-slavery agitators prevented Rose from being returned to the South. This is just the start of trouble caused by the Fugitive Slave Act. I think this sort of thing will become more common.*

11—J.J. Bagley and his friend, Daniel Scotten, become apprentices at Miller's Tobacco Company in Detroit. They will oversee the work of the women and children who roll cigars there. *That's Miller's—the "Horsy" cigar. I think there's a future for these boys.*

15—John William Draper is appointed professor of physiology at the University of New York.

17—Francis Galton, English scientist and cousin to Charles Darwin, begins his exploration of South Africa. *The exploration of Africa is growing. There's a missionary named Dr. Livingston in East Africa doing the Lord's work there. No one's heard from him in a while.*

18—Celebrations break out in San Francisco as the steamer Oregon brings the news of California statehood.

20—Grand Rapids, Michigan, settled in 1833 and incorporated as a village in 1838, is incorporated as a city to-day.

22—The individual provinces in British Australia are granted self-government in the Australian Colonies Government Act. Federal union of New South Wales, Victoria, Queensland, and the other colonies is still far off.

30—Construction of The Jenny Lind Theater is begun in San Francisco in anticipation of that singer's visit to the city next year.

November
The Great Railroad Conspiracy in Michigan comes to a head with the firing of the freight depot in Detroit. Farmers object to the railroad crossing their lands, killing their livestock, and upsetting their lives. They grease the tracks, shoot at the train crews, and generally fight rail expansion in Michigan. Grass Lake is the center of this activity.

The major banking institutions in Detroit are the Michigan State Bank, Charles C. Trowbridge, president, The Peninsular Bank, Charles Howard, president, and the Detroit Savings Institution, Elon Farnsworth, president.

2—The Detroit Musical Society is organized with O.T. Hown as president.

3—Voters in Michigan overwhelmingly approve the new state constitution. It outlaws public money for road construction, provides public votes on any banking laws, institutes borrowing limits, and cap public officials' salaries. Married women are granted control over all property they owned before marriage. Suffrage is granted not only to all white male citizens over 21 but to aliens who have declared their intention to become citizens, and to "civilized Indians". Free black men in Michigan are still denied the vote. Beginning five years after the adoption of the constitution at least three months of free public education is to be provided for all of the state's children.

—A referendum in Bird, Michigan in Hillsdale County changes the name of the town back to Ransom. In honor of former Michigan Governor Epaphroditus Ransom. *These folks just can't make up their minds.*

6—The Sisters of Charity open St. Mary's Hospital in Detroit. It had 150 patients. The newly constructed building is at Clinton & St. Antoine on land that was donated by Mrs. Antoine Beaubien. *Madam Beaubien is from a proud old French family and owns land on the Eastside of Detroit. I met her once. She's a nice lady.*

—Point San Jose, the Presidio, Goat Island, Angel Island, and Black Point in San Francisco are received by the Federal Government for military purposes. *I had an argument with a fellah from California about the way they pronounce places like San Jose. I was saying "San Jo-sy" with a J sound. He says it's San Ho-say, likes it's an h up front. He told me all Js ate pronounced as if they was Hs. I believed him 'til I met a fellah from New Hersey!*

7—At Olmutz, Prussia is pressured by Russia and Austria to renounce its earlier support of the Erfurt Union of Princes that would have given Prussia political and military dominance in the German countries. Instead, the revived German Confederation is instituted, assuring for a time shared power in Germany. The Prussians called this the "Humiliation of Olmutz".

—Nashville, Michigan is renamed Sparta Center.

11—A second convention of slave-holding states is held. It draws few delegates. The convention supports the right of states to leave the Union.

14—Trinity Evangelical Lutheran Church of Detroit calls its new pastor, the Reverend Mr. S.M.G. Schaller. The church was organized last year (1849) and currently meets in a building on Woodbridge Street in the rear of Christ Church.

18—Col. Charles L. Wilson announces the start of a plank toll road from San Francisco, California to Mission Delores. *I suppose this is to facilitate them men made rich in the gold fields going to confession to confess how they got rich.*

19—Anti-rail-road agitators burn the freight depot in Detroit. *Sheriff Cicotte is looking for Abel Fitch of Grass Lake for questioning in regard to this matter. Good old Abel is the leader of the anti-rail-road crowd there and quite the hero in these parts. He says he'd like to hire Senator William Seward of New York to be his lawyer if he can.*

20—Zion German Reformed Church of Detroit is incorporated. They meet at the City Hall.

24—The late president, Zachary Taylor's birthday is to-day. He would have been sixty-six years of age if he had lived. *He was elected when he was 64. We shoulda known he weren't gonna last being that old!*

25—A treaty of friendship and commerce between the United States and the Swiss Confederation is signed at Bern, Switzerland. *We need all the friends we can get—especially in Europe.*

27—The Detroit Young Men's Christian Association (YMCA) opens a new hall at the cost of $8,500.00. This puts the organization into deep debt. *They may have to raise their dues.*

30—The Child's Book of the Soul by Thomas H. Gallaudet is published.

To-day is set aside as a Day of Thanksgiving in California to celebrate its admission to the Union. *And a day of mourning for the rest of us.*

December

Piety Hill in Detroit is a great place to coast and sled. It is located in Detroit bounded by Randolph, Bates, Larned, and Michigan Grand Streets. *A good coast from the top of the hill can put you out on the Detroit River. Hope the river's frozen hard if you do that!*

The Detroit Musical Association is now presenting concerts in Detroit churches and public halls. *One of the most popular halls in Detroit is the City Hall. This is not a government building—that confuses some people. It is a privately owned hall that can be rented for meetings and concerts. I've heard concerts there. It is well lit with oil lamps and holds many people.*

The budget of the City of Detroit is $127,260 a year. That is $3.26 per capita on $321.00 per capita of property value. *That's about four days' income per person to run the city government! The federal budget is about a dollar per person, but, I guess, the city does more for folks that the federal government.*

Ever since the Fox sisters, Margaret and Leah, of Hydeville, New York heard "rappings" in their home in 1848 and began "communicating" with the one rapping, there has been a growing number of "spirit circles" in America. These are people interested in the new notion of Spiritualism that promotes contact with unseen spirits. *I'm not much for this sort of thing. At my age I know a lot of dead people and most of 'em I didn't like talking to in life. Why should I want to talk to 'em now?*

The Christmas season is being marked with family gatherings and church services by those who celebrate this holiday. More people are, especially the Roman Catholics and the Lutherans. The Methodists are still uneasy about what they consider to be a "Roman Catholic holiday".

1—The newly married Stephen Foster and his wife, Jane Denny McDowell, move from Pittsburgh, Pennsylvania to New York City. *This Foster fellah has written some great songs. They include "Oh Susanna", "Ring, Ring the Banjo" and others. He's quite the drinker, but that's a good thing. He writes a song and drinks up all the profits. That keeps him writing. If he were sober he probably would not write as much as he does.*

2—The Harmonie Society of Detroit presents a festival of German music at their hall.

5—Louis Kossuth (Kosoth Lajoth in the Magyar language), Hungarian patriot in the uprising of 1848, is given a rousing public reception in Washington. This shows the continued American support for the revolutions of 1848 in Central Europe. *Because of the 1848 revolt we're getting more Hungarian immigrants in America. In Michigan they're settling downriver from Detroit near the town of Belgrade on the Detroit River.*

6—The last edition of the Detroit Daily Herald is published. The newspaper was established on the 26th of last year (1849). *And I bought three-year subscription!*

—Godey's Magazine in London publishes a picture of the Royal Family around a Christmas Tree for the first time showing the German side of Albert and Victoria. *This could be bad. If people see them royals with a Christmas tree the idea may catch on here. Much too German, you know.*

10—The Hutchinson Family, the nation's most famous singing group, have announced the end of their touring career. Sister Abby is marrying. That leaves her brothers, Judson, Asa, and John on their own. The ten-year run of the quartet from New Hampshire was marked with controversy as the recent inclusion of abolition songs led to rioting at some of their concerts. *This is a real national tragedy. I saw the Hutchinsons perform once and found 'em to be wonderful. Abby's voice is strong and angelic. Her brothers carry a good tune, as well. But, times change, I suppose.*

—The Right Reverend Joseph Sadoc Antemany, Bishop of California, addresses worshippers in San Francisco in English, Spanish, and French.

13—A state convention in Georgia declares that although not all in Georgia agree with the Compromise of 1850, future action by the United States government to repeal the Fugitive Slave Law will be resisted by Georgia "even to the disruption of every tie that binds her to the Union". The convention is being held in Milledgeville, Georgia. *I don't see nothin' in our national Constitution that gives a state a way to leave the Union, but these folks from Georgia do. I have hope they're right. If there is a way we can get rid of a state, there's still hope to get rid of California!*

14—Locks are installed on the jail cells in San Francisco because too many prisoners are escaping. *Need I say anything more about California?*

—Captain Parker H. French's expedition reaches San Francisco overland from New York City. He left New York on May 13th, 1850.

—A storeowner in Detroit, Michigan hires a man dressed in a Santa Claus suit to stand in front of his store in order to lure in customers. *Shocking! The commercialization of Christmas! The public will not stand for it.*

15—Susan Warner, writing under the penname of Elizabeth Wetherell, has published a novel called *The Wide, Wide World*.

17—Famed actress, Lola Montez (real name Marie Dolores Elizia Rosanna Gilbert) arrives in California. The Irish-born adventuress was a sensation in Europe and was the mistress of Kind Ludwig of Bavaria until his abdication in 1848. Caught up in the revolutions of 1848 Lola Montez left Europe and will make a career on the stage in America. She does a "spider dance" that is well received among men. She intends to entertain the gold miners of Grass Valley, California. *This is one incredible woman. She's of lowly birth but rose to high places in the courts of Europe. She'll do well in California, I suspect.*

19—William Evart Gladstone's letters from Naples denounce the cruelty of the Neapolitan government. *Italy is all broken up into many countries. In the north there is Lombardy and Venice. Both are under the control of the Austrians. Also north is Savoy and Nice along with Piedmont and Sardinia, a united nation under Kind Victor Emanuel. This is the fellah some hope to make the king of a fully united Italy. Austria and France will never allow that. In the South of Italy is the Kingdom of the Two Silicies with King Fredinand in charge. Old Ferdi's not much for uniting with the north. Pope Pius IX holds lands in the middle and there are other small duchies and kingdoms, too. Last year there was an attempt to unify the whole place, but it failed. This was after the Pope renounced some of his liberal reforms and was made to flee Rome. One of the leaders of the uprising, Giuseppe Garibaldi lost his wife, Anita, in the fighting and, is now working as a ship's captain in New York. He hopes to go back to Italy someday.*

21—U.S. Secretary of State Webster defends American recognition of revolutions in Europe. This is a letter to Austrian Foreign Minister Chevalier Hulsemann. We had supported the revolt in Hungary in 1848 which was suppressed by the use of Russian troops In 1849 Russia and Austria defeated the Hungarian Republic that was set up and returned the region to the control of the Austrian Empire. *This may mean war. The Austrians are mad that we nosed into what they thought were their affairs. Webster maintains that it is our right, as the world's leading democracy, to hold out the hope of political freedom to any people. But, with Austria way over in Europe and that being a two or three-month sail from here, I don't think any war between us and them will be a big one.*

21—William Wallace Lincoln, the third son of Abraham and Mary Lincoln of Springfield, Illinois, is born. His parents will call him "Willie". *A nice family, this. Their son, Eddie, died earlier this year. I hope this birth will help 'em heal.*

23—Green Oak, Michigan changes its name to Warnerville in honor of its founder, George A, Warner.

25—Christmas Day is marked by those who celebrate it with family meals and church services. Most Americans count this as a minor holiday, if they observe it at all. *There is a growing celebration of Christmas what with all them Germans coming to America. This is a big day for 'em, you know. In fact, this year, 1850, a British magazine publishes a picture of the English Royal Family gathered around a Christmas Tree. This helps to popularize the idea of the Christmas Tree in America. Clement Moore's poem, "A Visit from Saint Nicholas", that was published a few years ago has helped popularize the notion of Santa Claus. Sadie and I enjoy a quiet meal with our family—after our overnight guests are seen to, of course.*

—The steamer Lot Whitcomb is launched into the Willamette River in the Oregon Territory. This steamer is 160 feet long with an enclosed cabin, a ladies parlor, and a dining saloon. The festivities are marred when a canon blows up, killing Captain Fred K. Morse. *I hate when that happens, don't you?*

THE UNITED STATES SENATE IN 1850

ALABAMA

William Rufus de Vane KING (1786-1853)—Democrat

Born in Sampson County, North Carolina was graduated by the University of North Carolina at Chapel Hill in 1803. Read law and admitted to the bar in 1806. Served in the Congress from North Carolina. Upon Alabama statehood in 1819 was elected to the Senate from Alabama as a Republican and a Jacksonian Democrat. Minister to France 1844-46. Appointed to the Senate in 1848 to fill the vacancy caused by the resignation of Arthur Bagley as a Democrat.

Jeremiah CLEMENS (1814-1865)—Democrat

Born in Huntsville, Alabama attended La Grange College and was graduated by the University of Alabama at Tuscaloosa in 1833. Read law at Transylvania University, Lexington, Kentucky. U.S. district attorney in 1836. Served in the War of Texas Independence and in the Mexican War. Unsuccessful candidate for Congress in 1848. Elected to the Senate to fill the vacancy caused by the death of Dixon H. Lewis November 1849.

ARKANSAS

Solon BORLAND (1808-1864)—Democrat

Born near Soffolk, Virginia attended school in North Carolina. Studied and practiced medicine. Settled in Little Rock, Arkansas. Served as a major in the Arkansas Volunteer Cavalry in the Mexican War. Elected to

269

the Senate in 1848 to fill the vacancy caused by the resignation of Ambrose H. Sevier.

William King SABASTIAN (1812-1865)—Democrat

Born in Centerville, Tennessee and was graduated by Columbia College, Tennessee in 1834.

Studied law and admitted to the bar in 1835. Became a cotton planter and prosecuting attorney and judge. Appointed to the Senate in 1848 at the death of Chester Ashley.

CALIFORNIA (admitted to the Union September 9, 1850)

William McKendree GWIN (1805—1885)—Democrat

Born near Gallatin, Tennessee and was graduated by Transylania University of Lexington, Kentucky in 1828. Practiced medicine in Mississippi. Elected to the Congress from Mississippi 1841-1843. Moved to California in 1849. Elected to the Senate upon California statehood in 1850.

John C. FREMONT (1813—1890)—Democrat

Born in Savannah, Georgia and the son-in-law of Senator Thos Hart Benton from Missouri. He studied at Charleston College and instructed in math in the U.S. Navy. Explored the American lands north of the Missouri River. More explorations followed for the Army where her was appointed Lt. Colonel of the U.S. Mounted Rifles in 1846. Acting Governor of California. Tried and convicted of mutiny by General Kearney but pardoned by President Polk. Settled in California and elected to the Senate upon statehood in 1850.

CONNECTICUT

Roger Sherman BALDWIN (1791—1863)—Whig

Born in New Haven and was graduated from Yale College in 1811. Studied law with his father and attended Litchfield College. Admitted to the bar in 1814. Governor of Connecticut. Elected to the Senate to fill the vacancy caused by the death of Jabez W. Huntington.

Truman SMITH (1791-1884)—Whig

Born in Roxbury and graduated by Yale College in 1815. Admitted to the bar in 1818. Member of the House of representatives and elected senator in 1849 after declining President Taylor's appointed as Secretary of the Interior.

DELAWARE

John WALES (1783—1863)—Whig

Born in New Haven and graduated by Yale College in 1801. Admitted to the bar in 1801. Moved to Philadelphia and then to Baltimore where he practiced law.
Removed to Wilmington, Delaware in 1815 and became president of a bank. Elected to the Senate in 1849 to fill the vacancy caused by the resignation of John Clayton who became the Secretary of State under Taylor.

Presley SPRUANE (1785—1863)—Whig

Born in Kent County, Delaware and engaged in manufacturing in Smyrna, Delaware. Elected to the Senate in 1847.

FLORIDA

Jackson MORTON (1794—1874)—Whig

Born near Fredericksburg, Virginia was gradated by Washington College (now Washington and Lee) in 1814. Moved to Pensacola, Florida in 1820 and engaged in lumbering. Elected Senator in 1849.

David Levy YULEE (1810—1886)—Democrat

Born David Levy in St. Thomas, Virgin Islands. Came to the United States at the age of nine. Studied law in St. Augustine and admitted to the bar in 1836. He changed his name to Yulee in 1846 and was elected to the Senate in 1845 at Florida statehood.

GEORGIA

William Crosby DAWSON (1798—1856)—Whig

Born in Greensboro, Georgia and graduated by Franklin College, Athens, Georgia in 1816. Admitted to the bar in 1816 and practiced law in Greensboro. Served in the Congress and as Governor of Georgia. Elected to the Senate in 1849.

John Macpherson BERRIEN (1781—1856)—Whig

Born at Rocky Point near Princeton, New Jersey and moved with his parents to Georgia. Graduated college at Priceton College in 1796 and admitted to the bar in Savannah in 1799.

Served as a judge and a captain in the War of 1812. Served in the Georgia legislature, the U. S. Senate, and as Attorney General under Andrew Jackson. Reelected to the Senate in 1841. Resigned to serve on the Georgia Supreme Court in 1845. Reelected to the Senate in 1846 to fills his own vacancy.

ILLINOIS

James SHIELDS (1806/10—1879)—Democrat

Born in Altmore, County Tyrone, Ireland in either 1806 or 1810. Immigrated to the United States in 1826 and studied law. Was admitted to the bar in 1832. At member of the Illinois Legislature and a judge. Commission brigadier general in the Mexican War. Governor or Oregon territory 1848—1849. Elected to the Senate in 1849 but his election was declare void due to his lack of citizenship for the required years. Reelected in October of 1849 and served.

Steven Arnold DOUGLAS (1813—1861)—Democrat

Born in Brandon, Vermont and educated in common schools. Became a cabinetmaker and moved to New York. Studied law at Canandaigua Academy and admitted to the bar in 1834 in Ohio. Moved to Illinois in 1834. Member of the state house. Elected to Congress and a judge of the Illinois Supreme Court. Elected to the Senate in 1847.

INDIANA

Jesse David BRIGHT (1812—1875)—Democrat

Born in Norwich, New York and admitted to the bar there in 1834. U. S. marshal for Indiana 1840—1843. Elected to the Senate in 1845. Reelected in 1850.

James WHITCOMB (1795—1852)—Democrat

Born in Windsor County, Vermont and attended Transylvania University, Lexington, Kentucky. Admitted to the bar in 1824. Member of the state legislature in Vermont. Practice law in Terre Haute, Indiana. Governor of Indiana 1843—1849. Elected to the Senate in 1849.

IOWA

George Wallace JONES (1804—1896)—Democrat

Born in Vincennes, Indiana and graduated by Transylvania University in Lexington, Kentucky in 1825. Admitted to the bar and moved to the Michigan Territory to be a miner and storekeeper. Served in the Black Hawk War. He was elected Delegate from the Michigan Territory and a Delegate from the Wisconsin Territory after Michigan statehood in 1837. Elected to the Senate from the new state of Iowa in 1848.

Augustus Caesar DODGE (1812—1883)—Democrat

Born in Ste. Genevieve, Missouri, moved to Illinois in 1827. Worked in his father's lead mines and served in the Black Hawk War. Elected delegate to Congress from Iowa. Elected to the Senate in 1846 at Iowa statehood.

KENTUCKY

Henry CLAY (1777—1852)—Whig

Born in Hanover County, Virginia attended public schools and law at Richmond, Virginia. Admitted to the bar in 1797. Began practice in Lexington, Kentucky. Elected to the Kentucky legislature and to the Senate in 1806. Speaker of The House and reelected to the senate. Secretary of State, candidate for president in 1824, 1832 and 1844.

Reelected to the Senate in 1849. Introduced his "Compromise Bills" in 1850 to save the Union.

Joseph Rogers UNDERWOOD (1791—1876)—Whig

Born in Goochland County, Virginia. Moved to Barren County, Kentucky in 1803 to live with his uncle. Was graduated by Transylvania College in Lexington in 1811. Studied law there. Served as a lieutenant in the War of 1812. Admitted to the bar in 1813. Elected to the state house of representatives and a judge. Elected to the Congress in 1835. Elected to the Senate in 1847.

LOUISIANA

Solomon Weathersbee DOWNS (1801—1854)—Democrat

Born in Montgomery County, Tennessee. Was graduated by Transylvania College in Lexington, Kentucky in 1823. Admitted to the bar in 1826. Practiced law in Bayou Sara, Louisiana, then in New Orleans in 1845. Elected to the Senate in 1847.

Pierre SOULE' (1801—1870)—Democrat

Born in France near Bordeaux. Exiled for anti-Bourbon activity in 1815 and pardoned in 1818. Studied law in Paris. Imprisoned in 1825 for publishing revolutionary articles. He escaped to England and went to Haiti. Moved to New Orleans to practice law. Elected to he Senate in 1846—1847 to fill the vacancy caused by the death of Alexander Barrow. Elected again in 1849.

MAINE

James Ware BRADBURY (1802—1901)—Democrat

Born in Parsonsfield, Maine and attended Gorham Academy. Was graduated by Bowdoin College of Brunswick, Maine in 1825Founded the first normal school in New England in New Hampshire in 1929. Admitted to the bar in 1830. Practiced law in Augusta, Maine. Elected to the Senate in 1847.

Hannibal HAMLIN (1809—1891)—Democrat

Born in Paris Hill, Maine and attended Hebron Academy. Worked as a surveyor in his family's firm which he led. Admitted to the bar in 1833. Member of the state house and Congress. Defeated for the Senate in 1846. Elected to the Senate in 1848 by the anti-slavery wing of the Democratic Party to fill the vacancy caused by the death of John Fairfield.

MARYLAND

David STEWART (1800—1858)—Whig

Born in Baltimore and attended Union College in Schenectady, New York. Attended the College of New Jersey (now Princeton University). Studied law and was admitted to the bar in about 1821. Practiced in Baltimore. Appointed to the Senate in 1849 to fill the vacancy caused by the death of Reverdy Johnson to January 12, 1850. Not a candidate for election he resumed the practice of law in Baltimore.

Thomas George PRATT (1804—1869)—Whig

Born in Georgetown, Maryland (now part of Washington D.C.). Attended Georgetown University and the College of New Jersey (now Princeton University). Admitted to the bar in 1823. Member of the state house and the state senate. Governor of Maryland 1845—1848. Moved to Annapolis in 1848. Elected to the Senate to fill the vacancy caused by the death of Reverdy Johnson.

James Alfred PEARSE (1805—1862)—Whig

Born in Alexandria, Virginia and was graduated by the College of New Jersey (nor Princeton University) in 1822. Admitted to the bar in 1824. Moved to Louisiana in 1825 and engaged in sugar planting. Returned to Maryland in 1828. Practiced law and elected to the Congress in 1835. Elected to the Senate in 1843.

MASSACHUSETTS

John DAVIS (1787—1854)—Whig

Born in Northboro, Massachusetts and attended Leicester Academy and was graduated by Yale College in 1812. Admitted to the bar and practiced law in Worcester in 1815. Elected to Congress and served as Governor of Massachusetts 1834—1835. Elected to the Senate in 1835. Resigned to run for Governor, again in 1841. Elected, again, to the Senate in 1847 to fill the vacancy caused by the death of Isaac C. Bates.

Daniel WEBSTER (1782—1852)—Whig

Born in Salisbury, Massachusetts and attended Phillips Exeter Academy. Was graduated by Dartmouth College, Hanover, New Hampshire in 1801. Admitted to the bar in 1805 and practiced in Bosawen near Salisbury, New Hampshire. Elected to the Congress in New

Hampshire in 1813. Moved to Boston in 1816. Represented Dartmouth before the U.S. Supreme Court, gaining national fame. Served in the Congress from Massachusetts. Elected to the Senate in 1827. Unsuccessful Whig candidate for president in 1836. Appointed Secretary of State by Presidents Harrison and Tyler. Elected to the Senate, again, in 1845. Resigned on July 22, 1850 to be appointed Secretary of State by Fillmore. His "7th of arch" speech in support of the Compromise of 1850 remains one of he greatest addresses presented on the Senate floor.

Robert Charles WINTHROP (1809—1894)—Whig

Born in Boston and graduated by Harvard University in 1828. Admitted to the bar in 1831 and practiced law in Boston. Elected to the state house in 1835 and to Congress in 1840. A protégé of Daniel Webster he was appointed to the Senate to fill the vacancy caused be the resignation of Webster on July 27, 1850

MICHIGAN

Lewis CASS (1782—1866)—Democrat

Born in Exeter, New Hampshire and attended Exeter Academy. Moved with his parents to Wilmington, Delaware and taught school there. In 1801 Cass moved to the Northwest Territory to farm near Zanesille, Ohio. He studied law and was admitted to the bar in 1802. Served in the Ohio state house and as U. S. marshal for Ohio. 1813—1814 served in the Army as a brigadier general. Was military and civil governor of the Michigan Territory 1813—1831. Settled in Detroit and explored the Michigan Territory leading to statehood. Appointed Secretary of War by President Jackson. From 1836—1842 he was Envoy Extraordinary and Minister Plenipotentiary to France. Elected to the Senate in 1845. Resigned in 1848 to run as the Democratic candidate for President of the

United States. Defeated by Taylor. Elected to the Senate to fill the vacancy caused by his own resignation.

Alpheus FELCH (1804—1896)—Democrat

Born in Limerick, Maine and studied at Phillips Academy. Was graduated by Bowdoin College, Brunswick, Maine in 1827. Admitted to the bar in 1830. Practiced law in Maine. Moved to Monroe, Michigan in 1833 where he continued to practice law. Member of the state house, auditor general, justice of the Michigan Supreme Court. Governor of Michigan 1846—1847. Elected to the Senate in 1847.

MISSISSIPPI

Jefferson DAVIS (1808—1889)—Democrat

Born in Kentucky he moved with his parents to a plantation near Woodville, Mississippi. Attended country schools and St. Thomas College, Washington County in Kentucky. Also attended Jefferson College and Wilkinson County Academy in Mississippi and Transylvania College in Kentucky. Graduated by the United State Military Academy at West Pointe in 1828. Served in the Black Hawk War. Promoted to first lieutenant in the First Dragoons in 1833. Resigned to his plantation "Brierfield" in Mississippi. Planted cotton. Elected to Congress in 1845. Resigned to serve in the Mexican War in command of the First Regiment of Mississippi Rifles. A hero at the Battle of Buena Vista. He was appointed to the Senate from Mississippi in 1847 to fill the vacancy caused by the death of Jesse Speight. Elected to the Senate in 1848.

Henry Stuart FOOTE (1804—1880)—Democrat

Born in Fauquier County, Virginia. Graduated by Washington College (now Washington and Lee University) in 1819. Admitted to the bar in 1823. Practiced law in Tuscumbia, Alabama. Moved to Mississippi in 1826 to practice law there. Elected to the Senate in 1847.

MISSOURI

Thomas Hart BENTON (1782—1858)—Democrat

Born at Harts Mill, near Hillsboro, New Hampshire. Attended Chapel Hill College (now the University of North Carolina) and William and Mary College, Williamsburg, Virginia. Admitted to the bar at Nashville, Tennessee in 1806. Practiced law in Tennessee and was elected to the state legislature. Served as the aide-de-camp to General Andrew Jackson and a colonel of the 39th U.S. Army Infantry 1813—1815. Moved to Missouri after the War of 1812 where he edited the Missouri Inquirer. Elected to the Senate upon Missouri statehood in 1821. He was defeated in a bid for reelection in 1850. He was also a well-respected muralist.

David Rice ATCHISON (1807—1886)—Democrat

Born in Frogtown, Kentucky and attended Transylvania College in Lexington, Kentucky. Was admitted to the bar in 1829. Member of the state house and a judge in Missouri. Elected to the Senate in 1843 to fill the vacancy caused by the death of Lewis F. Lynn.

NEW HAMPSHIRE

Moses NORRIS, jr. (1799-1855)—Democrat

Born in Pittsfield, New Hampshire and attended Pittsfield Academy and was graduated by Dartmouth College in 1828. Admitted to the bar in

1832. Member of the state house and the Congress. Served as the Speaker of the House of Representatives 1847—1848. Elected Senator on in 1849.

John Parker HALE (1806—1873)—Free Soil

Born in Rochester, New Hampshire and attended Phillips Exeter Academy. Was graduated by Bowdoin College in 1827 and admitted to the bar in 1830. Member of the state house and an U.S. Attorney in 1834. Elected to Congress in 1843. Removed by the state legislature because he refused to vote for Texas annexation in 1845. Elected to the State as a Free-Soiler in 1846.

NEW JERSEY

Jacob Welsh MILLER (1800—1862)—Whig

Born in German Alley, New Jersey and attended public schools. Admitted to the bar in 1823 and practiced in Morristown, New Jersey. Elected to the state council and to the Senate in 1840. Reelected to the Senate in 1846.

William Lewis DAYTON (1807—1864)—Whig

Born in Basking Ridge, New Jersey and attended Newark Academy. Was graduated from the College of New Jersey (now Princeton University) in 1825. Admitted to the bar in 1830. Practiced law in Freehold. Elected to the state council and became a judge of the state supreme court. Elected to the Senate to fill the vacancy caused by the death of Samuel L, Southeard in 1845.

NEW YORK

Daniel Stevens DICKERSON (1800—1866)—Democrat

Born in Goshen, Connecticut and moved with his parents to New York. Attended common schools and apprenticed to a clothier. Taught school and engaged in land surveying. Admitted to the bar in 1828 and practiced law in Guilford, New York. Moved to Binghamton and became the first president of that city. He was elected to the state senate and was lt. Governor of New York. Elected to the Senate in 1844 to fill the vacancy caused by the resignation of Nathaniel Tallmadge. Reelected in 1845.

William Henry SEWARD (1801—1872)—Whig

Born in Florida, New York and was graduated by Union College in 1820. Admitted to the bar in 1823 and practiced law in Auburn, New York. Served in the state house 1830—1834. Governor of New York 1838—1842. Elected to the Senate in 1849.

NORTH CAROLINA

George Edmund BADGER (1795—1866)—Whig

Born in New Bern, North Carolina and instructed by private teachers. Attended preparatory school in New Bern and Yale College in 1810 and 181. Admitted to the bar in 1814. Practiced law in New Bern. A member of the house of commons of North Carolina. Elected judge. Appointed Secretary of the Navy by Presidents Harrison and Tyler. Elected to the Senate from North Carolina in 1846 to fill the vacancy caused by the resignation of William H. Haywood.

Willie Person MANGUM (1792—18610—Whig

Born in Orange (now Durham) County, North Carolina. Was graduated by the University of North Carolina at Chapel Hill in 1815. Was admitted to the bar in 1817 and practiced law in Red Mountain, North

Carolina. A member of the state house and elected superior court judge. Elected to Congress in 1823. Elected to the Senate.

OHIO

Salmon Portland CHASE (1808—1873)—Whig

Born in Cornish, New Hampshire and schooled at Windsor School in Worthington, Ohio. Attended Cincinnati College and Dartmouth in New Hampshire. Taught school. Admitted to the bar in 1829 at Cincinnati. Elected to the city council. Helped form the Liberty Party in 1841 and Elected to the Senate as a Free-soiler in 1849.

Thomas CORWIN (1794—1865)—Whig

Born in Bourbon County, Kentucky. Admitted to the bar in 1817. A member of the Ohio state house and elected to Congress in 1831. Elected to the Senate in 1845. Resigned upon his appointed by President Fillmore to be Secretary of the Treasury on July 20, 1850.

Thomas EWING (1789—1871)—Whig

Born in West Liberty, Ohio County (now West Virginia). Was graduated by the University of Ohio at Athens. Appointed Secretary of the Treasury by President Harrison. Elected to the Senate in 1831. Appointed Secretary of the Interior by President Taylor. Reelected to the Senate in July of 1850 to fill the vacancy caused by the appointment of Thos Corwin to Secretary of the Treasury.

PENNSYLVANIA

James COOPER (1810—1863)—Whig

Born in Frederick County, Maryland and was graduated by Washington (now Washington and Jefferson) College of Washington, Pennsylvania in 1832. Admitted to the bar in 1834. Practiced law in Gettysburg and elected to Congress in 1839. Elected to the state house in 1843, 1846 and 1848. Elected to the Senate in 1849.

Daniel STURGEON (1789—1878)—Democrat

Born in Mount Pleasant, Pennsylvania and attended common school there. Moved to Western Pennsylvania with his parents in 1804. Was graduated by Jefferson College, Cannonsburg, Pennsylvania (later Washington and Jefferson College) in 1813. Practiced medicine in Uniontown and appointed coroner. A member of the state house and the state senate. Auditor General of Pennsylvania and state treasurer. Elected to he Senate in 1839 to fill the vacancy caused by the legislature's failure to elect. Reelected in 1844.

RHODE ISLAND

John Hopkins CLARKE (1789—1870)—Whig

Born in Elizabeth. New Jersey and privately taught. Admitted to he bar in 1812. A cotton manufacturer. Elected to the state house in 1836. Elected to the Senate in 1847.

Albert Collins GREENE (1792—1863)—Whig

Born in Greenwich, Rhode Island. Attended Kent Academy. Admitted to the bar in 1812. A brigadier general in the state militia 1816—1823. Elected to the Senate in 1845.

SOUTH CAROLINA

John Caldwell CALHOUN (1782—1850)—Democrat

Born near Calhoun Mills (now Mount Carmel), South Carolina. Attended common schools and private academies. Was graduated by Yale College IN 1804. Was admitted to the bar in 1807 and practiced law in Abbeville, South Carolina. A member of the state house and elected to the Congress in 1811. Appointed Secretary of War by President James Madison. Elected ice president in 1824 with President John Quincy Adams. Reelected in 1828 with Andrew Jackson as President. Resigned the ice Presidency in 1832. Elected to the Senate that year to fill a vacancy caused by the resignation of Robert Y. Hayne. Reelected in 1834 and 1840. Served as Secretary of State under President Tyler and reelected to the Senate in 1846. Died in that office on March 31, 1850. With Daniel Webster and Henry Clay, Calhoun formed the "Great Senate Triumbiate" of the three greatest orators of that body.

Andrew Pickens BUTLER (1796—1857)—Democrat

Born in Edgefish, South Carolina. Attended Dr. Waddell's Academy and was graduated by South Carolina College at Columbia in 1817. Admitted to the bar in 1818. A state senator and a judge. Elected to the Senate in 1848.

Robert Barnwell RHETT (1800—1876)—Democrat

Born Robert Barnwell smith in Beaufort, South Carolina. Admitted to the bar in 1824 and changed his name in 1838. A delegate to the Nashville Convention of Slave-holding States 5/7/1850. Elected to the Senate to fill the vacancy caused by the death of John C. Calhoun in 1850.

TENNESSEE

John BELL (1797—1869)—Whig

Born in Nashville, Tennessee and was graduated from the university of Nashville in 1814. Admitted to the bar in 1816. A state senator and member of Congress. Elected to the Senate in 1847.

Hopkins Lacy TURNEY (1797—1853)—Democrat

Born in Dixon Springs, Tennessee. An apprenticed tailor. Fought in the Seminole War in 1818. Admitted to the bar and elected to the state house. Elected to Congress in 1837 and to the Senate in 1845.

TEXAS

Samuel HOUSTON (1793—1863)—Democrat

Born at Timber Ridge Church near Lexington, Virginia. Moved with his widowed mother to Blount County, Tennessee. Attended Maryville academy (now Maryville University). Employed as a store clerk in Kingston, Tennessee. Enlisted as a private in the U.S. Infantry in 1813 and served under General Andrew Jackson in the Creek War. Rose to lieutenant and resigned the army in 1818. Admitted to the bar in 1818. Was district attorney and adjutant general of Tennessee in 1820. Elected to Congress from Tennessee. Governor of Tennessee 1827—1829. Resigned and moved to the Cherokee Nation (now part of Oklahoma). Worked as a trader and made a citizen of the Cherokee Nation by tribal council. Moved to Texas in about 1835. A member of the convention of San Felipe de Austin. Was made commander in chief of the Army of the Republic of Texas and defeated the Mexican Army at the Battle of San Jacinto in April of 1836. Became the first President of the Republic of Texas 1836—1838. Served in the Texas Congress and reelected as President in 1840. Elected to the Senate upon Texas annexation in 1845.

Thomas Jefferson RUSK (1803—1857)—Democrat

Born in Pendleton District. South Carolina was self-taught. Admitted to the bar. Moved to Nacogdoches, Texas in 1835 and practiced law there. A delegate to the Texas independence convention of 1836 and became the first Secretary of War of the Republic of Texas in 1836. He took command of the Texan forces at the Battle of San Jacinto. He served in the Texas Congress from 1838 to 1842. Elected to the United States Senate in 1845 upon Texas annexation to the U.S..

VERMONT

Samuel Shethar PHELPS (1793—1855)—Whig

Born in Lichfield, Connecticut and graduated by Yale College in 1811. Admitted to the bar in 1812 and practiced law in Middlebury, Vermont. Served in the War of 1812 as a paymaster and elected to the state house in 1821. A judge of the state supreme court. Elected to the Senate in 1839. Reelected in 1845.

William UPHAM (1792—1853)—Whig

Born in Leicester, Massachusetts and moved with his father to Vermont in 1802. Attended district schools and the Montpelier Academy and was privately tutored. Admitted to the bar in 1811. Practiced law in Montpelier. Elected to the state house in 1827. State's attorney for Washington County in 1929. Elected to the Senate in 1843. Reelected in 1849.

VIRGINIA

James Murray MASON (1798—1871)—Democrat

Born on Analostan Island in Fairfax County, Virginia (now Theodore Roosevelt Island, Washington, D.C.). Studied with a private tutor and at an academy in Georgetown, D.C.

Was graduated by the University of Pennsylvania at Philadelphia in 1818. Earned a law degree from William and Mary College at Williamsburg in 1820. Admitted to the bar in 1820. A delegate to the Virginia constitutional convention of 1829 and a member of the state house. A Democratic elector for Virginia in 1832. Elected to the Congress in 1837. Elected to the Senate

In 1847. Gave the final speech of he ailing John C. Calhoun in the Senate during the debate on the Compromise of 1850.

Robert Mercer Teliaferro HUNTER (1809—1887)—Democrat

Born at "Mount Pleasant" near Loretto, Essex County, Virginia and tutored at home. Was graduated by the University of Virginia at Charlottesville in 1828. Admitted to the bar in 1830 and practiced law at Lloyds. A member of the state assembly. Elected as a states-rights Whig to the Congress in 1837. Speaker of the House of Representatives. Unsuccessful candidate for reelection then elected to Congress, again. Elected to the Senate in 1846.

WISCONSIN

Isaac Pigeon WALKER (1815—1872)—Democrat

Born near Wheeling, Virginia (now West Virginia) and moved to Danville, Illinois in his youth. Attended common schools and was employed as a store clerk. Studied law and admitted to the bar in 1834. Practiced law in Springfield. Elected to the Illinois state house and an elector on the Democratic ticket. Moved to Wisconsin Territory in 1841. Practiced law there. Elected to the

Territorial legislature in 1847. Elected to the Senate upon Wisconsin statehood in 1848.

Henry DODGE (1782—1867)—Democrat

Born in Vincennes, Indiana and received limited schooling. Moved to Missouri in 1796 and settled at Ste. Genevieve. Elected county sheriff. Operated a lead mine. Moved to the Michigan Territory in what would become Wisconsin and settled near the present site Dodgeville in 1827.

Served in the Black Hawk War and other Indian wars. Left the Army as a colonel of the First United State Dragoons. Appointed Governor of the Wisconsin territory 1836. Elected to Congress. Governor, again, in 1845 to statehood in 1848. Elected to the Senate upon Wisconsin statehood.

Territorial Representatives to the United States Congress in 1850
MINNESOTA TERRITORY

Henry Hastings SIBLEY (1811—1891)

Born in Detroit, Michigan, the son of Solomon Sibley. Attended the Detroit Academy and studied under private tutors. Studied law and moved to Sault Ste. Marie, Michigan in 1828. Engaged in mercantile pursuits there. Moved to Mackinaw in 1829 to work for the American Fur Company. Served as the justice of the peace. Moved to the mouth of the Minnesota River in 1834 and engaged in fur trading. Elected a delegate from the Territory of Wisconsin to Congress and upon the formation of the Minnesota Territory he was elected to the Congress as delegate. He began his service on July 7, 1849.

OREGON TERRITORY

Samuel Royal THURSTON (1816—1851)—Democrat

Born in Monmouth, Maine and attended Wesleyan Seminary, Readfield, Maine and Dartmouth College, Hanover, New Hampshire. Was graduated by Bowdoin College, Brunswick, Maine in 1843. Studied law and admitted to the bar in 1844. Moved to Burlington, Iowa in 1845 to practice law there. Editor of the Iowa Gazette. Moved to Oregon City, Oregon Territory in 1849. Elected delegate to Congress from the Oregon Territory in 1949.

University of Michigan Officials in 1850
Board of Regents

President
John S. Berry, Governor of the State of Michigan

Regents (year appointed)

Austin E. Wing (1850—resigned in 1850)
Former Lt. Gov. Epaphroditus Ranson (1850)
Elon Farnsworth (1850)
The Rev. Elijah H. Pilcher
Eben N. Wilcox (1845)—Secretary of the Board
John J. Adam (1848)—Treasurer of the Board
Prof. Andrew Ten Brook, M.A. (1850)—Librarian of the Board

Professors in the Department of Literature, Science, and Arts

The Rev. George Palmer, L.L.D.—Mathematics and Physics (1841)

Abram Sager, M.D.—Botany & Zoology (1842)

The Rev. Andrew Ten Brook—Moral & Intellectual Philosophy (1844)

The Rev. John Holmes Agnew, D.D.—Ancient Languages & Literature (1845)

The Rev. Daniel D. Whedon, D.D.—History & Rhetoric (1845)

Louis Fasquelle, L.L.D.—Modern Languages & Literature (1846)

Silas Hamilton Douglass, M.A. M.D.—Chemistry, Geology & Mineralogy (1848)

Professors in the Department of Medicine and Surgery

Silas Hamilton Douglass, M.A., M.D.—Materia Medica, Pharmacy & Medical Jurisprudence (1848)

Abram Sanger, M.D.—Theory and Practice of Medicine, Obstetrics & the Diseases of Women and Children (1842)

Samuel Denton, M.D.—Theory and practice of Medicine and Pathology (1848)

Moses Gunn, M.A., M.D.—Anatomy (1848)

Jonathan Adams Allen, M.A., M.D.—Therapeutics, Materia Medica & Physiology (1850)

Benjamin Cocker, M.D. (1850)—Medical Ethics

THE WORLD IN 1850

Afganistan

Afganistan has been organized as an independent emirate since 1747

Albania

Albania is a provice of the Ottoman Empire

Algeria

Algeria was occupied by France in 1830 and officially became part of the Republic of France in 1848.

Angola

The coastal region of Angola is a Portugese colony. The central area is the nativist nation of Chokwe.

Argentina

Argentina is a nation in South America, Spanish speaking, and ruled by the Dictarorship of the Rosas. In 1850 the English and the French end their blockade of Montevideo harbor in support of Argintine claims against Uraguay.

Austrailia

Austrailia, founded as a penal Colony by England, is a growning region with settlements along the coast. The interior (the Outback) remains unexplored. In 1850 the British Parlement passes the

Austrailian Government Act of 1850 that organized some home rule for Austraian provemces.

Austria (see the German Countries)
Belguim

Belguim is a Kingdom with King Leopold as monarch. Leopold is married to the daughter of the former King of France, Loius Phillippe of the House of Orleans. From 1815 to 1830 Belguim was part of a united Netherlands with Holland. In 1830 Belguim revolted and formed their our country. The Treaty of London made Belguim independent in 1831.

Bolivia

Bolivia won its independence from Spain in 1825.

Bosnia

Bosnia is a province of the Austrian Empire

Botswana

The independent nation of Bamangwato.

Brazil

Brazil won its independence from Portugal in 1820. Brazil became the Empire of Brazil with Dom Pedro I as its emperor.. He was the son of the King of Portugal. In 1840 Pedro abdicated in favor of his son who is the current monarch, Dom Pedro II. Dom Pedro II's sister is the current Queen of Portugal.

Bulgaria

Bulgaria is padt of the Ottoman Empire.

Burundi

Burundi is an independent African nation

Burma

Burma has been rulled by the British since 1826.

Cambodia

Cambodia is the independent nation of Khmer and is resisting incursions by the British and the French.

Canada

Canada is part of the British realm since the Treaty of Paris in 1763. It is currently ruled by Queen Victoria. In 1841 the Provences of Upper Canada and lower Canada were united and they have a shared Parlement meeting at Montreal. Upper Canada is primarily English speaking while Lower Canda is primarily French speaking. The Queen is represented by the Earl Elgin who serves as Governor-General of Upper and Lower Canada. Government is formed in Parlement by Robert Baldwin and Louis Hippoltyte Lafontaine. Fur trapping remains a major industry and shipping at St. John's, Quebec City, Montreal, and Toronto is important, too.

There is a large number of Irish arriving in Canada due to the Potato Famine in Ireland..

Other provenices in British North America are New Foundland, Nova Scotia, Prince Edward Island, New Brunswick, British Columbia and

Vancouver. The areas between Upper Canada and British Columbia are controlled by the Hudson Bay Company, Chartered by the Crown. The western areas are known as New Caledonia.

The recent Upper Canada Rebellion and Patriots' War have caused Canadians to look toward unification.

George Brown publishes the Toronto Globe since 1843.

Chad

The African nation of Chad contains the independent states of Wadai and Darfur.

Chile

Chile won its independence from Spain in 1818 by revolts led by Bernardo O'Higgins and Jose' se San Martin.

China

China is an ancent empire now rulled by the Ching dinasty. The English recently defeated the Chinese in the Opium Wars to force the opium traded on China and to establish trading rights on the Chinese mainland. The English have a 100 year lease on Hong Kong. Sir John Bowring is the English Council at Hong Kong. In the Taiping Rebellion, begun in 1850, the Black Flags fight Foreign occupation while the Yellow Flags want peace.

The European nations have forced trading concessions at Canton and other Chinese ports.

The Imperial capitol is located at Peking. There the Emperor lives in the Forbidden City, a walled compound exclussive to his family.

Columbia

This is the nation of New Granada and has been independent from Spain since 1824. It includes mainland Columbia and the Panana ismus.

Congo

The headwaters of the Congo River contain the independent African nation of Chokwe.

Costa Rica

Costa Rica has been indendent since 1821. It is a republic with Jose' Maria Vastro as president.

Croatia

Croatia is a Province of the Austrian Empire.

Cuba

Cuba remains under Spanish rule. In 1849 ans in 1850 revolts and invations were led by Spanish general Narcisco Lopez to free Cuba from Spanish rule. This cause had great American support and hurt relations between the United States and Spain.

Cyprus

An island that is part of the Ottoman Empire.

298 • Silas Cully's Tavern Tales

Czech Republic

The Province of Bohenia, a part of the Austrian Empire.

Dahomey

Dahomey is an independent kingdon in Africa

Denmark

King Frererick VII, born in 1808, is the ruler of the Kingdom of Denmark since 1848. He is an archaeologist and a writer. Denmark is in the second year at war with the breakaway provinces of Schleswig and Holstein. They are at odds with Prusiia over this issue. The King is a descendant of Christian, Count of Olderburg in 1448.

The Act of Constitution established Denmark's modern Constitution June 5, 1849.

Denmark controlls Greenland and Iceland but lost Norway to Sweden in 1815.

Dominican Republic

The Eastern area of Hispanola Island is dominated by Haiti, France and Spain.

Ecudor

Ecudor gained its independence from Spain in 1830. Border disputes with Peru often leads to battles between those two countries.

Egypt

Egypt is a pashate of the Ottoman Empire currently undrer the control of Pasha Mohamet Ali.

El Salvidor

After the break-up of the Central American Union in 1839 El Salvidor became an independent country. A treaty of amity, navigation and commerce is signed between El Salvidore and the United States in 1850.

England

England is ruled by Victoria of the House of Hanover. She is married to her cousin, Albert of Saxe Coburg and Gotha, and has just borne her Seventh child, Arthur, created Duke of Connaught. Victoria became queen in 1837.

The Prime Minister of England is.Earl Russell, a Whig.

London, England is the largest city in the world with over a million in population.

William Makepeace Thackery's novel, History of Pendennis, is published. It follows his popular Vanityv Fair.

Engineer Izanbard Kingdom Brunnel's ship design, the Great Britain, is the largest steam ship ever built. It has screw propellors and an all metal hull—the first such ship. It is larger than Brunnel's Great Western.

Alfred Lord Tennyson publishes his In Moemoriam.

The late Prime Minister, Robert Peal, dies. Robert Peal was he head of the Metropolitan Police in London and it it from his name that members of the London Police force are called "Bobbies".

Wax museum owner and artist, Madam Tussand, dies in London.

Bill Perry, the Tipton Slasher, wins the heavyweight boxing champeonship in England.

England and the United States sign the Clayton-Bulwer Treaty to provide cooperation in building a canal in Central Ametica.

Philosopher Herbert Spencer publishjes his first important work in London.

Christian Socialist writer Charles Kingsley publishes his novel, Alton Lock, as well as essaies against the horid working conditions in the factories of Birmingham.

Bradshaw's Railway Guide is the prime sourse of travel information. It was first published by George Bradshaw in 1830. Thomas Cook, a bankrupt temerance organizer, is now publishing a guide to the Midland Counties Rail-road and organizing rail triups to Scotland.

Mary Carpenter, born in 1807, is a social reformer and teacher. She organized "ragged schools" and reformatories for girls.

Queen Victoria and Prince Albert are building a new castle in Balmoral, Scotland

Estonia

Estonia is under Russian control since 1721 at the defeat of the Swedes.

Ethopia

The kingdoms of Shoa, Tigri, Gojjam and others are pledged to the Emperor of Ethoepia of the Amharic dynasty. The emperor traces his anscetry to King David of Israel and the Queen of Sheba.

Finland

Finland is a Grand Duchy within the Russian Empire.

France

The Second Republic was established by revolution in 1848. The president of the Republic is Loius Napolean, the nephew of the later Emperor, Napolean Bonnepart.

Charles Louis Ambroise Thomas's opera, A Midsummer Night's Dream, opens in Parlis.

Dramatist Augutin Eugene Scribe presents his latest play, The Queen of Navarre, in Paris.

George Sand (nom de plumb of Madam Armatine Lucile Aurore Dupin Dudevant) publishes The Devil's Pool.

Pierre Joseph Proudhon is arrested after the government closes his bank and newspaper, The People.

Writer Honore' de Balzac dies in Paris.

Gabon (Gaboon)

The first French settlement was established in Gabon in 1839. Libreville is a trade port on the Atlantic Ocean.

Gambia

Gambia is a Crown Colony of Engla nd since 1843.

German Countries

Germany is a "geographic expression". Like Italy, Germany and the german speaking people are divided up among a many of countries. Each country has its own king, prince, duke or some other leader.. Among the many German countries are:

The Austrian Empire (Ostreich)

Foremost among the German speaking countries in Europe is the Austrian Empire. It is currently the main force against Prussian domination of Cenrteal Europe. The Austrian Empire presently is ruled by young Franz Joseph von Hapsburg who ascended the throne in 1848 upon the abdication of his uncle, Ferdinand I. Franz Joseph's premier is Felix, Furst zu Schwarzenberg whose uncle defeated Napoleon at the Battle of Leipzig in 1813. Austria is an empire that includes many nationalities. Among these ruled from Vienna are Hungarians, Chechs, Slovaks, Croatians, Slovenes, Muslim Bosnians, Dalamatians, Montenegrins, Poles, and others. In 1848 there were revolts in Hungary and other parts of the Austrian realm that led to the abdication of Emperor Ferdinand and the invasion of Hungary by the Russian Army to aid Austria in crushing the Hungarian Republic.

Louis Kossuth (Kossuth Lajos) was a leader of the Hungarian revolt against the Austrians in 1848 and in 1849 he took control of the revolution. When Kossuth declared independence on April 14, 1849 to form the Hungarian Republic, the Ausrtians called in Russian troops and Kossuth and other Hungarian leaders fled. Presently Lajos Kossuth is on tour and received a great welcome in America.

The Croats revolted against Ausrian control, too, setting up an independent government at Zagreb. This was overturned by Austrian force of arms.

Another leader of a people of the Ausrian Empire is Frantisek Palacky' who is writing a hisrtory of medieval Bohemia and has worked for a Slavic dominated Ausrian Empire. After the defeats of the revolts of 1848 Palacky' has tilted toward Russian-led Pan-Slavism.

Empror Frank Joseph married Elizabeth of Bavaria. She is called Cee Cee over there and she is respected by the Hungarians. Her presence beside F ranz Joseph helps brings peace to Hungary. Louis Kossuth on a tour of America intruced the "slouch hat" that is a style inspired by the kind of headgear he wore. It became widely popular..

Bavaria (Bayern)

Bavaria is a kingdom located in the south of the German states in mountainous regions. Its capitol is Munich (Munchen). Munich is a Roman Catholic nation that opposes the ambitions of the Protestant north and Prusiia to unite all the German countries under one ruler. The

King of Bavaria is King Maximillian II, having come to the throne in 1848 at the abdication of Louis (Ludwig). Maximillian is married to Princess Marie of Prussia and they have a son, Otto. Maximillian's father was Archduke Franz-Karl, the brother of the former Emperor, and his mother is Archduchess Sophie of Bavaria. King Ludwig resigned during revolts. His mistress, Lola Montez, left him to go to California.

Franconia

Franconia is a Lutheran area under the control of Roman Catholic Bavaria. It is from this region that the recent immigrants to Michigan came to found Frankenmuth, Frankentrost and Frankenlust, all towns along the Cass River near Flint.

Hanover (Hannover)

Hanover is located from Holland to the North Sea to the Harz Mountains in the North German plain. Sugar beets and wheat are crops in the rich soil called Borde. Rye and potatoes are grown outside of that fertile area. It is a Duchy with the capitol in the city of Hannover.

The current duke is Ernest Augustus (Ernst August), the Duke of Cumberland. King George I of England was a Hanavarian ruler. fellahs and the Kings of England have been the dukes of Hanover from 1714 to 1837. In 1837 Queen Victoria became queen of England and the Hanovarians demanded another morarch. They chose the queen's cousin, Ernie of Cumberland to be their duke. Right now Hanover opposes the ambitions of Prussia.

Mecklenburg

Mecklenburg is located on the Baltic Sea between the Elbe and the Oder Rivers. Its big cities are Rostock, Schwerin, Warnemunde and

Newbrandenburg. The country is divided into two grand duchies, Mecklenburg-Schwerin and Mecklenburg-Strelitz. Each is ruled by a grand duke.

Prussia (Prosen)

Prussia is a country in the east of Germany at the Mark of Brandenburg. It is a kingdom currently ruled by the Holenzoleran family. The current monarch is King Frederick William IV (Koenig Fredrich Wilhelm IV) who became King of Prussia in 1840. He survived the uprising of 1848 and in 1849 he declined the crown of a united Germany offered by the Frankfurt Parliament. In 1850 the King led changes in the 1848 constitution to strengthen the voting power of the rich by a three tier voting system The German Parliament meeting in Frankfort wanted to make the King of Prussia the King of a united Germany. He knew that a crown offered by a parliament was worth little. What a parliament gave it could take back. If the princes offer him the crowd he might take it. There is a rising star in Prussia, Otto von Bismarck.

Westphalia (Westfalen)

Westphalia is located in west-central German between the Rhine River and the Weser River. It is south of Hanover. Its major cities are Dortmund, Duisburg, Dusseldorf and Essen. Until 1803 the Archbishop of Cologne was the head of the Westphalian State. Since 1803 Westphalia has been a duchy under the control of Prussia. There are many Westphalians in Michigan. Freedom Township north of Clinton near Manchester, Michigan was founded by Westphalians.

Some Germans to watch—

Robert Schumann who has just published his Faust.

Richard Wagner who with Franz Liszt as producer has presented a new opera, Lohengrin.

Franz Liszt, a Hungarian, now works in Weimar where he is the director of the State Theater.

Ghana (The Gold Coast)

This is a British colony since 1820.

Greece

Greece began independent of the Ottoman Empire after a revolt in 1827. Prince Otto of Bavaria was called to the throne of the Kingdom of Greece and rules as Otho, King of the Hellenes.

Guatemala

Guatemala has been a republic since 1839.

Guinea

This is part of French West Africa.

Haiti

A republic that gained independence from France by revolt led by Toussaint L'Ouverture in the 1790s.

Honduras

Honduras has been independent of Spain since 1838

Hungary

Hungary is part of the Austrian Empire. Louis Kossuth (Kojoshj Lojos) and others led a revolt against the Austrians in 1848 and 1849 but it was crushed by Russian troops on behalf of Austria.

Iceland

Iceland is a part of Denmark since the Union of Kalmar in 1483.

Iran (Persia)

An independent Empire.

Iraq (Mesopotamia)

A part of the Ottoman Empire.

Italy

Like Germany Italy is divided with many small countries occupying the Italian Peninsula. Among the Italian countries are:

Ancona

A small state near Romagna.

Lombardy (Lombardia)

Lombardy is a country in northern Italy that, although nominally independent, is under the control of the Austrian Empire.

Modena

A small state near Parma.

Nice

A small state to the west of Savoy. In the Mediterranean coast.

Parma

A small state in the north-central area of Italy.

Piedmont and Sardinia

The Kingdom Piedmont and Sardinia is comprised of a mainland holding in northwest Italy and the island of Sardinia in the Mediterranean Sea. The king is Victor Emanuel of the House of Savoy.

Romagna

A small state on the eastern coast of the Italian Peninsula.

Rome (Roma) and the Papal States

Rome and much of central Italy remains under the direct command of the Pope of the Roman Catholic Church, Pius IX. The Pope is the sovereign in this region and was a force in the repudiation of the "Risorgimento" (national rebirth), a movement to unite all of Italy under a liberal parliamentary monarchy with the House of Savoy as the rulers. In 1849 the Pope was forced to flee Rome when Mazzini and others established the short-lived Roman Republic. He is mow back in Rome.

Savoy

A small state to the West of Piedmont, loyal to Victor Emanuel of Piedmont and Sardinia.

The Kingdom of the Two Sicilies

The Kingdom of the Two Sicilies is composed of a large mainland component that includes the city of Milan (Milano) and the island of Sicily in the Mediterranean Sea. Its current monarch is King Ferdinand of the House of Bourbon. It remains opposed to Italian unification.

Tuscany (Tuscana)

A small state in the north of Italy.

Venice (Venetia)

A rich trading country in the north of Italy fully under Austrian control.

There are several Italian notables. They are—

Giuseppe Mazzini, a writer who inspired the drive to make Italy one country with Rome as the capitol. He founded Giovine Italia (Young Italy), a patriotic republican organization. He is now in London.

Vincenzo Gioberti, was the leader of the Risorgimento.

Giuseppe Garibaldi, a leader of the 1848 revolt in Italy who wears a gaucho costume ever since he fought in the Italian Legion in South America. After his forces were defeated in Rome last year, Garibaldi is working as a ship's captain in New York.

Giuseppe Verdi who writes opera music. His Chorus of the Hebrew Slaves from his opera Nabucco is a theme song for the Italian patriots. Every time it is played all the Young Italians stand up and sing.

Ivory Coast

In 1842 the French are granted trade concessions here in 1842.

Jamaca

Jamaica is a British possession. The slave trade there was abolished in 1807 and emancipation came in 1833.

Japan (Nihan)

Japan has two rulers. One is the hereditary empire, the Mikado and the other is a military ruler, the Shogun. The capitols are Kyoto and Edo. There is no trade with foreign countries with the sole exception of a Dutch trading mission at Nagasaki.

Kenya

The coastal regions are part of the Sultanate of Zanizbar. Inland there are several nativist nations including Buganda and Karagwe. Deep in this region is English explorer and missionary, Dr. David Livingston.

Korea

The Lee Dynasty controls the Korean Peninsula.

Laos

Laos was seized by Siam in 1827.

Latvia

Latvia is part of the Russian Empire since 1795.

Liberia

Liberia is an independent state established by the American Colonization Society in 1821 as a homeland for freed slaves and other blacks in America. Abolitionists and ex-slaves settled there. The capitol, Monrovia, is named for American President James Monroe.

Freed slaves are still going to Liberia.

Libya

Libya is a part of the Ottoman Empire controlled by the Bey of Tripoli.

Lithuania

Since 1795 Lithuania has been part of the Russian Empire.

Luxembourg

Luxembourg is a grand duchy since 1815. In 1839 the Treaty of London gave the western part of Luxembourg to Belgium.

Malagasy (Madagascar)

This is an independent nativist nation. The separate country of Marina lies in the center of the Madagascar Island.

Mali

This area contains the trade city of Timbuktu and the Samori nation.

Mauritania

This is a French ruled area.

Mexico

Mexico is a republic, gaining independence from Spain in 1810. In 1836 Mexico lost the province of Texas to a revolt. In 1846 it went to war with the United States and lost the American West in 1848. Leaders of reform in Mexico are Emilio Zapata and Benito Jarez.

Middle Eastern States

All of the Middle East states are parts of the Ottoman Empire. These include Syria, Lebanon, Israel, Jordan, Arabia, Kuwait and others.

Turkish (Ottoman Empire) Assyriologist Hormuzd Rassam is excavating ancient Ninevah, capitol of the Assyrian Empire.

Mongolia

Mongolia accepted Manchu rule in 1689 and has been ruled by the rulers of China ever since.

Morocco

Morocco is an independent sultanate but is a French protectorate..

Mozambia (Mozambique)

The coastal regions are a Portuguese colony with Beira as a trade port. The Yao chiefs control portions of the inland regions.

Nepal

Nepal is an independent Gurkha controlled nation that has recently allowed English settlement in Kathmandu.

Netherlands (Holland)

Holland is a kingdom with Leopold of the House of orange as monarch. The liberal constitution of 1848 is in effect with Jan Thorbeck as Prime Minister.

New Zealand

New Zealand has been a British possession from 1840.

Nicaragua

An independent republic, Nicaragua has a road and river route to connect the Atlantic and the Pacific used by those going to California.

Nigeria

This area is composed of the Ibo state, the Yorba states and the Fulani Empire that contains the trade cities of Gordo and Sokota.

Norway

Since 1815 Norway is a part of the Kingdom of Sweden. It's largest city is Christina.

Pakistan

This is a principality of India.

Panama

Panama is part of New Granada. The isthmus provides passage from the Atlantic to the Pacific.

Paraguay

Paraguay became independent of Spain in 1811.

Peru

Peru became independent of Spain in 1824.

Philippines

The Philippines has been under Spanish rule for 250 years.

Portugal

Portugal is a kingdom with the sister of Brazilian Emperor Dom Pedro II as queen. Slowly losing its empire and trade status Portugal has slipped into a period of dynastic quarrels.

Romania

Romania is a kingdom with King Michael as monarch.

Russia

Russia is an empire with Tsar Nicholas of the House of Romanov as ruler. Nicholas is entering into a period of reaction to the revolts of 1848 and sent troops to suppress the Hungarian Republic in 1849. Russia and

England are coming to a dispute about the Russian use of the Dardanelles and entry into the Mediterranean Sea from the Black Sea.

Rwanda

Rwanda is an independent nation.

Senegal

Senegal is a French possession.

Slovakia

A province of the Austrian Empire.

Slovenia

Slovinia is a province of the Austrian Empire.

South Africa

England gained control of the Cape Colony in 1814. They freed the slaves of the Boer (Dutch settlers). The Boers remain strong in the Transvall and Orange States. The native population is being suppressed. The English army is fighting the Zulus in Natal. The Zulus are under their king, the grandson of the great Zulu chief Shaka.

South and Central American Colonies

In Central America the English hold British Honduras.
In South America the English hold British Guyana. The French hold French Guyana. The Dutch hold Dutch Guyana.

Spain

Queen Isabella II rules the Kingdom of Spain. Born in 1806 she is the daughter of Maria Christina who was the daughter of Ferdinand I, King of the Two Sicilies. Isabella married Ferdinand VII in 1829. She serves as Queen-Regent. Spain, although losing most of its vast empire in the first half of the 19th Century still holds Cuba, the Philippines, Puerto Rico and colonies in Africa.

Sweden

Sweden's king, Oscar, descends from Jean Bennedotte, a marshal of France under Napoleon who was called to be the Swedish king. Sweden gained control of Norway in 1815.

Swiss Confederation

In 1848 the Roman Catholic Cantons of the Swiss Confederation left to form Sondeland. A new confederation was begun in 1848, modeled after the United States. Neufchatel has left Prussian control to join the Swiss. A treaty is signed in Bern in 1850 between the United States and the Swiss Confederation for friendship and cooperation.

Tanzania

The coastal area of Tanzania is part of the Sultanate of Zanzibar.

Thailand (Siam)

The kingdom of Siam is often at war with the Burmese and the Cambodians. England gained trade concessions in Siam in 1824.

Tunisia

This is an independent state within the sovereignty of the Ottoman Empire. It is now controlled by France.

Turkey

Turkey is the seat of the Ottoman Empire. Disputes are arising between the Ottoman Empire and Russia over the control of the Dardanelles and control of Christian holy sights in Anatolia.

Trinidad-Tobago

This has been a British possession since 1803.

Uganda

This area was first visited by European explorers in 1844. Arab traders are active there.

Uruguay

A republic, Uruguay has been involved in a border dispute with Argentina that led to the British and French blockade of Montevideo.

Venezuela

This is a republic free from Spain since 1821. Until 1830 it was federated with Columbia (New Granada) and Ecuador.

Vietnam

This area is composed of the independent nations of Tongking, Annam and Chochin.

Yugoslavia

Serbia and Montenegro are independent kingdoms.

Zambia

This contains the nativist kingdoms of Ndebele and Barotse.

ABOUT THE AUTHOR

Bert George Osterberg was born 1943 in Michigan. He was reared in Detroit and still lives in Michigan. Mr. Osterberg has had a love of history since his school days and has authored several books on a variety of historic subjects. His works include **Forgotten Heroes: Detroit's Fight for Freedom, 1850— 1910, One-hundred Years in America, A Black Family Story and 1850: A Year in the Life of America.** He is currently writing a novel, **Our Silent Song,** the story of an African-American family in America from 1750 to 1910.

After working for almost thirty years for the Detroit Water Department where he became the Telecommunications Manager, Bert Osterberg retired and began writing more frequently. He soon had taken a job at Dearborn, Michigan's Henry Ford Museum and Greenfield Village portraying the historic character of the Eagle Tavern barkeeper, Silas H. Cully. In this role, Bert entertains and informs visitors to the eighty-acre outdoor museum while serving beverages authentic to the 1850s at the Eagle Tavern, an 1850's stagecoach stop.

In addition, the author was certified as a Lay Minister by the United Church of Christ and regularly provides preaching services to congregations both within and without that denomination. Bert also gives talks and first-person historical presentations to school and civic groups in the Detroit area.

Bert Osterberg is married to the former Armaine Yvonne Lacene who is "Sadie" in his stories. He is the proud father of three children, Bert Osterberg, Jr., Lisa Lazar, and Margaret McFarlane. He also has seven grandchildren. One of them, Kayla McFarlane, often helps him in his Greenfield Village job by playing the part of Nettie Cully, his historic character's granddaughter.

Bert and Armaine have always provided homes for animals. They currently share their home with dogs, Champ and Wolf; cats, Shadow, Patches, Treasure, and Boo; a bird named Buddy; and several unnamed goldfish.

0-595-18297-6